*Moscow and the Global Left
in the Gorbachev Era*

Moscow and the Global Left in the Gorbachev Era

Edited by

Joan Barth Urban

Cornell University Press

Ithaca and London

Contents

Acknowledgments

Preparations for this book began in 1987 when Heinz Timmermann and I decided to organize a panel, "Gorbachev and the Global Left," for the 4th World Congress of Soviet and East European Studies, held at Harrogate, England, in July 1990. All five contributors participated on that panel, at which the Timmermann, Gelman, and MacFarlane chapters first appeared as papers.

In the Department of Politics at the Catholic University of America, Patricia Cioppa, Timothy E. Sifert, and Timothy J. Vickey were most helpful in processing various drafts of the Argentieri, Timmermann, and Urban chapters. Oleg V. Yaroshin provided invaluable research assistance. Laszlo K. Urban helped with the translation of the Timmermann chapter from the original German.

J. B. U.

Contributors

FEDERIGO ARGENTIERI teaches sociology at Loyola University (Rome Center) and is a research fellow at the Centro Studi di Politica Internazionale in Rome and a co-founder of the Institute for the History of the 1956 Hungarian Revolution in Budapest. He writes on East European politics and is the author of *L'Ottobre Ungherese* (Rome: Valerio Levi, 1986).

HARRY GELMAN is a senior staff member at the RAND Corporation in Santa Monica, California. He writes on Soviet politics and foreign policy and is the author of *The Brezhnev Politburo and the Decline of Détente* (Ithaca, N.Y.: Cornell University Press, 1984).

S. NEIL MACFARLANE is a professor of political science at Queen's University in Canada. He teaches Soviet government and foreign policy and is the author of *Superpower Rivalry and Third World Radicalism: The Idea of National Liberation* (Baltimore: Johns Hopkins University Press, 1985).

HEINZ TIMMERMANN is a senior staff member of the Bundesinstitut für ostwissenschaftliche und internationale Studien in Cologne, Germany. He writes on Soviet politics and foreign policy and the West European left and is the author of *The Decline of the World Communist Movement: Moscow, Beijing, and the Communist Parties in the West* (Boulder, Colo.: Westview Press, 1987).

[x]   *Contributors*

JOAN BARTH URBAN is a professor of political science at the Catholic University of America in Washington, D.C. She teaches Soviet government and foreign policy and is the author of *Moscow and the Italian Communist Party: From Togliatti to Berlinguer* (Ithaca, N.Y.: Cornell University Press, 1986).

Abbreviations

AFD	Alliance of Free Democrats
ANC	African National Congress
CC	Central Committee
CPSU	Communist Party of the Soviet Union
EC	European Community
FMLN	Faribundo Marti National Liberation Movement
FRG	Federal Republic of Germany
GDR	German Democratic Republic
HSP	Hungarian Socialist Party
HSWP	Hungarian Socialist Workers' Party
INF	Intermediate-range nuclear forces
MPLA	Popular Movement for the Liberation of Angola
PCF	French Communist Party
PCI	Italian Communist Party
PDS	Democratic Party of the Left
PLO	Palestine Liberation Organization
PRC	People's Republic of China
PUWP	Polish United Workers' Party
ROAD	Civic Movement–Democratic Action
SACP	South African Communist Party
SED	German Socialist Unity Party
SI	Socialist International
SPD	German Social Democratic Party

SWAPO	Southwest African People's Organization
UNITA	National Union for the Total Independence of Angola
USSR	Union of Soviet Socialist Republics
ZAPU	Zimbabwe African People's Union

*Moscow and the Global Left
in the Gorbachev Era*

Introduction

Joan Barth Urban

This book explores Soviet policy toward the global left during the half decade of what we call the "Gorbachev revolution"—in contradistinction to the democratic revolution that overturned the seven-decades-old Soviet order in the aftermath of the failed coup of August 1991. When we speak of the global "left," we have in mind the term as customarily understood in the West: social democracy in Europe, the nonruling communist parties in the developed world, the radical liberation movements in the Third World, the People's Republic of China along with other indigenous Leninist regimes. In other words, we refer to political movements and entities that have been considered leftist by virtue of self-definition, not by virtue of Soviet domination, as was the case in the Kremlin's erstwhile East European empire. For the sake of clarity, it should be kept in mind that we have chosen this traditional usage of the term "left" notwithstanding the current Russian attribution of "leftist" to radical democratic groups and "rightist" to hard-line communist elements. In the same vein, our time frame of 1985–90 embraces the period when one could still speak of a "Soviet" policy, when Moscow was the acknowledged seat of a centrally administered Union of Soviet Socialist Republics (USSR) and Mikhail Gorbachev was the unchallenged head of that Union.

The kaleidoscopic transformation of the Soviet polity triggered by

Gorbachev's policies of *glasnost* and *perestroika*—of intellectual openness and restructuring of the political and economic systems—has gripped the attention of Moscow-watchers around the world. In English alone countless volumes have been written on the stages, facets, and vicissitudes of domestic Soviet reform, on the Pandora's box of ethnic and national tensions that the reform process has opened, and on the startling changes in East-West relations spawned by Gorbachev's "new thinking" in foreign policy, the collapse of communism in East-Central Europe, and the end of the Cold War. One topic, however, has been neglected in the outpouring of commentaries on the Gorbachev era: Moscow's policy toward the global left on the eve of the 1990s. It is this unexamined slice of recent history that this volume seeks to address.

The importance of the USSR's ties to leftist movements around the world derived from the centrality of Marxist-Leninist ideology to the Soviet system. The ideology, so the Soviet people were told, legitimized both the Communist Party's monopoly on power and the nationalized command economy. Yet the ideology also proclaimed the inevitability of a global march toward socialism. Thus, whatever a given Soviet leadership's actual belief in Marxism-Leninism—and this is a much-debated question among Western analysts—the Kremlin always sought to bolster the doctrine's validity in the public mind by showing evidence of a global revolutionary advance.

Historically, therefore, the global left occupied a key position in the international and domestic political calculations of the successive Soviet leaderships. Lenin, through the creation in 1919 of the Third Communist International, or Comintern, sought to harness European Marxism and nascent Third World liberationism to his vision of the world revolutionary process. Stalin, despite his use of the international communist movement to advance his personal power and the political interests of the Soviet state, did not stint on revolutionary rhetoric in the early 1930s and the late 1940s. Khrushchev, undaunted by the East European anti-Soviet upheavals of 1956, hoped to restore unity and vitality to the world communist movement through multilateral interparty consultations at which communist parties deviating from Moscow would be brought into line by a pro-Soviet majority rather than by Kremlin *diktat*.

Brezhnev, during his long hold on power, saw the virtual disintegration of the global communist left into publicly feuding constellations, yet he still clung to the multilateral party conferences in what appears to have been an attempt to shore up his regime's waning ideological credentials in the eyes of its own people. For while the fractiousness of world and regional communist conferences made headlines in the West, it was concealed from the Soviet public. Instead, the very convening of such gatherings was portrayed in the USSR's domestic media as evidence of both foreign communist support for Moscow and of international proletarian unity in the global march toward socialism.

For Gorbachev, too, relations with the global left figured prominently in his domestic and foreign policy designs of the second half of the 1980s. Early on, he made clear his interest in overcoming the Kremlin's decades-old split with the People's Republic of China as well as its estrangement from the Italian Communist Party (PCI), the world's largest nonruling communist organization. Gorbachev's normalization of ties with two of the most important components of the international communist movement gave him a handle in dealing with hard-line domestic critics for whom "new thinking" abroad and reforms at home represented ideological capitulation to the class enemy. Reconciliation with the PCI and Beijing (prior to the 1989 crackdown in Tienanmen Square) also provided the Soviet innovators with access to information and advice regarding various aspects of their own reform proposals. Last but not least, these conciliatory moves enhanced the USSR's international leverage by breathing new life into the triangular relationship among Washington, Beijing, and Moscow, on the one hand, and by providing the Soviet Union with a bridge to West European social democracy, on the other, through the PCI's successfully cultivated common policies and growing contacts with members of the Socialist International.

Even more dramatic in its implications than the attempted reconstruction of world communist unity was the Moscow reformers' reassessment, on a theoretical as well as a practical plane, of Western social democracy. For the first time since the schism between socialism and communism engineered by Lenin in 1920 at the Second Comintern Congress, the Soviet Communist Party (CPSU) began to acknowledge that social democracy represented a legitimate current, indeed a mainstream, of the European Marxist movement. To be sure, from the earliest days of Soviet rule the Kremlin had periodically called for short-term, or tactical, cooperation between communist and social democratic parties. But under Gorbachev, CPSU theorists revised Marxist-Leninist doctrine to the point of conceding that the original split between the two mainstreams of the Marxist tradition was the result not of historical inevitability (let alone social democratic betrayal) but of the particular situation that existed in Europe during the early twentieth century. These conceptual overtures to the communist movement's historic competitor on the left facilitated Gorbachev's policy of détente with the many countries in Western Europe where socialist or social democratic parties played a major role. But they also opened up an avenue of doctrinal renewal, even inspiration, for CPSU thinkers who saw their own ideological moorings being rapidly undermined by revelations of the damage done to their compatriots and fatherland by the purveyors of orthodox Marxism-Leninism.

The CPSU reformers' reassessment of social democracy is the subject of the first contribution to this volume, written by Heinz Timmermann. The title of Timmermann's chapter, "Rendezvous with Revisionism: CPSU Reformers and International Social Democracy," captures the gist of his argument. He relates how by 1988 establishment intellectuals close to the Gorbachev leadership began to write openly about the growth potential of capitalism and the capacity of Western democracy to serve the public interest. From this reappraisal of contemporary capitalist society, it was but a short step to a radical reinterpretation of the theory and history of social democracy. In a nutshell, Eduard Bernstein, father of the reformist Marxist notion of evolutionary democratic socialism, had been right, if only in the long run! It was thus incumbent on Moscow to seek closer ties with its one-time revisionist adversaries, the social democratic parties of Europe, not just to advance Soviet foreign policy interests but also to enhance the CPSU's programmatic vision, to enable it to learn how to mesh socialism and democracy. In the process, those nonruling communist parties that refused to adjust to this new approach would be consigned to political isolation and terminal irrelevance.

Timmermann finished his contribution to this volume at the close of 1990, when portents of the abortive hard-line coup that occurred in August 1991 were everywhere to be seen. He thus concluded on a pessimistic note, uncertain whether the Slavic heartland would embrace the Westernizing impulses represented by social democracy or succumb to a "backwards-turning inner dynamic" of crackdown and authoritarianism. In retrospect, however, Timmermann's findings on the "social democratization" of the CPSU's reform wing go far in explaining both the orthodox Leninist coup attempt of August 1991 and the postcoup commitment by erstwhile Russian Communist reformers to full-scale democratization.

Timmermann's chapter is followed by my "Gorbachev and the Italian Communist Party: From Breach to Embrace," which addresses the transformation that occurred in Moscow's relations with the PCI during the mid-1980s. In 1982, shortly before Leonid Brezhnev's death, the Kremlin had denounced the Italian Communists as traitors to the cause of socialism. From the very start of Gorbachev's tenure as general secretary, he set out to mend this breach (or *strappo*, as the Italians called it) in relations between the two parties. He repeatedly conferred with PCI general secretaries, lauded their policies, and feted them in Moscow. Firsthand accounts of Gorbachev's many conversations with Italian Communist leaders from 1984 through 1989 indicate, moreover, that he turned to them as interlocutors and advisers with regard to his "new thinking" on social democracy, the European Community, and East-West relations.

If the collapse of communism in East-Central Europe in the second half of 1989 had the effect of intensifying ethnic and national liberationism within the USSR itself, it also plunged the PCI into a searing crisis of identity. Indeed, by March 1990 a two-thirds majority of Italian Communists had resolved to transform their party into a noncommunist democratic formation, a step taken at the 20th (and last) PCI Congress in early 1991. Still, during the halcyon days of Gorbachev's leadership, from mid-1985 through mid-1989, the entente that emerged between the CPSU reformers and the PCI suggested the virtual Eurocommunization of the Kremlin.

In Chapter 3, "Gorbachev and Sino-Soviet Normalization," Harry Gelman analyzes the process whereby the Soviet Union and the People's Republic of China (PRC) normalized relations after almost three decades of bitter hostility. While Brezhnev had signaled interest in overcoming the Sino-Soviet split the year before his death, it was Gorbachev who decisively altered the terms of discourse between Moscow and Beijing. From the start he called for an improvement in relations between the two communist powers and parties. Then in mid-1986 in Vladivostok he linked an appeal for a rapprochement with China to the announcement that discussions had begun on a pullback of Soviet forces from Mongolia, a key Chinese requirement for normalization and a harbinger of further concessions to come.

Thereafter, several of the USSR's most widely hailed geopolitical retreats represented breakthroughs on the path to Sino-Soviet reconciliation as well as superpower détente. For example, during the negotiations leading to the December 1987 Soviet-American treaty banning intermediate-range nuclear weapons—the focal point of which had been arms reductions in Europe—Moscow also agreed to remove all such missiles deployed along the Sino-Soviet frontier in Asia. By the same token, the early 1988 agreement on the withdrawal of Soviet troops from Afghanistan by mid-February 1989 served to placate the USSR's critics in Beijing as much as those in Washington. Gorbachev was thus able to facilitate the restoration of ties between the CPSU and the Chinese Communist Party at a summit in Beijing in May 1989, just before the crackdown on students in Tienanmen Square and the rise to power in the PRC of a hard-line military-ideological coalition. Though the new Chinese leaders were dismayed by Gorbachev's forbearance toward the democratic revolutions that swept Eastern Europe the following autumn, they did not let it unduly affect subsequent Sino-Soviet dealings.

If geopolitical retreat on the periphery of China enabled Gorbachev to attain the restoration of CPSU ties with Beijing, the USSR's retrenchment in the Third World was a precondition for genuine détente with Washington. In "Moscow's 'New Thinking' on Third World Liberationism," S. Neil MacFarlane relates how the CPSU reformers altered, in fact de-ideologized, the conceptual foundations of Soviet policy toward the Third World. Orthodox Soviet Marxism-Leninism had furnished the cognitive rationale for the Brezhnev regime's activist support of militant Third World liberationism: with the help of the world socialist community (read Soviet bloc) and local communist vanguards, said the ideologues of the Brezhnev era, the transition from colonial underdevelopment to developed socialism could be expedited and the stage of bourgeois capitalism avoided altogether. According to the "new thinking" of the men around Gorbachev, on the other hand, capitalist entrepreneurship, political pluralism, and integration into the global bourgeois economy were essential ingredients of Third World modernization. Soviet disengagement from the regional conflicts spawned by radical liberation movements was a logical corollary of such rethinking. MacFarlane focuses his discussion, however, not on specific foreign policy developments but on the causes of this reconceptualization, on the reasons why Soviet establishment analysts in the late 1980s concluded that capitalism, not socialism, was the order of the day in the Third World.

The USSR's geopolitical retrenchment in the Third World and withdrawal from the borders of China, however spectacular, paled in comparison to its retreat from Eastern Europe. From the inception of this volume, the contributors considered the Soviet Union's relations with its Warsaw Pact allies to be beyond our purview, as the communist regimes in that region were the products of the Kremlin's hegemonic drive rather than the work of an indigenous left acting on its own. Indeed, local reform communists had failed over the years to win national independence from Moscow even when they enjoyed widespread popular support, as in Hungary in 1956 and Czechoslovakia in 1968.

It was only in 1989, when it became clear to the world that Moscow had abandoned its hold on the destiny of East-Central Europe, that the left in that region became an appropriate topic for inclusion in this book. By then, however, it was also becoming clear that even communist reformers committed to national independence, such as the Imre Pozsgay group in Hungary, had lost their ability to win the support of the people. This turn of events raised two fundamental questions: first, why were the independence-minded and democratically oriented leftists unable to muster in 1989–90 the same kind of following they appeared to have had at earlier junctures in postwar East European history; and second, to what extent was the failure of reform communism in East-Central Europe a portent of the failure of the Gorbachev revolution in the Soviet Union?

While the latter question is touched on in the conclusion to this volume, the former is addressed by Federigo Argentieri in his chapter "The Role and Limits of Reform Communism in East-Central Europe." After an analysis of the past experiences of reform communism, especially in Hungary, Czechoslovakia, and Poland, he concludes that the historic role of communist reformers was to extricate their countries from Stalinism and open the way to democratization, but not to preside over the actual creation of democratic orders. Reform communism could at best constitute only a transitional stage on the path to Western-style pluralist democracy. Not only that, but the legacy of communist rule was such that scarcely anything remains of the left in the areas where it once prevailed.

In the conclusion, or "Afterthoughts in Light of the August 1991 Coup," I relate the findings of this book to the political dynamics that culminated in the abortive attempt by reactionary circles in the Soviet Communist Party to reverse the democratic revolutionary process. I venture an assessment of the political profile of Mikhail Gorbachev. The role played by ideological commitment in the Soviet president's decision to reject the "real, existing socialism" of the Brezhnev period in favor of a humane and democratic vision of socialism is a theme I find particularly fruitful to explore. I also discuss the growing complexity—as of the summer of 1991—of dealing with the question of Moscow's relations with the global left. For by mid-1991 the emergence in the USSR of several social democratic parties as well as the factionalization of the CPSU itself resulted in the differentiation of the Soviet left along lines that paralleled the spectrum of the global left, ranging from Western social democracy to the hard-line Chinese Communist leadership. Most ominous in this regard was the apparent entente that developed from May 1990 onward between those in power in Beijing and the coup plotters in Moscow. I conclude, finally, with some reflections upon the parallels and differences between the evolving postcommunist orders in East-Central Europe, on the one hand, and the territories of the former USSR on the other.

The diversification of the Soviet left was a reflection of the broader pluralization of politics in the USSR that won a new lease on life in the spring of 1991 after a winter of political backsliding and economic reversals. The contributions to this volume were largely completed during that earlier period, the fall and winter of 1990–91, when a hard-line military-ideological backlash against the efforts to radically transform Soviet society seemed to gain the upper hand under cover of the crisis in the Persian Gulf. Gorbachev's unexpected rejection in mid-autumn 1990 of the "500 days plan" for the marketization of the Soviet economy, Foreign Minister Eduard Shevardnadze's sudden resignation on December 20, 1990, in protest over what he perceived as the looming threat of dictatorship, and the bloody if contained military crackdown in Lithuania on January 12–13, 1991, were but the most visible signs of that overall process of retrenchment.

The stalemate between reform and reaction was broken only on March 28, 1991, when the Kremlin proved unwilling or unable to order the 50,000 Russian troops it had mobilized in the center of the capital to prevent Russian citizens from demonstrating in the streets in favor of democracy. Within weeks of that singular turning point, the decision was made to elect by direct popular ballot the president of the huge Russian Republic, while Gorbachev and the chief contender for the Russian presidency, Boris Yeltsin, reached an agreement providing for the resumption of the democratization, marketization, and federalization of the USSR. On June 12, 1991, Yeltsin was elected president of Russia by a three-fifths majority of the popular vote.

The catalyst for the abortive coup attempt two months later was the projected signing by nine of the fifteen Soviet republics of a new union treaty worked out by the Gorbachev-Yeltsin team, a treaty that would have retained the union structure but shifted extensive political and economic power from the central government to the republics. But on a deeper level the coup signified the recurrence at the very core of the CPSU of the historic split between Leninism and social democracy which had rent the European Marxist movement asunder in the aftermath of the Bolshevik Revolution. This theme will be elaborated in the "Afterthoughts."

The political zigs and zags of 1991 underscored the difficulty of analyzing the recent past and present (let alone predicting the future) of the Soviet Union. They also vindicated our decision to focus in this volume on relations between Moscow and the global left during the years 1985–90, a period which represented the last hurrah of the internationalist mystique that was so central to the Soviet Communist experience. These were also the years when the systemic structures

Gorbachev inherited from his predecessors as well as his control over them still remained largely intact. The following pages thus recount the Gorbachev reformers' "new thinking" and conduct toward the global left in the heyday of *perestroika*.

[1]

Rendezvous with Revisionism:
CPSU Reformers and
International Social Democracy

Heinz Timmermann

On the eve of the 1990s the USSR's multidimensional domestic crisis, the problems arising from the transformation of an empire at home and abroad, the efforts needed to achieve reconciliation and cooperation with the Western community—all this was more than enough to absorb the Soviet leadership's full attention. Thus it is no surprise that the "world communist movement" lost significance and weight as a determining factor in Moscow's reform policies.[1] Documents of the Soviet Communist Party (CPSU) as well as party diplomacy indicate that the Western fraternal parties no longer played more than a marginal role. With regard to the traditionalist type of communist parties such as those in France, Portugal, and West Germany, the CPSU reformers apparently considered relations with them to be rather burdensome.[2]

It was to be expected that communist parties still guided by outdated patterns of thought and action would receive ever less of the

1. Important evidence for this is that the International Department of the CPSU Central Committe (headed since October 1988 by CC member Valentin Falin) began to put the major emphasis on international diplomacy, attaching only minor importance to relations among communist parties.

2. See in this connection my article "Die KPdSU und das internationale kommunistische Parteiensystem. Paradigmenwechsel in Moskau," *Beilage zur Wochenzeitung Das Parlament* (Bonn), no. 12 (March 17, 1989):20–28.

preferential treatment to which they had been accustomed. Organizations of this type no longer mattered very much to Moscow. They would continue not to matter at least as long as the Soviet leadership continued its radical open-door policy within and without, its critical examination of the history of the Soviet Union as well as Marxist-Leninist ideology, its renunciation of the CPSU's monopoly on truth, and the translation of these positions into concrete political practice.

The growing distance between the Soviet leadership and the ortho-dox communist parties, however, did not imply that Moscow had lost all interest in the West European left. Rather, it meant that more attention was being paid to international social democracy and, most of all, to social democratic parties in Western Europe. This interest, in turn, signaled a radical change of direction in the CPSU's relations with the two historical mainstreams of the international workers' movement.

The reappraisal can be explained in part by the fact that the social democratic and socialist parties belonging to the Socialist International (SI) started early on to support the reorientation of Soviet foreign policy in its central aspects and tried to influence their governments' conduct accordingly. But this is not the key point, for even before Gorbachev the SI welcomed Soviet initiatives on détente and disarmament.

The Soviet reformers' change of mind vis-à-vis the two basic streams of the West European left was prompted above all by their belief that the social democratic concept of combining socialism *and* democracy could well supply useful examples for their projected internal *perestroika*. Symptomatic here was the writer Chingiz Aitmatov's remark—later repeated in many versions by Soviet publicists—that true socialism was built not in the Soviet Union but in states "thriving under the rule of law" like Sweden, Austria, Finland, Norway, and other West European countries.[3] It is well known that in these countries social democrats exert substantial influence on the direction of national development.

Thus the CPSU in its draft platform for the 28th Party Congress of

3. Central Soviet Television, June 5, 1989 (speech to the Congress of People's Deputies). Deputy Aitmatov was appointed in April 1990 to Gorbachev's Presidential Council.

July 1990 logically abandoned its preference for relations with the communist parties of the West. Instead, it claimed to be "open to cooperation with communist and workers' parties, socialist and social democratic, liberal and national democratic parties, with all organizations and movements standing for peace, democracy and social progress." Most remarkable in this context was the CPSU's mention of a possibility that would have been dismissed as out of the question only a few years earlier, namely, the possibility of "overcoming the historical split in the socialist movement, of its renaissance as a world movement on a modern basis."[4]

For the time being, these words reflected little more than a blurred vision. On the one hand, splitting tendencies were emerging within the CPSU itself to the point where it was difficult to foresee its programmatic development and its future role in society. On the other hand, the Soviet party's bid for a reconciliation with Western socialists, or "the return of the prodigal son into the harmonious socialist family," as one Soviet author put it, was not without problems for the SI. As that author rightly remarked, "Of course, they are happy to see him return but welcome him with caution—they do not yet know what he has brought with him and how he is going to behave; they only know where he has been and what he has done during the time of going astray."[5]

Still, the CPSU reformers were to be taken seriously when they pointed out the possibility of "overcoming the historic split in the socialist movement." Such a perspective fit into their plans to integrate the Soviet Union as a constructive partner into the world's cultural, political, and economic life. It was also consistent with their reevaluation of the UN's role, their recognition of universal human and civil rights, and their wish to take part in the economic summits of the seven Western industrial powers. In Europe the CPSU reformers envisaged a transition from antagonism to cooperation on the state level, from class struggle to coevolution on the societal level. As a consequence, it was plainly in their interest to look for preferential relations with formations such as the SI parties, which not only

4. *Pravda*, February 13, 1990, 1.

5. L. Ionin, "Soziale Architektur," *Neue Zeit* (Moscow-German edition of *Novoe Vremya*), no. 36 (1989):36.

supported these goals but were also guided by the perspective of a "humane, democratic socialism" that the CPSU wanted to incorporate into its program.[6]

In the following pages I shall describe some aspects of the intellectual framework on the basis of which Soviet reformers reoriented their relations with the West European left. That framework includes not only a reassessment of Western systems, their functional mechanisms, and foreign relations, but also a reevaluation of the history of the international workers' movement. Against this background, the CPSU's changing relations with the left's two mainstreams will then be described and the motives behind that change analyzed.

The present study concentrates on the policies of the moderate reformers around Gorbachev during 1985–90 and leaves aside the more extreme positions within the CPSU, such as the polemical conservative protests against the CPSU's alleged caving in to social democratic positions[7] and the positions of radical reformers who already felt themselves to be democrats and were by 1990 trying to push the CPSU in that direction.[8] The balance of power between these two groups in the CPSU was then very delicate and threatened a split in the party at any time. Because of this, the following analysis considers only overall tendencies and comes to no more than a provisional conclusion.

Tentativeness regarding the prospects of the moderate CPSU reformers was all the more valid from the summer of 1990 onward when the conservative elements regrouped and started to exercise growing influence on their country's policies. Faced with economic chaos and a disintegrating empire, Gorbachev—having been vested with broad authority as president and CPSU general secretary—began to rely ever more upon those forces that promised to create law and order: the CPSU apparat, the military and internal security establishments, and the defense industry. Should the counteroffensive of

6. The quoted words were the title of the draft platform for the 28th CPSU Congress (see note 4).

7. E.g., Politburo member Yegor Ligachev in an interview with *Selskaya Zhizn* (Moscow), April 8, 1990.

8. This reference is to the many exponents of the "Democratic Platform" group in the CPSU. Their program of radical renewal was published in *Pravda*, March 3, 1990, 3.

the military-ideological complex—inspired by the Communist Party nomenklatura—prevail, resulting in an authoritarian regime or even the "dictatorship" forecast by Eduard Shevardnadze in December 1990, that would surely torpedo the USSR's/Russia's incipient reorientation toward Europe. It would also cripple the CPSU's attempt at a rapprochement with international social democracy and undermine any efforts to include the USSR or Russia in the European process of growing integration and interdependence.

If the attempted reorientation toward Europe and toward international social democracy is nevertheless analyzed below in detail, it is because it signifies a serious and, in the future, potentially effective effort on the part of the Westernizing political and intellectual elites of Russia to lead their country out of its historical isolation. Only the future will tell whether this undertaking will be successful in the long run or whether a great part of what is described below as the concepts and vision of the "Western" and "democratic socialist" elements within the CPSU should already be consigned to the ash heap of history.

New Appraisal of the West

New thinking and acting vis-à-vis the West European left grew out of the CPSU reformers' conviction that general human values must be given priority over class interests. This premise was based on the argument that in the face of an ever growing global interdependence and all the tasks that must be fulfilled by the whole of mankind, the struggle between systems could only be carried on as peaceful competition. Both sides needed to concentrate on finding a kind of cooperation that did not put each other's system to the test.

Representatives of Social Progress

Moscow's reformers had in mind not only state diplomacy. In their view, even on the social level "many previous distinctions between different sections of the forces of progress do not make sense any longer." Each element had to relinquish "the claim to possess omniscience" as well as the attempt to play the leading role in everything. Faced with new tasks, the dividing line between the forces of progress and the forces of reaction no longer totally coincided "with the historic borders between countries and blocs or even classes and parties." The overall forces of progress were no longer delineated by resistance against a common opponent. Rather, they developed out of "common positive ideas aimed at guaranteeing mankind's survival, overcoming the crisis of civilization, and moving toward a world without violence."[9]

This basic thesis put forward by the CPSU reformers warrants our attention because it signaled not only a reassessment of the objective conditions for mankind's survival but also a radical change of mind with regard to the social forces representing civilization and progress. It involved the disavowal of communist parties that continued to follow traditional Marxist-Leninist reasoning and saw themselves as the historically ordained vanguard of a revolutionary march toward a better world.

The CPSU reformers' change of mind seemed all the more convincing since their strategic reorientation toward interdependence, dialogue, and cooperation with all progressive forces was based on a reassessment of "capitalism" and a de-demonization of "imperialism." In other words, the CPSU's shift away from traditional communist parties toward international social democracy accelerated as the reformers began to perceive Western systems to be capable of carrying out reform and maintaining peace. The social democratic strategy was gaining in weight because Moscow no longer considered it to be a stabilizing factor in "state-monopolistic capitalism." Rather, social democratic concepts were seen as a positive force that could serve as an example in many respects for a CPSU orienting itself to *perestroika*.

Functional Mechanisms of Western Democracies

The Soviet reappraisal of the West that was a precondition for the change of attitude toward the West European left can only be briefly described here. "Capitalism," so we heard in Moscow, used to be seen

9. Members of the CPSU CC Institute of Social Sciences, "Sotsialnyi progress v sovremennom mire," *Kommunist,* no. 7 (1988):90.

by communists as an incurable crisis-prone system. Communists, therefore, were to take a wait-and-see attitude, confident of living to see the system's ultimate collapse. This strategy turned out to be wrong. Capitalism proved to possess more stability and more flexibility and ability to innovate than expected, not least because of the pressure applied by the reform-minded left. But CPSU reformers believe that this development also came about for other reasons.

First of all, a structure of institutions that achieves consensus while allowing comprehensive pluralism guarantees a system that is both acceptable to the population and open to changes in economic, social, and other values. Typically enough, as early as 1988 the CPSU's chief ideologue, Vadim Medvedev, protested against a "nihilist relationship" with bourgeois democracy and stressed: "It would be unacceptable sectarianism and political narrow-mindedness to refuse to critically and creatively examine and utilize democratic forms that are the result of social progress and, as such, actually the *common property of human civilization.*"[10]

Second, market mechanisms and mixed forms of property secure high economic efficiency and technological innovation. In addition, they create the preconditions necessary for building an efficient social security system. As Medvedev put it, "Given our present circumstances, the market is an irreplaceable means of flexibly adjusting economic production to constantly changing needs, an important instrument of social control over the quality of the goods and the cost of their production. The market without its speculative aberrations is *one of the greatest achievements in the development of human civilization.*"[11]

Finally, the welfare state is the result of a balance of group interests, of a lasting and generally accepted compromise between employers and employees. Involving a combination of state regulation, workers' economic participation, and social institutions of partnership, the modern welfare state of the West European type has little in common with capitalism as it was at the turn of the century.

On the whole, therefore, Moscow's reformers came to the conclu-

---

10. Vadim Medvedev, "K poznaniyu sotsializma," *Kommunist,* no. 17 (1988):12; emphasis in the original. Politburo member Medvedev was at the time the head of the Ideological Commission of the CPSU CC.

11. Ibid., 16–17; emphasis in the original.

sion that in Western industrialized countries the state could no longer be regarded as simply the agent of monopoly capital. Instead, the state should be seen as an institution that could be used by reform-minded forces to bring about radical changes of structure, and to promote extensive political rights and social improvements. This reappraisal of the functional mechanisms in Western societies almost inevitably led the CPSU to shift its priorities vis-à-vis leftist formations in Western Europe. Parties striving for evolutionary change within the system, like social democratic parties, were given preference. Parties that continued to adhere to a strategy aimed at breaking with the system, as did orthodox communist parties, were of less and less interest to Soviet reformers.

Rejection of Lenin's Theory of Imperialism

The above trend received additional impetus from the new Soviet evaluation of Western foreign policy. For a long while Lenin's theory of imperialism as aggressive by nature and unable to protect its own interests in the long term prevailed. By the late 1980s, however, this theory increasingly gave way to another argument: capitalist economic systems are in principle capable of making progress even without the militarization of the economy, society, and politics. They are capable of organizing peace and cooperation not only among themselves but also with the other side.

A good example of this reappraisal was the change in thinking and acting with regard to the rapidly integrating European Community (EC), a central field of action for the West European left.[12] Until well into the 1980s the CPSU denied the possibility of a lasting compatibility of interests among rival capitalist states and considered the EC as a bridgehead of U.S. imperialism. By the eve of the 1990s, however, this picture had completely changed. As "one of the leading centers of the present-day world," the EC came to be seen in Moscow as an efficient partner for the modernization of the Soviet economy and

12. See in this connection my article, "Sowjetunion und Westeuropa: Perzeptionswandel und politische Neuausrichtung," in Hannes Adomeit, Hans-Hermann Höhmann, and Günther Wagenlehner, eds., *Die Sowjetunion unter Gorbatschow* (Stuttgart: Kohlhammer, 1990), 329–58.

as an influential and constructive factor in developing pan-European structures.[13] Furthermore, successful EC integration was presented as proof that the majority of the people accepted this community. Despite all the contradictions and difficulties, especially in the social field (for example, unemployment), the EC was credited with many achievements such as "the creation of modern international, supranational judicial and ethical norms and mechanisms, the overcoming of national introversion, the mutual enrichment of cultures." All this was said to have happened as a result of the "internationalization of the forces of production, the creation of powerful incentives for the scientific-technological revolution, the optimization of production creating the elements necessary for its 'socialization.'"

It is obvious that the Soviet reappraisal of Western systems and their ability to develop modern forms of cooperation and integration between the blocs contributed to the CPSU's change of attitude toward the different streams of the West European left. This trend was further reinforced by a parallel development: the traditional Soviet interpretation of the history of the workers' movement was subjected to a radical revision that found forceful expression in an ever more positive evaluation of the social democratic Second International (1889–1923) at the expense of the communist Third International (1919–1943) and its successor organizations.

Reevaluating the History of the International Workers' Movement

In their reassessment of Soviet history, the CPSU reformers arrived at a point where Lenin's central patterns of thought and action (his views on violence, for example) were submitted to critical examina-

---

13. For this and the following points, see V. N. Ierusalimskii and A. F. Pankin, "Novyi etap zapadnoevropeiskoi integratsii i poiski demokraticheskoi alternativy, *Rabochii klass i sovremennyi mir* (Moscow, henceforth *RKSM*), no. 5 (1989):15–25. Both authors were working in the CPSU CC Institute of Social Sciences. The article reflects the substance of a symposium of Soviet and communist-oriented West German analysts. See also Yuriy Borko, "Architektur des Einvernehmens: Erfahrungen bei der Integration Westeuropas," *Neue Zeit,* no. 46 (1989):16–17. Borko is head of a department of the USSR Academy of Sciences' Institute for Europe.

tion or denounced altogether.[14] It then became impossible to avoid taking aim at the Bolshevik-dominated Comintern. This criticism, in turn, contributed to the alienation between the CPSU and traditional communist parties in Western Europe like the French Communist Party. These parties saw themselves as linked to the Comintern through the unbroken continuity of traditions and categories supposedly forming the historically ordained revolutionary countermovement against the "revisionism" and "nationalism" of the social democratic parties. Starting from this assumption, they continued to believe that they were in possession of the one and only correct concept for building a more just society.[15]

Criticism of the Comintern

CPSU reformers began to assess the Comintern and its strategy toward the communist movement in a much more differentiated way than before. As they saw it at the close of the 1980s, the ideological and organizational split in the international workers' movement in 1914 was not at all dictated by historical necessity. Nor could it be attributed solely to "subjective" factors such as "faults and errors committed by top-ranking officials of the workers' parties." On the contrary, this split now appeared to be mainly the result of a "chauvinistic wave" that engulfed even the workers at the time and helped to break up proletarian solidarity.[16]

This new interpretation was remarkable in the sense that it considered the split in the workers' movement to be the result of a specific situation at a given historical moment. Rather than following Lenin,

14. Cf. in this connection the statements by Politburo member Aleksandr Yakovlev, who was formally speaking about the 200th anniversary of the French Revolution but in fact referring to the October Revolution and its consequences; "Velikaya frantsuzskaya revolyutsiya i sovremennost," *Sovetskaya kultura* (Moscow), July 15, 1989.

15. For the analogous former interpretation in Moscow, see Vadim Zagladin, "Velikii Oktyabr i kommunisticheskoe dvizhenie: proshloe i nastoyashchee," *Voprosy Istorii* (Moscow), no. 11 (1980):13–30. Zagladin was in the late 1980s a member of President Gorbachev's staff of consultants.

16. Yuriy Krasin, "Sotrudnichat, ne dramatiziruya proshloe," *Kommunist*, no. 12 (1989):120–22. See also "100-letie II Internatsionala i nekotorye problemy sovremennogo rabochego dvizheniya," *Mirovaya ekonomika i mezhdunarodnye otnosheniya* (henceforth *MEMO*), no. 11 (1989):5–16.

who had accused the "workers' aristocracy" of betraying the movement's original goals, this new view saw the founding of the Comintern and the establishment of communist parties as having been a temporary affair. These events were the products of an era when capitalism still meant fierce class struggle and imperialist wars instigated periodically as the only means of solving internal contradictions. Many West European communist parties, in contrast, were still influenced by basic patterns of an analysis that regarded the noncommunist left in all its variations as part of an overall capitalist-imperialist system.

After Gorbachev's assumption of office, Moscow intensified its criticism of this orthodox interpretation, not the least in recalling its own past. For example, we find criticism of the Comintern's total fixation on the strategy of Stalin's CPSU as an error that led directly to the "Comintern's tragedy."[17] Included in this condemnation was the policy line that allowed "cooperation with workers organized in social democratic parties only on the condition that they adopt consistent revolutionary positions and break off with their original organizations."[18]

Furthermore, there was criticism not only of the Comintern's 6th World Congress of 1928, including its sectarian motto of "class against class," but also of the 7th World Congress of 1935 with its strategy of building a comprehensive workers' front against fascism. Until this day, orthodox communist parties keep praising that strategy. But at the time, an authoritative CPSU spokesman explained in 1988, communists merely pretended to unite with democratic forces. In reality they "aspired to hegemony and considered these forces not as independent and equal partners but only as special reserves in the proletarian class struggle."[19]

17. See L. A. Latyshev, "Istoriya mogla byt inoi. Tragediya Kominterna," *Molodezh Estonii* (Tallinn), June 23, 1988. Latyshev was then a professor at the Higher Party School in Moscow.

18. Fridrikh Firsov and K. K. Shirinya, "Komintern: Opyt deyatelnosti," *Kommunist*, no. 10 (1988):109. Firsov was then head of a department and Shirinya a consultant at the CPSU CC Institute of Marxism-Leninism. Cf. my article, "Geschichte der Komintern in neuem Licht. Ansätze zu einer Umwertung in Moskau," *Deutschland Archiv* (Cologne), no. 12 (1988):1285–92.

19. Yuriy Krasin, "Marksizm i novoe politicheskoe myshlenie," *Politicheskoe obrazovanie* (Moscow), no. 18 (1988):7.

As a last example, during the 1970s polemics were hurled at Eurocommunism for supposedly infiltrating dangerous revisionist ideas into the communist movement. But in the late 1980s Moscow's reformers voiced views like those of the Italian Communist Party, which had as early as 1981 declared that the October Revolution and its creation, the CPSU, had "exhausted their propulsive force." In Soviet publications, one could read more and more self-critical reflections on Moscow's centralism of the Stalin-Brezhnev type and how it actually harmed the communist movement and communist parties in the West, thwarting their development at home.[20]

Reevaluating the Second International's Program and Policies

Parallel to the Third International's devaluation, including its patterns of thought and action, ran a clear reevaluation of the Second International and its successor organizations. In contrast to previous assessments, the fact that the Second International united programmatically different parties and currents of Marxist mold and led them to common actions in the interest of the workers came to be viewed positively. Let me quote, for example, a late 1989 statement by Yuriy Krasin, rector of the Institute of Social Sciences of the CPSU Central Committee:

> At this moment, we see clearly the continuity with one of the more valuable traditions of the Second International, namely, the tradition of democracy and pluralism, unity in diversity. The Second International combined representatives of different countries at different levels of

---

20. See the following examples: Gorbachev to PCF General Secretary Georges Marchais, TASS, September 22, 1989; Aleksandr Bovin, "Perestroika i sudba sotsializma," *Izvestiya,* July 11, 1987; Yuriy Krasin, "Marksizm," 3–11 (see note 19); M. N. Gretskii, "My i marksisty zapada," *Voprosy filosofii* (Moscow), no. 7 (1989): 100–111. In addition, see the following self-critical roundtable discussions by Soviet analysts with representatives of Eurocommunism: "Problemy kommunisticheskogo dvizheniya i perestroika v SSSR," *Kommunist,* no. 5 (1989):52–59; "Wichtige Anregungen auch für unsere Zeit: Zu Palmiro Togliattis Vermächtnis von Jalta," *Probleme des Friedens und des Sozialismus* (henceforth *PFS;* German edition of *World Marxist Review*), no. 7 (1989):951–61; "Wir brauchen die ganze Wahrheit über den Stalinismus," *PFS,* no. 1 (1990):49–63 (in the annex); "Eurokommunismus: Positive und negative Erfahrungen," *PFS,* no. 2 (1990):276–86.

socio-economic and political development. The concrete tasks to be solved by the parties united there involved substantial differences. Heated discussions flared up on all important questions concerning the theory and political practice of the workers' movement. The organizational framework of the Second International was large enough to make room for diverse forces all united in behalf of one common goal: to stand up for the interests of the workers. In spite of all the internal clashes, the drive for unity won the upper hand for some time over centrifugal forces.[21]

Given present circumstances, this assessment can be interpreted as an expression of the CPSU reformers' interest in joining the Socialist International at some point later on. In the tradition of the Second International, SI member parties offer a great variety of programs. Time has blurred the categorical choice between revolution and evolution. As Krasin put it: "In comparison to a theoretical scheme that came into the world during quite a different epoch, life has proven to be much more complicated than that."[22]

This ideological reorientation toward international social democracy and its representatives also found expression in another area. Historical theoreticians and leaders of the workers' movement who were previously criticized or polemically attacked began to receive ever more positive reviews. Among them were the Russian Georgii Plekhanov, the Austrians Victor Adler and Otto Bauer (the latter concerning problems of the nation and nationalities), the Frenchman Paul Lafargue, the Italian Filippo Turati, the Spaniard Pablo Iglesias, the Belgian Emile Vandervelde, and the Germans Eduard Bernstein and Karl Kautsky.[23]

It is worth noting that Soviet scholars and the media increasingly paid special attention to the arch-revisionist Eduard Bernstein. He supported a concept of reform socialism aimed at implementing workers' self-determination in the existing state, economy, and society. At the same time, he declared the "movement" and not the

---

21. Contribution to a joint 1989 symposium in Moscow of social democratic and communist analysts on "The Second International: Past and Present." This part was left out of the published version of the statement; see Krasin, "Sotrudnichat" (see note 16).

22. Krasin, unpublished manuscript (see note 21).

23. "100-letie II Internatsionala" (see note 16).

"final goal" to be the key factor. Until recently, orthodox communist parties fiercely attacked Bernstein. In their opinion he was the most influential protagonist of a current within the international workers' movement that allegedly kept the proletariat from carrying out the class struggle while attempting to integrate it into the capitalist system. Dogmatically oriented communist parties in the West have continued to maintain this view. The Moscow reformers, however, pointed to the fact that many of Bernstein's ideas proved to be correct and forward-looking.

It was Krasin, member of the CPSU's Commission on Ideology as well as rector of its Institute of Social Sciences, who played a prominent role in this reappraisal. Krasin's analysis carries even more weight if we remember that the institute he heads was considered the think tank of Aleksandr Yakovlev, a leading reformer. Yakovlev, a member of the CPSU Politburo from 1987 to 1990, head of the Central Committee's Commission on International Affairs from 1988 to 1990, and a member of Gorbachev's Presidential Council in 1990, exerted great influence on Moscow's ideological and programmatic reorientation.

According to Krasin, Bernstein's only error was to be actually ahead of his time and to fail to include in his analysis the possibility of the revolutionary explosions that occurred after World War I. As a practical politician he was not up to Lenin, but as a theoretician he correctly analyzed long-term tendencies in the economic and sociopolitical development of modern capitalism and devised an appropriate strategy for the workers' movement. Krasin explained in early 1990 that Bernstein

> pointed out the possibility of a radical modification of capitalism and was of the opinion that changes in the social structures of capitalist society would not lead to the polarization of classes but to an increase in the specific weight of the middle class. He maintained the view that the dictatorship of one class had to be the product of an insufficiently developed political culture. Bernstein warned of a socialist public ownership that ignored the principle according to which "all administrative units and mature citizens must assume economic responsibility." Without comprehensive self-administration based upon this principle, Bernstein wrote, "so-called public ownership of the means of production could

well lead to an unrestrained destruction of the forces of production, to a meaningless indulgence in experiments and aimless violence."[24]

Elsewhere Krasin went even further by characterizing socialism as a historical process and not a ready-made model, not a concrete goal toward which the workers' movement must direct its strategy. Recalling the negative experiences with Stalin's model of Marxist-Leninist socialism, Krasin endorsed Bernstein's opinion that setting up complete models can end in utopias utterly disastrous for the people. Krasin even detected a kernel of truth in Bernstein's long-denounced slogan: "Movement is everything, the final goal nothing." Taken seriously, this slogan could prevent the danger of pursuing socialist ideals removed from reality.[25]

This striking reappraisal of Bernstein not only indicated the extent of Moscow's ideological-programmatic rethinking, but also signaled a radical revision of traditional interpretations of the history and strategy of the international workers' movement. By characterizing Bernstein's concept of evolutionary social transformation as forward-looking, the CPSU reformers implicitly condemned the Bolshevik strategy aimed at violent revolutionary ruptures as a tragic error dictated by the circumstances of their time.

Reduced Involvement with International Communism

As an organizational consequence of its conceptual rethinking, the CPSU reduced its activities within the traditional communist party system. In April 1990, for example, the Prague magazine *Problems of Peace and Socialism* ceased to appear.[26] Founded in 1958, this monthly periodical was at the end published by sixty-nine communist

24. Yuriy Krasin, "Leninskoe nasledie: potrebnost v novom videnii," *MEMO*, no. 4 (1990):11–12. The quotations are from Bernstein's 1899 book, *Die Voraussetzungen des Sozialismus und die Aufgaben der Sozialdemokratie*, which became known as the "bible of revisionism." Krasin made similar statements at a session of the CPSU CC's Ideological Commission, a summary of which, called "Leninism and Perestroika," was published in *Pravda*, February 1, 1990. See also Krasin's interview, "Sovmestno reshat globalnye problemy," *Ekho planety* (Moscow), no. 43 (1989):9–11.
25. A. I. Volkov and Yuriy Krasin, "Sotsializm vchera i zavtra: tot zhe samyi ili drugoi?" *Kommunist*, no. 7 (1990):14.
26. Reported by the Prague news agency, CTK, May 22, 1990.

parties, under a Soviet editor-in-chief, and distributed in forty-one languages to 140 countries.[27] A journal that had long been an outlet for Soviet orthodoxy rather than open discussions, it had obviously become obsolete at a time when the CPSU was opening up to different intellectual currents.

The same was true for the World Peace Council, founded in 1950. Originally one of its central tasks was to create publicity for Soviet foreign and security policy in the West. But in 1989–90 the Moscow reformers criticized the organization's one-sidedness and its inability to reorient itself toward the problems of mankind, which now took priority over class interests, and to cooperate with dissenting groups and currents in the peace movement.[28] For these reasons the CPSU significantly reduced its political commitment to the Council. Moreover, it no longer seemed willing to shoulder the financial burden of the organization, as could be seen from the CPSU's request that the Council restructure its activities "on the principle of self-financing."[29]

The clearest sign of conceptual revision, however, was that Gorbachev, in his best-selling *Perestroika,* refrained from acknowledging the international communist movement.[30] After two years of hesitation, moreover, the new CPSU leadership gave up any intention of convening a communist party world conference. Instead, on the occasion of the 70th anniversary of the October Revolution (November 1987), an informal meeting of representatives of some 178 diverse parties and movements from 120 states was organized in Moscow. It was attended by one hundred communist parties, twenty-nine socialist and social-democratic parties, forty parties and movements from the Third World, and such parties as the Indian National Congress, the Finnish Center Party, and the Greens from the Federal Republic of Germany.[31]

27. Roland Bauer, "Ein internationales Forum für die Fortschrittskräfte," *Horizont* (East Berlin), no. 7 (1988):11.

28. Wladimir Orjol, "Orientierung auf Morgen: Ist der Weltfriedensrat den Herausforderungen der Zeit gewachsen?" *Neue Zeit,* no. 12 (1990):40–41.

29. Wladimir Orjol, "Weltfriedensrat: Was weiter?" *Neue Zeit,* no. 15 (1989):12–13.

30. M. Gorbatschow, *Perestroika. Die zweite russische Revolution. Eine neue Politik für Europa und die Welt* (Munich: Knaur, 1987).

31. See Juri Shilin, "Potential des Friedens, der Vernunft, des guten Willens," *Neue Zeit,* no. 50 (1987):26–27. The individual statements are published in *Treffen der Vertreter von Parteien und Bewegungen, die an den Feierlichkeiten zum 70. Jahrestag der Grossen Oktoberrevolution teilnahmen,* 2 vols. (Moscow: APN, 1988).

The CPSU considered the meeting to be a breakthrough in the dialogue the party had sought with the largest possible number of participants, not the least with those of differing views. It was in fact an alternative to the traditional narrowly constituted world communist conferences, and for Moscow it served as a pilot project and model for further engagement in positive competition among different intellectual and political currents in the East and West.

But the CPSU reformers' real interest lay in enlarging and intensifying bilateral and multilateral contacts with international social democracy. Social democracy in all its various forms served as an increasingly important point of reference and orientation for the reformers in their endeavor to adapt *perestroika* to the model of "democratic socialism" and to treat their international partners as equals.

Most Favored Partners: International Social Democracy

In recent years the CPSU greatly intensified its contacts with the Socialist International and its member parties, with whom it also undertook a dialogue on common future tasks. Here it bears mentioning that the Italian Communist Party (PCI) did likewise. The PCI was, accordingly, accepted and courted by the CPSU as an integral and constructive part of the West European reform-minded left ("Euroleft"). According to Soviet data, by the middle of 1989 the CPSU maintained relations with forty social democratic, socialist, and labor parties, especially those in Western Europe.[32] At SI conferences the CPSU began to participate as an "observer," as did most of the former governing communist parties of Eastern Europe, now transformed into "socialist parties."

Gradual Rapprochement with the Socialist International

In contrast to the ex-communist parties of Hungary and Poland, as of 1990 the CPSU deemed it too early to apply for membership in the Socialist International. Moscow was realistic enough to know that the

32. Karen Brutents, *Pravda*, June 25, 1989, 5; CC candidate member Brutents was then deputy head of the International Department of the CPSU Central Committee.

SI would not answer such an application with a list of precise conditions analogous to the famous "21 conditions" for admission to membership in the Comintern; but the SI would certainly use delaying tactics and wait with a decision until the CPSU had further clarified its own situation. Another reason for Moscow's hesitation was the view that more common ground regarding content had to be found before it made sense to set up a unified organization. Points of contact could be found, for example, at bilateral and multilateral conferences and seminars for the CPSU and SI members or through more CPSU participation in SI commissions. For Soviet authors, the CPSU's cooperation with the SI consultative council on disarmament and the CPSU–German Social Democratic Party (SPD) study group on the "common European home" were promising steps and a solid basis for such organizational unity later on.[33]

Gorbachev and Willy Brandt (as chairman of the Socialist International) met in October 1989 to clarify the substance of these Soviet ideas. According to some Soviet insiders, Gorbachev himself was rather skeptical about social democracy and familiarized himself only reluctantly with its policy and program.[34] Nonetheless, during this meeting Gorbachev confirmed the CPSU's willingness to critically examine the experiences of the two streams of the workers' movement and to look "into the past, present, and future openly and without prejudice or passion." Gorbachev went on to say that the future development of socialism had to be judged in connection with the overall development of contemporary civilization. To this end, one had to make good use of the experiences of other societies and social movements and all that was acceptable to socialism and that served the people. Thus the general secretary invited the SI to send a high-ranking delegation to Moscow to further discuss the form and content of a regular exchange of views between the CPSU and the SI.

33. See the dialogue between the Swiss Social Democrat, Jean Ziegler, and the Soviet expert on social democracy, Alexander Veber, in "Kommunisten und Sozialdemokraten.—Es ist an der Zeit, alten Hader zu begraben," *PFS*, no. 8 (1989):1081–91. Veber was then a consultant in the International Department of the CPSU Central Committee.

34. Stanislav Shatalin, "Chto znachit byt sovetnikom prezidenta," *Moskovskie novosti*, no. 14 (1990):6. The economist Shatalin was appointed to the Presidential Council by Gorbachev in March 1990. See also Chapter 2 herein.

Apart from the traditional issues of peace and disarmament, Gorbachev named as possible fields of future cooperation such topics as "the economy and ecology, the scientific-technological revolution, information, North-South conflicts, and perspectives on socialism and civilization as a whole."[35]

This list of topics indicates that the Moscow reformers hoped to reactivate those relations with representatives of socialism in Western Europe which had been consciously cut off by Lenin and his successors. High-ranking advisers to Gorbachev assessed the prospects of such a rapprochement quite optimistically. Georgii Shakhnazarov, for example, wrote in early 1989 that the main reasons for the split in the European left would disappear if only the CPSU concentrated henceforth on the concept of evolutionary transformation and centered its *perestroika* policy on combining socialism and democracy.[36]

At the same time, however, Gorbachev's catalogue of subjects suggests that by intensifying its relations with international social democracy, the CPSU had other objectives in mind than a simple reunification of the workers' movement. The reformers in Moscow considered social democracy a programmatic and political force in Western Europe that would greatly influence not only their immediate environment but also the dynamic process of pan-European cooperation and integration. Furthermore, they anticipated that close contacts with social democrats in Western Europe, including institutionalized ties, would prove helpful to the Soviet leadership's attempt to integrate their country as a civilized and respected partner into the political, cultural, and economic life of a Europe that was growing ever closer together. Gorbachev and his reform-oriented "Westernizers" saw this as the only alternative to a USSR uncoupled from Europe and pushed back toward Asia under the slogan of Europe "from Brest to Brest."

In the SI's declaration of principles we find a passage confirming its willingness to constructively support the process of liberalization and democratization, the creation of decentralized market mechanisms,

35. *Pravda*, October 18, 1989, 1. For more details, see S. Yastrzhembskii, "Povorot k novomy kachestvy," *Sotsialisticheskaya industriya* (Moscow), November 3, 1989, 3. See also Chapter 2 herein.

36. Georgii Shakhnazarov, "Vostok—Zapad: K voprosu deideologizatsii mezhdunarodnykh otnoshenii," *Kommunist*, no. 3 (1989):67–78.

the conduct of an open-door policy, and the protection of human rights in the Soviet Union and Eastern Europe. In the past this passage would have been strongly condemned as illegitimate interference in the internal affairs of the Soviet Union and its East European allies,[37] but at the close of the 1980s it met with the approval of CPSU reformers, who were guided by the same indispensable principles and norms of European tradition and civilization.

The Foreign Policy Dimension

With regard to international relations, the Soviet reformers were interested not only in the social democratic concepts regarding a "common security policy" for East and West but even more in the West European reformist left's ideas and initiatives relating to the future shape of Europe. In their positive reappraisal of the European Community, the reformers emphasized the "Euroleft's" successful drive for a social and ecological foundation on which to base Europe's internal integration. Even more important, however, was Moscow's hope to have the reformist left as a reliable ally working for the EC's greater opening to the East and as a constructive partner for building the projected "common European home."

Reflecting their concept of a "new internationalism," the Moscow reformers not only considered social democrats as representatives of the West's support of further integrating the Soviet Union into Europe, but as influential partners in trying to keep Eastern Europe's transition to democracy peaceful and in creating an all-European architecture of cooperation and mutual security. In the reformers' view, the political pluralization of Eastern Europe presented international social democracy with new and important tasks. In this regard, *Izvestiya* published a remarkable article in April 1990 which seemed to reflect a significant tendency within the new thinking.

The nature of Eastern Europe's transformation, according to the article, depended essentially on "how soon we succeed in creating guarantees for a peaceful transition free of violence and in neutraliz-

37. Sergei Yastrzhembskii, "Zayavka no globalnuyu missiyu," *MEMO*, no. 11 (1989):17–23. The basic declaration of the SI is in *Socialist Affairs* (London), no. 1–2 (1989):28–35.

ing the influence of nationalist and other forces of the extreme right." In this situation measures must be implemented to prevent an uncontrollable international process threatening constructive change and relations of trust in Europe. Here social democrats could play an especially stabilizing role since they had "gathered experience for more than a century in a non-confrontational political culture." To be sure, because of complicated political and economic circumstances it was not expected that revived social democratic parties would immediately attract too many followers. Still, it was certainly in the Soviet interest to see these currents develop into long-term "intellectual and political centers of gravity" participating to a large degree in the government's decision-making process.[38]

The growing attention paid by CPSU reformers to social democrats in Eastern Europe is noteworthy especially if one remembers how the reform-minded left was broken up by Moscow after World War II. This change of attitude was further underscored by Moscow's appeal to Western social democratic parties to "make good use of their solid potential for influencing the situation in Eastern Europe in a constructive way" and thus to contribute along with their SI sister parties there to a peaceful change of system.[39] To win over European social democracy in the East and West as an influential partner of the Soviet Union for crisis-management in Eastern Europe as well as for developing concepts and initiatives aimed at building cooperative structures in the whole of Europe—this was an important motive behind Moscow's new conciliatory approach.

"Social-Democratization" of the CPSU?

The CPSU reformers, however, maintained the view that the Soviet Union would be able to fully participate in European integration only if its leadership consistently promoted an internal transformation oriented toward the traditional norms and values of European civili-

38. Marina Pavlova-Silvanskaya and Sergei Yastrzhembskii, "Vostochnaya Evropa: Probil chas sotsial-demokratii?" *Izvestiya*, April 3, 1990, 5. The authors were working at the Moscow Institute for the Economy of the World Socialist System (headed by Oleg Bogomolov).

39. Ibid. See also Gorbachev's dialogue with Willy Brandt in *Pravda*, October 18, 1989, 7.

zation. That the reformers referred first of all to social democracy as one of the main intellectual-political currents of that tradition was certainly due to the fact that both their history and that of the social democrats went back to common roots in the international workers' movement.

On the other hand, the reformers considered social democracy a force that could in many respects serve the CPSU as a programmatic point of reference for its goal of a "democratic socialism" that successfully combined democracy and social justice, market and state regulation, economic growth and conservation. To this end, in 1988 Politburo member Medvedev specifically asked Soviet politicians to "earnestly look into the practice and concrete activities of today's social democratic parties" when organizing social and economic life. It should be noted that the CPSU's chief ideologue referred not only to the social democrats' success in social fields but also to "the general democratic achievements" gained through their hard struggle.[40]

When Soviet experts demanded, "We need our own Godesberg,"[41] they were not only expressing their wish to see the CPSU radically revise its program in a *formal* analogy to the famous SPD Congress of 1959 in Bad Godesberg (where the SPD formally relinquished Marxism in favor of a leftist people's party oriented to basic human values and a social market economy with mixed forms of property); implied also was the suggestion to carefully examine the *content* of social democratic programs and to use it for *perestroika* under Soviet conditions.[42]

In line with this resolve, reformers began studying social demo-

40. Vadim Medvedev, "Sovremennaya kontseptsiya sotsializma" (speech to sociologists of the "Socialist Community"), *Pravda*, October 5, 1988, 4. See also Karen Brutents's address at a conference in the Soviet Foreign Ministry, "Sotrudnichestvo i dialog s politicheskimi partiyami i dvezheniyami," *Mezhdunarodnaya zhizn* (Moscow), no. 10 (1988):37–42. Cf. my contribution, "The Communist Party of the Soviet Union: Reassessment of International Social Democracy: Dimensions and Trends," *The Journal of Communist Studies* (London), vol. 5, no. 2 (1989):173–84.

41. Boris Orlov, "Wir brauchen unser Godesberg. Zum Problem der Ausarbeitung eines neuen theoretischen Kurses der KPdSU," *Osteuropa* (Aachen), no. 2 (1990):95–104. See Volkov and Krasin, "Sotsializm vchera i zavtra," 15 (see note 25). In the authors' view the Godesberg Program of the SPD, which was formerly criticized as reformist, represents a central document in the changing paradigms of socialist thinking and acting.

42. Volkov and Krasin, "Sotsializm vchera i zavtra" (see note 25).

cratic concepts with great care. The CPSU theoretical organ *Kommunist* spread social democratic ideas down to the party base by publishing detailed excerpts from the latest SI program as well as from the draft of a new SPD program of general principles.[43] This was all the more remarkable because the CPSU's own revised program of 1986 was considered obsolete and was therefore hardly mentioned any more. Furthermore, researchers and publicists from Central Committee institutes and the Academy of Sciences worked intensively on the history, programs, and policies of international social democracy. Most noteworthy were the discussions and conclusions published by the Council for Research on Social Democracy established in 1987 by the Institute of Social Sciences of the CPSU CC. Experts from different institutes were members of this research council.[44] This high tide of articles, theses, and analyses on social democracy reached its peak in June 1989 when the Socialist International celebrated its centennial at its 18th Congress in Stockholm. The Soviet Union accepted an invitation to send a delegation as observers.[45]

43. For extracts from the new SI basic declaration, see *Kommunist*, no. 16 (1989): 116–21; for extracts from the SI resolution on environmental protection, see *RKSM*, no. 1 (1990):104–20. Essential parts of the SPD draft program are to be found in *Kommunist*, no. 9 (1989):107–14.

44. Institut obshchestvennykh nauk pri Tsk KPSS (henceforth ION), ed., *Sotsialdemokratiya v sovremennom mire* (Moscow: Laboratory paperbacks, 1989). The central part of this book is a discussion by experts on "Social Democratic Ideology in the Present Stage," with an introduction by Boris Orlov, 14–65. Also the book discusses inter alia aspects of Austro-Marxism and contemporary French socialism. Materials of the ION Research Council were published under the title "100-letie II Internatsionala" (see note 16).

45. In addition to sources in note 44, see ION, ed., *K 100-letiyu II Internatsionala* (Moscow: Laboratory paperbacks, 1989); I. M. Krivoguz, "Soznatelnyi rabochii nikogda ne otrechaetsya: K 100-letiyu Vtorogo Internatsionala," *Politicheskoe obrazovanie*, no. 10 (1989):89–95; Sergei Yastrzembskii, "Zayavka na globalnuyu missiyu," (see note 37); Krasin, "Sotrudnichat" (see note 16). More contributions are to be found in *Kommunist*, no. 12 (1989), 116–20, as well as in *RKSM*, no. 5 (1989), 49–75. See also A. A. Galkin and Yuriy Krasin, "K novomy kachestvy dialoga," *MEMO*, no. 2 (1989):87–92; this article refers to a symposium of representatives of European communist and socialist parties in December 1988 near Bonn, where the SPD–German Socialist Unity Party (SED) paper on "The Controversy of Ideologies and Common Security" was discussed. See also the positive assessments in the CPSU Central Committee greetings to the 18th SI Congress, in *Pravda*, June 20, 1989, and those by A. B. Veber in his summary, "K novomu urovnyu vzaimoponimaniya," in *Pravda*, July 20, 1989. Not without justification, the antireformist leadership of the Chinese Communist Party blamed the CPSU for its betrayal of Marxism-Leninism and its shift to

The conclusions about social democracy reached in these publications may be briefly summed up as follows.[46]

First of all, when conceiving their policies and putting them into practice, social democrats do not let themselves be guided by a binding ideology or a ready-made model. They rather orient themselves to certain fundamental values like freedom, equality, justice, and solidarity, and adapt their policies accordingly to any given circumstance. This approach not only has the advantage of doing away with "the idea that 'socialism' consists of a catalogue of 'definite characteristics' (like social ownership of the means of production, a planned economy, the leading role of the party, etc.),"[47] but also creates the basis for transforming social democratic parties into leftist people's parties where representatives of different social groups and ideological orientation can find their place.

Second, democracy does not merely serve as an instrument for implementing policies aimed at realizing fundamental values, but rather marks the path *and* goal of a "democratic socialism." Social demo-

---

positions of "social democratism under new historical conditions." As a secret memorandum of the Beijing Politburo correctly put it, "The essence of this lies in the denial of the class struggle in the international framework, the transformation of the character of communist parties and the pursuit of the policy of Western parliamentary democracy" (*Zheng Ming* [Hong Kong], April 1990); see *Die Tageszeitung* (West Berlin), May 31, 1990.

46. For examples of the examination of social democratic programs and policies by Soviet analysts, see, in addition to the above cited works: "Sotsial-demokratiya i sovremennyi mir" (Theses by experts of the Academy of Sciences' Institute for the International Workers' Movement, Moscow), *RKSM*, no. 1 (1989):21–30; Sergei Peregulov, "Sotsial-demokraticheskaya model obshchestvennykh otnoshenii," *MEMO*, no. 5 (1990):5–20. Also see the comprehensive works by Boris Orlov, especially: "Perestroika i teoreticheskie podkhody sotsial-demokratii," *RKSM*, no. 5 (1988):125–31; "Sotsial-demokratiya: Portret bez chernoi retushi," *Kommunist Estonii* (Tallinn), no. 11 (1989):53–71; "Wer hat Angst vor der Sozialdemokratisierung?," *Neue Zeit*, no. 6 (1990):24–25. In spring 1990 the Moscow "Politizdat" press published a book on "modern social democracy" which for the first time in the Soviet Union described the history and the ideological and political development of the social democratic movement. It also contained detailed descriptions of the SI and its member parties as well as biographies of former social democratic politicians of the 1970s and 1980s; reported by the East German news agency, ADN, March 6, 1990.

47. Volkov and Krasin, "Sotsializm vchera i zavtra," 15 (see note 25). See German Diligenskii in a roundtable discussion, *Pravda*, January 21–22, 1990. For Diligenskii, a department head at the Institute of the World Economy and International Relations of the Academy of Sciences, "socialism is first of all a system of values which are humanistic in their essence."

crats work for the democratization of all areas of life so that the right of the individual will be guaranteed equally with social justice for all groups of society.

Third, the state and its institutions in the West are not one-sidedly determined by capital but play an autonomous role and are arenas of contention. Depending on the respective balance of power, they may serve the workers' movement as levers to secure far-reaching political rights and social improvements. This has been achieved especially in Scandinavia but also in the Federal Republic of Germany and Austria.

Fourth, social democrats have moved away from the postulate that state property is the highest form of social property. They have convinced themselves of the advantages of well-functioning market mechanisms. They have successfully developed and practiced ways to lead their economies onto the path of progress by using various methods and combinations of state regulation, workers' participation, and institutions based on social partnership.

Finally, the welfare state is the social democrats' "greatest contribution to world civilization."[48] At the same time, social democrats are developing promising concepts to fight the negative consequences of an industrialization one-sidedly aimed at achieving quantitative growth (at the expense of environmental damage and inhumane technology). The market economy is to become compatible with ecological and humane values. By reconciling traditional interests of the workers' movement with those of "post-materialistic" social groups, social democrats have a good chance to assert themselves as an influential political force in the face of rapid changes in the economy, values, and the whole of society.

On the whole, in other words, Western Europe's reform-minded left has not at all capitulated to the interests of capital, we read in an impressive Soviet analysis of "functional socialism" in Sweden, "functional democracy" in Austria, and "productive democracy" in West Germany. Through a combination of partnership and strong social opposition, it is said, the left since World War II has succeeded in winning very strong positions within the overall structure of society. This has led to a "qualitative change" in the situation of the working

---

48. Orlov, "Sotsial-demokratiya," 64 (see note 46).

class and its organizations with regard not only "to material but also to legal and political conditions."[49]

Common Tasks

The next logical step after this positive reappraisal was the CPSU's turning away from its former most favored partners, the traditionalist communist parties, and toward social democratic, socialist, and reform-oriented communist parties (such as the PCI). Clearly, the search for what the latter groups had in common with the CPSU was becoming more and more important. By the beginning of the 1990s, references to continuing ideological-programmatic differences, obligatory in the past, were seldom made.

Indicative of the CPSU reformers' orientation toward international social democracy was a detailed catalogue of topics in three problem areas set forth in 1989 by the innovative Council for Research on Social Democracy as worthy of discussion and conducive to further rapprochement.[50]

The first area was the history of the workers' movement, with the following topics slated for investigation: "the positive and negative experiences of communist and social democratic parties in governmental activities"; "an assessment of the Second International's most prominent leaders and their influence on theory"; and an evaluation of "crucial points in the history of the workers' movement" (that is, international social democracy's conduct in 1914, the October Revolution and the schism in the workers' movement, and the breaking up of East European social democratic parties after 1945).

A second complex of topics was of a more current practical political nature. According to the Soviet experts it should include, apart from central aspects of foreign and security policy, the following: "democratization of all areas of social life and a reliable system for

---

49. Peregulov, "Sotsial-demokraticheskaya model," 15 (see note 46). Peregulov was at the time a department head at the Institute of the World Economy and International Relations.

50. "100-letie II Internatsionala," 13–14; see Krasin, "Sotrudnichat," 122 (for both, see note 16).

securing fundamental human rights"; "protection of religious, ethnic and intellectual-political minorities and their democratic rights"; and "creation of a close alliance between the workers' movement and new democratic movements."

The most difficult tasks, the analysts believed, arose from the third area, which concerned the joint formulation of guidelines for political action. The topics included: "new criteria for and paths to social progress"; "cooperation and mutual interaction between both socio-political systems"; "optimization of the relationship between spontaneity and consciousness in the development of today's world"; and "*perestroika* of socialist society and the evolution of both streams of the workers' movement."

The authors of this list of topics for discussion among Soviet reform communists and European social democrats pointed out that it should be augmented by other problem areas. Still, the catalogue as it is provides us with a good idea of the dynamics and depth at that time of Moscow's reorientation toward the West European reform-minded left. This change of outlook becomes even more evident when one looks at the CPSU's concomitant criticism of and increasing distance from Western Europe's orthodox communist parties.

Turning Away from Orthodox Western Communist Parties

When Vadim Zagladin, the Soviet expert on Western affairs, announced in April 1986 that the CPSU considered itself an "integral part of the European left" just like the PCI, Western media reactions ranged from disbelief and amazement to derisive caricatures.[51] The ideological-political gap between the CPSU and the West European reformist left torn apart by Lenin and his successors was too deep for anyone to take this announcement seriously.[52]

51. "Anche il Pcus è sinistra europea," interview with Zagladin in *la Repubblica* (Rome), April 12, 1986. The most biting cartoon was in the April 14 issue of the PCI daily, *l'Unità*.

52. The relations between the CPSU and the reformist left since the October revolution are a central topic of my book, *The Decline of the World Communist Movement* (Boulder, Colo.: Westview Press, 1987).

The PCI as a Bridge to Europe

This view greatly changed following the transformation of the CPSU itself. Looking back, it seems no accident that Zagladin gave this surprising signal precisely at the 17th Congress of the PCI, a party that had been criticized repeatedly and sharply by the CPSU during the Brezhnev era because of its programmatic revisionism and foreign policy inclination toward the West.[53] With the advent of Gorbachev, the pro-European PCI, which insisted that the EC combine its internal integration with an opening to the East as the Soviet Union also desired, came to be highly regarded in Moscow as the biggest and most influential communist party in Western Europe. Furthermore, Moscow viewed the PCI as an example of innovative communist party thinking for having long propagated a revision of central Marxist-Leninist doctrines within the communist movement.

Against this background the PCI was seen in Moscow as an important additional bridge to Europe—a political bridge to the Europe of the EC and a programmatic bridge to international social democracy and its concepts. And the PCI bridge also played an important role in Soviet domestic affairs. It was after all much easier to confront one's conservative opponents at home when one was able to justify new thinking and acting by pointing to the similar concepts and goals of the biggest communist party in the West. It was thus only consistent that, as Joan Barth Urban recounts in Chapter 2, Gorbachev met with PCI leaders on a number of occasions during the second half of the 1980s and evaluated their strategy positively.[54] Typically enough, the

53. See Joan Barth Urban, *Moscow and the Italian Communist Party: From Togliatti to Berlinguer* (Ithaca, N.Y.: Cornell University Press, 1986).

54. See, for example, the results of the visit to Moscow by PCI general secretary Achille Occhetto in March 1989, in *l'Unità*, March 1–2, 1989. For Moscow's radical reassessment of PCI policy, see Vladimir K. Naumov, "IKP pered sezdom," *Kommunist*, no. 1 (1989):102–12; L. B. Popov, "Tribuna marksistskoi mysli IKP," *Kommunist*, no. 4 (1989):118–22. Characteristically, beginning in 1989 the Prague-based, Soviet-dominated periodical, *Problemy mira i sotsializma* (*Probleme des Friedens und des Sozialismus* in the German version) gave high-ranking PCI officials the opportunity to present in detail the past and present line of the PCI: e.g., the theorist Giuseppe Vacca (no. 7, 1989); the foreign policy expert Antonio Rubbi (no. 4, 1989), and the Directorate members Fabio Mussi (no. 8, 1989) and Massimo D'Alema (no. 1, 1990). See also Antonio Rubbi, *Incontri con Gorbaciov* (Rome: Riuniti, 1990); here the leader of the PCI's Foreign Department describes the substance of the seven CPSU-PCI summit meetings held between 1984 and 1989. See also Chapter 2 herein.

constructive role of the SI was emphasized during these discussions and the PCI expressed its intention to join that organization as a full member as soon as possible.

Western Europe's Orthodox Communist Parties Sidelined

This politico-programmatic rapprochement with the PCI and the West European reform-minded left made the CPSU's growing distance from communist orthodoxy all the more obvious: for it increasingly turned away from the communist parties of France, Portugal, and Greece, all still relatively strong with 10 percent of the vote, and also from communist party sects in the Federal Republic of Germany (FRG), Austria, and Denmark. In their striving for a socialism removed from real life, these parties were still able to communicate with each other by using a "jargon of abstract ideals," Krasin wrote. "But outside the circle of those initiated into the secret mythology, nobody understood a jargon that ignores reality with all its dark sides and contradictions."[55]

In all probability the CPSU is going to maintain its relations with these communist parties but at a greatly reduced level and with an ever louder accompaniment of mutual polemics.[56] This requires a difficult balancing act not only by the CPSU but also by the Western communists. In the past, they more or less uncritically followed Soviet orthodoxy, drawing strength and self-confidence from the knowledge that they belonged to a world revolutionary movement and would be, finally, the victors of history. On the threshold of the 1990s they had to seek their salvation in a highly problematic demarcation from the CPSU while at the same time emphasizing their own specific historical conditions and national characteristics.[57] In this way, the traditional

55. Yuriy Krasin, *Perestroika i problemy teorii sotsializma* (Moscow: ION, 1988), 27. The book comprises instruction materials for the CPSU CC Institute of Social Sciences.

56. See Timmermann, "Die KPdSU und das internationale kommunistische Parteiensystem" (see note 2). Also, CPSU material aid to its supporters among the Western communists seems to have ended. An example of this is the drastic reduction in sales of the British Communist Party daily, *The Morning Star,* from 12,000 to 3,000 copies; see the French news agency AFP, October 25, 1989, and *Le Monde* (Paris), January 9, 1990, 4.

57. See the recent book by PCF general secretary Georges Marchais, *Démocratie* (Paris: Messidor, 1990), and his essay, "Der Sozialismus und wir," *Probleme des*

communist parties contributed their part to the liquidation of communism as an international movement even though they were forced to keep conjuring up its existence because their identity depended on it.

It was rare, however, for the Moscow reformers to criticize orthodox West European communist parties directly, and even then such criticism was always accompanied by a sharp condemnation of the CPSU's former hegemonism vis-à-vis these parties. Gorbachev, in his conversation with PCF General Secretary Georges Marchais in September 1989, confined himself to remarking that differences of opinion on the new thinking "seem to come from underestimating the fundamental changes in the development of civilization."[58] Earlier that year, Politburo member Yakovlev had warned the communists of the FRG in much clearer terms "not to deceive themselves and look for comfort in the illusion that the infallibility of a dogma is more important than development and that it stands above life." The only ones who can allow themselves this attitude, Yakovlev explained, are those "who study Marxism without relating it to reality and who bear no responsibility for the fate of mankind."[59]

In the meantime, the media and scholarly publications in Moscow clearly spelled out the deficiencies of these Western communist parties. They cited their clinging to "étatism," to quantitative growth, and to projected collectivism and their uncritical optimism with regard to progress, as well as their basic assessment of foreign relations as an ongoing class struggle between "socialism" and "imperialism." Because of this traditional outlook, said the CPSU reformers, Western communist parties overlooked the new tasks and new challenges facing the West European left. Overcoming these deficiencies required, among other things, a redefinition of the role of the state, especially with regard to the extent and nature of its role as a regulator of the

---

Friedens und des Sozialismus, no. 2 (1990):151–56; as well as the related collection of articles, "PCF: Cheminement d'une stratégie," in the PCF theoretical organ *Révolution* (Paris), no. 525 (March 23, 1990). Politburo member Charles Fiterman meanwhile sharply criticized the anti-*perestroika* policy of his party; see his speech to the PCF CC in *Le Monde,* October 18, 1989, 10.

58. *Pravda,* September 23, 1989, 1.

59. Greeting message to the Congress of the West German Communist Party, in *Pravda,* January 7, 1989, 4.

economy; dealing with the scientific-technological revolution and its structural consequences in production and services; a redefinition of the term "progress" to include ecological imperatives; taking into account the changes in society and values as well as the growing concern for individualism; thinking and acting beyond national borders in an all-European dimension; and awareness of the increasing interdependence in international relations.

Yuriy Krasin's analyses of the programs and policies of orthodox Western communists were prime examples of such a negative evaluation. As early as 1988 he sharply criticized orthodox West European communist strategy with regard to domestic affairs. By ignoring the rapid changes in Western societies and values, he argued, these parties incurred the danger of "being pushed into the peripheral position of defending corporate issues." They thus ran the risk of "falling into the role of *ouvrièrism*," a role in which "loyalty to the class positions of the proletariat takes on a dogmatic character, remote from life." But now, Krasin said, the communists "must throw off the blinkers of obsolete ideological clichés and see reality as it is."[60]

This sally was directed against the French Communist Party (PCF), the hard core of Western Europe's traditional communism with its anti–social democratic, pseudo-revolutionary, ultra nationalist strategy (the PCF was at the time more and more side-lined and in the process of disintegration). The national Bolshevik line of the PCF and the communist parties close to it was also criticized in Moscow because it was combined with a fundamentalist opposition to the process of EC integration. In the view of the CPSU reformers, European unification could no longer be characterized according to Lenin's theory of "ultra-imperialism" as the path to "international counterrevolution." Rather, it was seen as an outgrowth of objective developments whereby national borders were being overcome and Europe as a whole was called upon to "play a creative role in history," and as corresponding to the subjective wishes of a great majority of the population. Apart from purely economic considerations, "historical, cultural, socio-political and geostrategic motives" were of great im-

60. Yuriy Krasin, "Rabochee dvizhenie v poiskakh demokraticheskoi alternativy," *Kommunist*, no. 14 (1988):68. See also Krasin, "Marksizm," 11 (see note 19).

portance. Those who ignored these aspirations, who only counted on protecting the interests of certain groups like peasants or workers in dying industrial areas, were going to be pushed onto the defensive with regard to European integration as well as in their own countries.[61]

In line with this argument, reformers in Moscow identified specifically with the PCI's concept of following "a European path to socialism." On this path, wrote Krasin, all components of the "Euroleft"—social democrats, reform-oriented communists, and alternative movements—should meet under the banner of pluralism and reciprocal tolerance and push the community toward progressive policies. The traditional West European communists were asked to give up their patterns of thought and transform "their mainly class-oriented confrontational policy into a mainly constructive participation in building the European community."[62]

Tendencies and Prospects

By late 1990 the rapid process of regrouping, erosion, and disintegration within the CPSU as well as the disappearance of a binding Soviet ideology of "socialism" made it highly difficult to predict the course of future developments in relations between the CPSU and the West European left. This was all the more true since inside and outside the former monopoly party social democratic-oriented groups were being formed that considered West European and international social democracy as their programmatic and political point of reference and that were entering into competition with the CPSU.[63]

A prognosis regarding future tendencies in some areas could nev-

61. See Ierusalimskii and Pankin, "Novyi etap zapadnoevropeiskoi integratsii," 22 (see note 13).

62. Ibid., 24.

63. The Social Democratic Association of the USSR was founded in mid-January 1990 in Tallinn; see Grant Gukasov, "Sotsial-demokraty," *Moskovskie Novosti*, no. 4 (1990):7. In May 1990 the Social Democratic Party of the Russian Republic was founded; see *Moskovskie Novosti*, no. 5 (1990). For the goals of this party, see the article of its co-chairman, Oleg Rumyantsev: "Über die autoritäre Modernisierung und die sozialdemokratische Alternative," *Die Neue Gesellschaft/ Frankfurter Hefte* (Bonn), no. 1 (1990):15–23. In March 1990 Rumyantsev was elected a member of the Congress of People's Deputies of the Russian Republic.

ertheless be ventured. It seemed rather probable that Gorbachev and his reformers would leave the orthodox communist parties in Western Europe to their fate just as they had done with the former ruling parties in Eastern Europe. Conceptual divergences between the CPSU and its former most favored partners would be likely to increase, especially since the changes in Moscow had in the meantime spread even into terminology. In CPSU documents one could no longer read terms like "dictatorship of the proletariat," "proletarian internationalism," or "two camps," terms that used to express the traditional identity of the international communist movement. Instead, terms like "revisionism," "pluralism," and "democratic socialism" were being used in a positive sense. CPSU reformers also spoke of creating a "civil society" as well as of a "new internationalism" at a time of growing "interdependence." Such changes in the central terminology of a system as decisively determined by ideology as Marxism-Leninism had to have far-reaching consequences. Bearing this in mind, we can appreciate how deep the ideological rift between the CPSU and the traditionalist current in Western communism must have become.

At the same time, CPSU reformers were likely to intensify their relations with Western Europe's social democratic parties not only for foreign policy reasons but also because of a programmatic rapprochement. This trend could be expected to accelerate insofar as the reformers continued to characterize Lenin's ideological-political teachings as the outgrowth of a particular situation at a particular time, or to revise them on the ground that they had become outdated and invalidated by the course of history. By 1990 Soviet documents no longer claimed that social democrats had "nowhere succeeded in building socialism." In the past, this standard argument had served the CPSU as an instrument to sharply demarcate the ideological difference between the communist movement and social democracy. Traditional communist parties in the West continued to advance this argument. Instead of drawing such a demarcation line, CPSU reformers oriented themselves toward concepts that had developed historically in West European countries under the influence of social democratic parties and that had provided employees with the opportunity for comprehensive participation.

Against this backdrop, a further "social-democratization" of the

CPSU (or a large part of it) seemed as possible as the SI's willingness in principle to support this change from the outside. SI member parties might, for instance, integrate reform-minded currents of the CPSU step by step into the Socialist International. This, in turn, could help Gorbachev and his "Westernizers" in their efforts to bring Russia closer to European traditions and to integrate the country into pan-European developments.

Whether or not this could be done, however, depended not only on the good intentions of reform-oriented elites in East or West, but on whether the population in the Slavic heartland and its political representatives would in the long term be able and willing to join this process with all its consequences. After all, as a CPSU protagonist of *perestroika* put it, "social-democratization is the sign of a higher culture in politics, economics, and life. It is very hard for people to adapt to it who are used to living by the rule: received-distributed, ordered-obeyed. It is as difficult as algebra or higher mathematics for people who prefer their abacus to a computer."[64]

Viewed in this context, intensified contacts between the CPSU reformers and Western socialists might be able to effectively support the transformation process in the Soviet Union. The transformation itself, however, had to grow out of the heart of the country. The prospects for success in this regard were, on the eve of 1991, very uncertain indeed. In point of fact, developments were by then characterized less by an orientation toward Europe and outreach by reform communists toward international social democracy than by a backward-turning inner dynamic, by a condition of growing tensions and sharpening conflicts. Was this trend irreversible or could those reform forces still prevail which aimed to transform the Soviet Union into a federation of sovereign states and launch it on the path of a "civil society"? The future character of relations between Soviet reform communism and international social democracy ultimately depended on the answer to this question.

64. Orlov, "Wer hat Angst vor der Sozialdemokratisierung?," 25 (see note 46). In much the same sense, Gorbachev stated on several occasions that in the USSR "political culture" and the "culture of economic performance" were underdeveloped.

[2]

Gorbachev and the
Italian Communist Party:
From Breach to Embrace

Joan Barth Urban

The dramatic turnabout in Moscow's relations with the Italian Communist Party (PCI) in the first years of the Gorbachev era, the shift from breach to embrace, was a harbinger of the revolutionary changes that were to engulf Soviet domestic and foreign policy on the eve of the 1990s.

In January 1982 Soviet-PCI ties were on the verge of rupture. The Soviet-backed imposition of martial law in Poland prompted Enrico Berlinguer, PCI general secretary from 1972 until his sudden death in 1984, to declare that the October Revolution had "exhausted its propulsive force," its ability to build a society with legitimacy at home and drawing power abroad. Moscow reacted with a barrage of scathing press attacks, charging the PCI leadership with betraying Marxism-Leninism under the guise of "innovation" and speaking the language of "Reagan, Haig, Weinberger, and Brzezinski" in its foreign policy pronouncements. The end result was a brief but intensely polemical breach in relations, or *strappo* as the Italians called it, between the two parties.[1]

Just four years later the *strappo* had become a distant memory. In

---

1. For details, see Joan Barth Urban, *Moscow and the Italian Communist Party: From Togliatti to Berlinguer* (Ithaca, N.Y.: Cornell University Press, 1986), especially 315–21.

January 1986 Berlinguer's successor, Alessandro Natta, and several of his associates were the honored guests of the new Soviet leadership. At the end of two days of freewheeling and wide-ranging talks, Gorbachev hosted the Italians at an unprecedented banquet attended by all the members of the CPSU Politburo then present in Moscow.[2] Over the next few years numerous top-level meetings took place between the Soviet and PCI leaderships. By the end of the decade the Gorbachev reform team had launched a series of foreign policy initiatives and domestic transformations that could well have been scripted by Leonid Brezhnev's Eurocommunist critics in the PCI.

What light did these developments shed on the earlier Soviet-PCI *strappo?* What impelled Gorbachev to launch a virtual courtship of the PCI from the very start of his tenure as CPSU general secretary? To what extent did we see the "Eurocommunization" of Soviet domestic and foreign policy during the heyday of the Gorbachev revolution? Finally, how did the PCI respond to the truth so starkly brought home by the revolutions of 1989: that reform communism in the East was but a transitional stage on the path to a democratic political order in which the people's choice was overwhelmingly anticommunist? These are some of the questions that will be addressed in the following pages.

Reflections on the *Strappo*

The Soviet-PCI breach of January 1982 was a culmination of tensions that had been evident since 1956 and had worsened dramatically after the Soviet-led invasion of Czechoslovakia in 1968. The Italian Communists were increasingly alienated from the Soviets on a number of issues: Moscow's heavy-handed domination of Eastern Europe; the political repressiveness, economic inefficiency, and anti-

---

2. An account of this Soviet-PCI summit, as well as all other top-level CPSU-PCI meetings from 1984 through 1989, has been provided by Antonio Rubbi in *Incontri con Gorbaciov: I colloqui di Natta e Occhetto con il leader sovietico* (Rome: Riuniti, 1990). As head of the PCI's Foreign Affairs Section, Rubbi was involved in the preparation of the meetings with Gorbachev as well as in keeping the stenographic account of their proceedings.

human rights policy of "real, existing socialism" in the USSR; the militarization of Soviet policy in the Third World along with the Kremlin's power political rivalry with the United States in all areas of international concern; Moscow's criticism of West European integration; and, last but not least, the CPSU's unremitting efforts to impose an ideological straitjacket on the international communist movement.

On this last account if no other, the PCI was in a position to thwart Soviet wishes. Well before 1968 it had begun to obstruct the CPSU's efforts to forge a unified, Moscow-centered communist movement. In the 1970s, under the rubric of a "new internationalism" (the term the PCI juxtaposed to the CPSU's tired slogan of "proletarian internationalism"), the Italians called for an open-ended dialogue with non-Marxist center-left forces in Europe as well as with all communist parties, even those like the Chinese that were hostile to the USSR. By the beginning of the 1980s the crux of their "new internationalism" had become a push to mend the decades-old schism between communism and social democracy. Under these circumstances, the crushing of Solidarity in Poland actually worked to the PCI's advantage: it provided the impetus and justification for Berlinguer to reject the very idea of an international communist movement separate and distinct from other left-wing forces.

The Brezhnev Kremlin, on the other hand, used the occasion of the PCI's broad-gauged criticism of the crackdown in Poland to declare the Italian party leadership beyond the political pale. Long incensed by the Italian Communists' challenge to the CPSU's ideological credentials and international conduct, the Soviet leadership had *Pravda* and *Kommunist* denounce them in January 1982 as heretics and traitors to the international communist cause.

Some Western analysts speculated at the time that Moscow's violent polemical assault bespoke fear of the contagious impact of the PCI's innovative ideas within the Soviet Union. Just as one could at that time hypothesize the existence of tens of thousands of "closet Sakharovs" in Soviet society, one could readily suppose the presence of "closet Eurocommunists" in the CPSU apparatus.[3] If this actually

---

3. The author spoke of both possibilities in her university lectures during the early 1980s.

was the case, the media tirades were certainly comprehensible from the Brezhnev group's perspective. In fact, at least one Soviet expert on PCI affairs, Vladimir K. Naumov, testified in 1989 that the anti-PCI polemics of early 1982 became an integral part of the theoretical baggage and official judgments of the Brezhnev regime. As such they were used to discredit any effort to critically analyze Soviet social development or foreign policy. If anyone even hinted at such criticism, he was "immediately saddled with the label 'Italian,' as if to say 'dissident,' or worse."[4]

While there is no hard evidence on the extent to which PCI views and criticisms had penetrated the Soviet political establishment at the beginning of the 1980s, by the end of that decade it seemed fair to cite the old saw that actions speak louder than words. As will be discussed below, from the autumn of 1987 through the spring of 1990 one saw what amounted to the virtual Eurocommunization of the Soviet policy agenda. The reform team around Gorbachev not only had multiple contacts with PCI policymakers during the late 1980s; it also took steps, wittingly or not, to bring Soviet practice into line with long-standing Italian Communist positions on a whole range of issues.

Soviet insiders began to speak openly, moreover, of the eagerness with which a circle of young CPSU specialists and functionaries sought contacts with the PCI through the editorial offices of *Problems of Peace and Socialism* in Prague during the 1960s. After 1968 this Soviet-controlled outlet became the exclusive preserve of apparatchiks preoccupied with glittering accounts of "real, existing socialism" and jargon-laden polemics against anti-Sovietism of any kind. But from 1958 through 1964, under the editorship of Khrushchev's protégé, Aleksei M. Rumyantsev, the journal offices provided a forum for searching, eclectic debates among communist scholars and experts on a wide variety of themes relating to the post-Stalin communist movement.[5]

It is entirely plausible that ruling communists seeking to improve their exercise of power and nonruling communists seeking to come to

---

4. Vladimir Naumov, "Il Kommunist risponde," *Rinascita* 46, no. 10 (March 18, 1989):23.

5. Lilly Marcou, *Les pieds d'argile: Le communisme mondial au présent, 1970–1986* (Paris: Ramsay, 1986), 274, 291–93.

power by democratic means would have found common cause in the need to reform "real, existing socialism." It is not surprising, then, that a number of Gorbachev's closest associates during the heyday of *perestroika* were among those Soviet specialists reportedly in touch with the PCI through the Prague-based journal: notably Ivan Frolov, after 1985 editor of *Kommunist* and then of *Pravda* as well as adviser to Gorbachev on CPSU programmatic issues; Anatoliy Chernyaev, personal aide to Gorbachev in his post as general secretary from early 1986;[6] and Yevgeniy Ambartsumov, a specialist at the Institute for the Economies of the World Socialist System (now the Institute for International Economic and Political Studies) who was one of the first establishment intellectuals to publicly criticize the Soviet invasions of Czechoslovakia and Afghanistan.[7]

Vadim Zagladin reportedly also belonged to this circle. A longtime functionary of the CPSU's International Department, Zagladin was an enigmatic figure. As Soviet-PCI relations deteriorated in the late 1970s, he stood out as one of the Kremlin's most visible ideological watchdogs vis-à-vis the Italians. He nonetheless continued to serve as first deputy head of the International Department under Anatoliy Dobrynin and, from the autumn of 1988, as a foreign policy adviser to Gorbachev in his new post of President. Gorbachev himself, at a meeting with PCI leader Natta in March 1988, explained this paradox rather facetiously. According to an eyewitness account, as Zagladin and Chernyaev entered the room, Gorbachev quipped: "This would be the time to change them both. . . . They have a monopoly on relations with various parties . . . but we wouldn't know whom to substitute for them. . . . [W]e haven't bothered to prepare for replacements."[8] Such indeed may have been the crux of the matter. During the CPSU's polemics with Eurocommunism in the second half of the

6. According to Roy Medvedev, Chernyaev "had been one of Ponomarev's aides in the Department of International Affairs, but he was an honest and competent person, in no way tied to the Brezhnev group. He had entered politics through the Khrushchev apparat, and was a member of what we call 'the generation of the Twentieth Congress';" Roy Medvedev and Giulietto Chiesa, *Time of Change: An Insider's View of Russia's Transformation* (New York: Pantheon, 1989), 72.

7. Ibid., 70; see the interview with Ambartsumov in *Rinascita* 43, no. 42 (November 1, 1986):18; cf. *l'Unità*, July 9, 1988, 4.

8. Quoted from Rubbi's notes on the meeting in *Incontri*, 165–66 (see note 2).

1970s, not to mention the period of the *strappo,* contacts with the PCI and other Western communist parties could be safely maintained only by compliant and tested Brezhnevites. Thus Gorbachev remained dependent on the technical expertise of the old-line functionaries, even while seeking a new type of relationship with nonruling communists.

The recent suggestion of a particular interest in PCI thinking among Soviet specialists involved with *Problems of Peace and Socialism* in the 1960s, while plausible, may simply be a reflection of the great esteem in which the Italian Communists were held by the Gorbachev reformers two decades later. Indicative of that attitude was a highly laudatory article on the PCI by the above-cited V. K. Naumov which appeared in the January 1989 issue of *Kommunist.*[9] Soviet press coverage of Gorbachev's frequent meetings with Natta had up until that time avoided any mention of the *strappo.* Naumov proceeded to set the record straight. While the bulk of his article was devoted to the PCI's "wealth of intellectual potential and innovation," scattered throughout were also explicit or implicit admissions of the validity of the Italians' earlier criticisms of Soviet reality and expressions of regret over the CPSU's 1982 press attacks on the PCI leadership. There was, to be sure, no explicit reference to the Polish crisis that triggered the polemics or to Italian Communist denunciations of other aspects of the Kremlin's foreign policy such as the war in Afghanistan. But Naumov did specify that the PCI had argued that "socialism as a social system began to lose its attractiveness at a certain moment," an allusion to Berlinguer's famous statement that the October Revolution had "exhausted its propulsive force." And he went on to note, wryly, that if this assessment was accurate, "it was hardly fair to blame [the Italian party] for it."[10]

Naumov's article created quite a stir in Italy, where it was translated in full in the PCI's weekly, *Rinascita.*[11] Prior to its publication there, Antonio Rubbi, then head of the Italian party's Foreign Affairs Section, interpreted the *Kommunist* piece as part of the broader struggle being waged within the CPSU and the communist world in general

9. V. K. Naumov, "IKP pered sezdom," *Kommunist,* no. 1 (1989):102–12.
10. Ibid., 109.
11. "La perestrojka e le ragioni del Pci," *Rinascita* 46, no. 3 (January 28, 1989):27–30; both the title and subtitles in the Italian version were added by *Rinascita.*

between reformers and conservatives.[12] To this Naumov replied that he actually had "much more modest aims" in mind when he wrote the article: by clearing the PCI's record he hoped to contribute to the removal of the ideological and bureaucratic constraints upon Soviet social scientists studying international issues and questions relating to the communist movement. "It is no secret to anyone," he flatly declared, "that in the past, in the course of innumerable conferences, seminars, and meetings on such themes, the condemnation of the PCI for its 'revisionist' theoretical elaborations and ideological conceptions, and in particular for its criticisms of Soviet reality, of 'real socialism' in the period of stagnation . . . was not only 'in fashion' but was put forward as proof of 'loyalty' to Marxism-Leninism on the part of the speaker."[13]

Naumov was presumably in a position to know of what he spoke. A member of the Department of World Politics and International CPSU Activities of the CPSU Central Committee's Academy of Social Sciences in the 1980s, he had in the 1970s written a book on the PCI entitled *The Communists of Italy*. The first edition, which came out in 1972, concentrated on PCI domestic activity from 1956 through 1971, touching only indirectly on the party's long-term goal of socialist pluralism and not at all on contentious international issues such as the PCI's denunciation of the Warsaw Pact invasion of Czechoslovakia in 1968.[14] The second edition went somewhat further in its treatment of sensitive topics. Published in 1977, it gave a positive account of both the "historic compromise" policy of cooperation with Italian Christian Democrats in the mid-1970s and the PCI's accommodation to NATO, describing them as understandable adaptations to national conditions.[15] Nevertheless, large gaps and distortions remained in Naumov's discussion of international questions. In

12. Umberto de Giovannangeli, "A chi parla il Kommunist: Intervista a Antonio Rubbi," *Rinascita* 46, no. 2 (January 21, 1989):14.

13. Naumov, "Il Kommunist risponde," 23 (see note 4).

14. V. K. Naumov, *Kommunisty Italii* (Moscow: "Mezhdunarodnye Otnosheniia," 1972). Published in an edition of 6,000 copies, the book quickly sold out. In January 1973 this writer searched in vain for a copy in the bookstores of Moscow and Leningrad and was finally obliged to read it in the Leningrad State Public Library.

15. Carlo Benedetti, "Uno studioso sovietico sulla 'via italiana'," *l'Unità*, November 26, 1977, 3.

general he seems to have gleaned PCI sources for quotes to demonstrate the Italian party's unswerving support for Soviet foreign policy while saying nothing whatsoever about Eurocommunism or other points of obvious disagreement. Whether this approach denoted implicit criticism of the PCI, as suggested in the preface to the 1978 Italian edition (written by Enrico Berlinguer's brother, Giovanni),[16] or was simply an effort to avoid guilt by association with the Italian "revisionists," is difficult to discern. Whatever the case, to this writer's knowledge Naumov's byline never appeared on an article openly critical of the PCI.

Gorbachev's Courtship of the PCI

During his first year as CPSU general secretary, well before launching his policies of *glasnost* and *perestroika,* Gorbachev made abundantly clear his interest in a reconciliation with the Italian Communists. There were probably several reasons for his overtures to the PCI. The first had to do with the impact upon him of Enrico Berlinguer's funeral on June 13, 1984. As head of the CPSU delegation, Gorbachev saw firsthand the spontaneous outpouring of grief by a million and a half Romans crowded into Piazza San Giovanni as well as the many gestures of respect accorded to Berlinguer by the noncommunist Italian political establishment, including the transport of his coffin from Padua to Rome in the official jet of President Sandro Pertini. Seated next to the Chinese liberal reformer, Zhao Ziyang, in the front row of the tribune, from which all the highest state and government dignitaries of Italy also viewed the two-hour ceremony, Gorbachev came, saw, and comprehended that the PCI enjoyed genuine grassroots support and political legitimacy.[17] This must have

16. Vladimir Naumov, *Il Pci visto da Mosca* (Milan: Teti, 1978), 6.

17. Chiara Valentini, *Berlinguer* (Milan: Arnoldo Mondadori, 1989), 472–76; Rubbi, *Incontri,* 24–25, 27 (see note 2). Gorbachev, who led the CPSU delegation to the 11th Congress of the Portuguese Communist Party in 1983, must have also been struck by the contrast between the PCI's national stature and the isolated position of the sectarian Portuguese Communists in their country's political life; see Carlos Gaspar, "Portuguese Communism since 1976: Limited Decline," *Problems of Communism* 39, no. 1 (January–February 1990):61, note 111.

given pause to a Soviet leader who was soon to have reason to question whether the communist regimes in Eastern Europe or even the USSR enjoyed either.

Gorbachev also began early on to reach out to center-left, social democratic forces in Western Europe in order to muster support for his arms control initiatives and overall détente policy. But the success of those overtures hinged in part on Soviet readiness to acknowledge the social democrats as political and ideological equals, and the Kremlin could hardly project a credible image on that score if it refused to respect the independent views of the continent's largest nonruling communist party. The dilemma Gorbachev faced recalled the dilemma Khrushchev confronted in the mid-1950s vis-à-vis the Third World: Khrushchev could hardly expect to win friends in the emerging nonaligned movement while continuing to ostracize Tito's Yugoslavia, a founding member of that movement. Thus, just as Khrushchev had hastily patched up the Soviet-Yugoslav dispute on Tito's terms, Gorbachev moved toward a speedy rapprochement with the PCI on its terms.

From the start of his encounters with the PCI leaders, moreover, Gorbachev displayed an eagerness to learn from them. He invited their views, explanations, and advice on a wide range of issues, from European integration to conventional arms control to the vitality of the Italian economy. He wanted, of course, to benefit from the ties the Italian Communists had been developing with European socialists and social democrats since the 1970s. But in addition, as will be detailed below, he sought to understand not simply how to build bridges to center-left sectors of European political opinion but what policies to pursue once those bridges were built.

Early Overtures, 1984–1985

Gorbachev's presence at the head of the CPSU delegation to Berlinguer's funeral was in itself significant because the upcoming Soviet leader had not been involved in any way with the *strappo*. Indeed, he had met Berlinguer only once for ten minutes during a vacation trip to Italy in the late summer of 1972. At that time Gorbachev and his wife Raisa were, according to their Soviet interpreter, Viktor Gaiduk, enchanted by a two-week stay in Sicily near Palermo and subsequent tour of Rome, Turin, Florence, and Venice. It was at the national festival of the communists' daily newspaper, *l'Unità*, in Turin that the Gorbachevs were introduced to Berlinguer, only recently promoted to general secretary of the PCI.[18]

The Soviet media's coverage of Berlinguer's death captured the ambiguity of Moscow's attitude toward the PCI at that moment. The news of his stroke on June 8, 1984, was played down or ignored until June 11, the day he actually died. That evening, on the other hand, the "Vremya" telecast devoted eight minutes to the deceased leader and the next day *Pravda* announced his death on the front page, printed CPSU general secretary Konstantin Chernenko's telegram of condolences on the second, and carried a three-column biographical article on the fourth. But the gist of all the tributes was the distorted message that Berlinguer had been a faithful comrade devoted to the USSR and its role in the world.[19]

Whatever the lingering hesitancy of the Brezhnev-era functionaries in the Kremlin, Gorbachev was noncombative and forthcoming during this first encounter with members of the PCI leadership. The evening after the funeral, the Soviet ambassador to Italy hosted a dinner for Gorbachev, Zagladin (also a member of the CPSU delegation), and several Italian Communist figures closely associated with the USSR over the years. The latter group included Giancarlo Pajetta, Paolo Bufalini, and Rubbi, who was responsible for the stenographic accounts of this and subsequent meetings between Gorbachev and the PCI.[20]

During the dinner Gorbachev steered the conversation away from the highly charged controversy over intermediate-range nuclear forces (INF) in Europe to the domestic Soviet scene. Zagladin and the others had initially broached the question of Berlinguer's abortive efforts earlier that year to persuade Moscow to accept the idea of a mutual Soviet-American freeze on further INF deployment as a prerequisite for the resumption of negotiations over their reduction.[21] Instead,

18. "Quelle conversazioni in Sicilia nel '72," *l'Unità*, December 1, 1989, 4; Rubbi, *Incontri*, 18 (see note 2).

19. Rubbi, *Incontri*, 20–21.

20. Ibid., 99, 166.

21. Ibid., 27–29.

Gorbachev suddenly launched into a discussion of the Soviet economy. To the astonishment of the Italians, he spoke of the need for profound changes in the structure of the economic system in terms that echoed the "Novosibirsk Memorandum" of reform-minded Soviet economists which, though still not officially in the public domain, had made its way into the hands of the PCI leadership. And he concluded with an even more surprising reference to the nationality question in the USSR, saying that it had been simply put aside, not resolved, and that some abuses had actually gotten worse.[22] While the subject of the Soviet-PCI *strappo* did not come up, Gorbachev plainly shared the Italians' judgment that something was rotten in the land of "real, existing socialism."

Before the Soviet delegation's departure the next day, Bufalini did briefly touch on his party's differences with Moscow, pointing out that they involved not just specific incidents but concepts, strategies, and values. Replied Gorbachev, "We can discuss even this and, who knows, we may find points of convergence."[23]

Upon becoming general secretary right after Chernenko's death in March 1985, Gorbachev promptly began to reach out to the PCI. The remainder of that year saw several signals of his interest in a reconciliation.

The Italian Communist delegation to Chernenko's state funeral was, first of all, particularly well treated. Composed of Natta, Rubbi, and Emanuele Macaluso, whom Gorbachev had met during his 1972 trip to Sicily, it was the first group of nonruling communists to be received by the new CPSU leader the day after the funeral, in a meeting that lasted over one hour. As was the case at Berlinguer's funeral, during their conversation Gorbachev stressed the urgency of making sharp changes in domestic policy (much to the consternation of International Department head, Boris Ponomarev, who was also present) but touched very little on foreign policy. He did, however, speak of the need to begin an entirely new chapter in Soviet-PCI relations, to create the conditions for dialogue and mutual understanding; and to this end it was agreed that a top-level meeting of the two parties should take place as soon as feasible.[24]

22. Ibid., 31–34.
23. Ibid., 37.
24. Ibid., 50–56.

A further sign of Gorbachev's receptivity to the Italian Communists was his unscheduled meeting of seventy minutes toward the end of May 1985 with Gianni Cervetti of the PCI *Direzione,* the Italian party's top policymaking body. Cervetti, an acquaintance of the Soviet leader from their student days together at Moscow State University,[25] was in Moscow in his capacity as chairman of the communist group in the European Parliament. In response to Cervetti's suggestion that the European Community (EC) be viewed in political (rather than ideological) terms, Gorbachev indicated his interest in normalizing relations between the EC and the Soviet trade bloc, Comecon.[26] This was a step long favored by the PCI but hitherto rejected by Moscow.

Likewise indicative of Gorbachev's openness to the PCI was his use, the following October, of words very similar to those of the longtime Italian party leader, Palmiro Togliatti, to describe the character of the international communist movement. In his speech introducing a revised version of the CPSU Program to the Central Committee, Gorbachev spoke of "a dialectical unity of diversity," a clear reference to Togliatti's idea of "unity in diversity."[27] This public show of deference to the PCI was all the more notable in that it followed by one day Natta's castigation during a visit to Beijing of the two superpowers' push for "superiority" and "hegemony."[28] In other words, in response to an innuendo that would have enraged the Kremlin in the days of Brezhnev, Gorbachev turned the other cheek.

The January 1986 Soviet-PCI Summit

This conciliatory demeanor was to characterize the new Soviet leadership's attitude toward every aspect of the precedent-breaking two-day summit with the PCI that was finally scheduled for January 27–28, 1986. When Rubbi went to Moscow in mid-December to arrange details of Natta's forthcoming visit, he was already struck by the cordiality and flexibility of his Soviet counterparts. He was

---

25. See the articles by Dino Messina and Claudio Schirinzi in *Corriere della sera,* December 2, 1989, 5, 34.
26. See Giulietto Chiesa's interview with Cervetti in *l'Unità,* May 22, 1985, 4.
27. Text of speech in *Pravda,* October 16, 1985, 2.
28. "Il ringraziamento del segretario generale del Pci," *l'Unità,* October 15, 1985, 5.

warmly welcomed by old friends who had only recently shied away from seeing him socially. The PCI's request for a working summit of only two days (shorn of ceremonial sightseeing), as well as the news that the Italian general secretary would not attend the CPSU's upcoming 27th Congress, were received with equanimity. Only Rubbi's proposal that the customary joint communiqué be replaced by an exchange of post-banquet "toasts," the texts of which would be published in full by each party (a procedure followed during Natta's visit to Beijing earlier that autumn), met with some resistance. But the next day it too was accepted, apparently after deliberation at higher levels.[29]

The Gorbachev-Natta meeting of January 1986 was the first Soviet-PCI summit since October 1978, if one discounts the brief encounters at the Kremlin's three state funerals between 1982 and 1985. In 1978 relations between the parties were already very tense. To this writer it appeared that Berlinguer had gone to Moscow at that time to bolster his party's revolutionary credentials in the eyes of Italian militants who were increasingly restive over the PCI's participation in a parliamentary majority dominated by the Christian Democrats. Indeed, he seemed to have cut a deal whereby the Italians would refrain from undertaking a rapprochement with the Chinese Communist Party in return for Soviet polemical restraint vis-à-vis the PCI.[30] Rubbi, in his account of the 1986 meeting, recalled the 1978 summit as "the most stormy in which I ever took part," describing Brezhnev-era ideologue Mikhail Suslov as beside himself with rage at Berlinguer's criticism of the repression and forced expatriation of Soviet dissidents.[31]

The character of the 1986 meeting was dramatically new and different.[32] This was clear at the outset when Ponomarev, soon to be replaced by Anatoliy Dobrynin as head of the International Department, did not appear at Gorbachev's side. Instead of Ponomarev's doctrinal scrutiny and "pedantry,"[33] Gorbachev took charge of the

---

29. Rubbi, *Incontri*, 71–73.

30. Urban, *Moscow and the Italian Communist Party*, 301–2 (see note 1).

31. Rubbi, *Incontri*, 82.

32. Ibid., 77–102; cf. Giulietto Chiesa's report from Moscow in *l'Unità*, January 28, 1986, 1, 20.

33. This was the term used by Gorbachev in his after-dinner speech to describe the character of past Soviet-PCI relations. See "Così i brindisi di Natta e Gorbaciov," *l'Unità*, January 29, 1986, 7; cf. *Pravda*, same date, 2.

talks, investing the daily four-hour sessions with an air of conversational informality. Indeed, Pajetta, who—along with Rubbi and Renato Sandri—accompanied Natta on this visit, reported afterwards that he was "amazed by the flexibility, the absence of that pedagogical, almost missionary approach" he had encountered in meetings with Soviets for some thirty-odd years.[34]

When differences arose, moreover, they were resolved to the satisfaction of the Italians. On the first day, for instance, Rubbi was startled by the wooden and outdated quality of the draft text of Gorbachev's after-dinner speech, or "toast." The next day he was shown a revised version which, though still not entirely reflecting the mood and ideas actually projected by the Soviet leader during the talks, was nonetheless a considerable improvement.[35] In the same vein, the Soviet draft of the joint introduction that was to precede the texts of the two after-dinner speeches carried a number of one-sided formulations, such as the omission of any allusion to independent political positions, a notion the Italians successfully insisted on including in the final text.[36]

As for the substance of the talks, Gorbachev again discussed the problems of the Soviet economy and the nationality question and spoke of the need for *glasnost*, for truth at all levels of the society, remarking that "disinformation has flourished throughout the country."[37] He likewise stressed his commitment to "new thinking" in international relations and to far-reaching arms reductions. But he did not broach the kind of deep political and institutional reforms the PCI had been calling for since 1982, and he still displayed overriding preoccupation and intransigence toward the U.S. strategic defense initiative, describing how he nearly got up and walked out of his talks with President Reagan at the Geneva summit of November 1985 on this account. Moreover, he clung to the concept of an international communist movement separate and distinct from social democracy and, needless to say, more ideologically and historically correct. In this regard he urged the PCI to consider the merits of a world con-

34. *Panorama*, February 3, 1986; cf. *l'Unità*, February 9, 1986, 2.
35. Rubbi, *Incontri*, 84–86, 96.
36. Ibid., 83–84.
37. Quoted in ibid., 81.

ference of communist parties; while conceding that conditions were not yet ripe for such a gathering, he stressed the intrinsic value of this kind of multilateral forum.[38]

On balance, therefore, it was not so much Gorbachev's concrete ideas as his candor, conviviality, and readiness to listen to others which most impressed the members of the PCI delegation. With respect to this last attribute, the Soviet leader specifically asked the Italians to help him better understand the structure, functioning, and policies of the European Community.[39] It was indeed this willingness to listen and learn that was to prove crucial from the PCI's point of view.

From the 27th CPSU Congress to the Seventieth Anniversary of the October Revolution

In his report to the 27th CPSU Congress on February 25, 1986, Gorbachev was even more ambiguous with respect to his policy agenda, as Western analysts widely noted. This was true not only of domestic and foreign policy but also policy toward the global left, an area of direct concern to the PCI. On the one hand, the Soviet leader defined the unity of the communist movement in a manner long advocated by the Italian party: "Unity has nothing in common with uniformity, with hierarchy, with interference by some parties in the affairs of others, with the striving by any party to have a monopoly on truth." On the other hand, he spoke of social democracy in terms wholly unacceptable to the Italians: "It goes without saying that the ideological differences between communists and social democrats are deep; their experience and achievements are not the same and are not of equal value."[40] If from the time of the *strappo* the PCI had denied the existence of an international communist movement—after Berlinguer's death rejecting even the notion of Eurocommunism—it now sought to identify itself with the social democratic "Euroleft." In fact, the rallying cry of its forthcoming 17th Congress was the assertion

38. Ibid., 91–95.
39. Ibid., 89.
40. *Pravda*, February 26, 1986, 8.

that the PCI was an "integral part of the European left," a point Natta made clear to Gorbachev in January.[41] Gorbachev's denigration of social democracy was thus wholly out of line with PCI policy.

Still, the Italian Communist delegation to the 27th CPSU Congress was treated with considerable warmth and respect, even though its composition was rather provocative. Led by Secretariat member Ugo Pecchioli, the group included historian Giuseppe Boffa, whose commentaries on the Soviet Union over the previous decade had often been derogatory, and who even following the 27th Congress published a series of articles in *l'Unità* which were notably cautious on the prospects for reform under Gorbachev.[42] Because of his criticisms of the USSR dating back to Soviet policy toward China in the late 1960s, Boffa had been ostracized by the Kremlin and had not been able to visit the USSR for a number of years. According to PCI insiders, however, his two-volume *History of the Soviet Union*—a work of Western-style scholarship—had appeared shortly before the 27th Congress in a restricted Russian edition and had been read by Gorbachev himself.

At a 1989 Soviet-PCI summit in which Boffa participated, Gorbachev confirmed this. After expressing his pleasure at finally meeting the Italian historian, he explained the emergence of a group of reform leaders in the Soviet Union in the following way: "We prepared ourselves in silence for years, and reading foreign works that the Progress publishing house printed in a very limited number of copies and distributed only to a restricted circle of leaders helped us very much. In this way, Comrade Boffa, I got to know your writings."[43]

In addition to the symbolic importance of Boffa's inclusion in the 1986 PCI delegation, Pecchioli—one of the first foreign guests to address the 27th Congress—alluded critically to the Soviet invasion of Afghanistan and called for a political settlement of regional conflicts in Southeast Asia (the Vietnamese-Cambodian War) as well as Central America.[44] That he could do so was also a sign of the changing times, for at the previous CPSU congress in 1981 the Soviets had exercised pre-censorship to prevent Pajetta from delivering an address

41. See the text of Natta's speech in *l'Unità,* January 29, 1986, 7.
42. See *l'Unità,* March 8 and 30, 1986; and April 1, 2, and 4, 1986.
43. Quoted in Rubbi, *Incontri,* 242; see also 243.
44. See text in *l'Unità,* March 2, 1986, 5.

to the congress similarly critical of Soviet foreign policy.[45] Now, Pecchioli's remarks notwithstanding, the PCI delegates—personally hosted by Politburo member Mikhail Solomentsev—were much sought after by Soviet TV and press reporters.[46]

After their two-day summit in January 1986, Gorbachev and Natta did not meet again until the seventieth anniversary of the October Revolution in November 1987. In the meanwhile, however, not only were there numerous lower-level Soviet-PCI exchanges,[47] but Gorbachev had now begun to define *perestroika* as the "radical reform of Soviet society."

The Soviet leader had also come close to accepting the PCI's redefinition of the global left. Thus all the parties of the Socialist International, along with several other center-left formations, were invited to attend the formal seventieth anniversary celebration on November 2–3 as well as informal roundtable talks to be held immediately afterward. As it turned out, 178 diverse political groups from 120 countries, including representatives of twenty-nine socialist and social democratic parties, accepted the invitation;[48] and of the sixty-five speeches delivered at the roundtable discussions on November 4–5, twenty were given by delegates from the "non-communist Western left," according to Giorgio Napolitano, head of the PCI's International Affairs Commission and a member of his party's delegation.[49]

The Kremlin's acquiescence to the PCI's conception of the European left came about gradually and with some equivocation. This was evident in the CPSU's reaction to the Italian party's 17th Congress, which took place in Florence in April 1986. The dominant theme of that conclave, as noted above, was that the PCI was "an integral part of the European left." A place of honor was thus accorded the German Social Democratic Party (SPD), which for the first time sent an official delegation. Seated in the front row at the opening session beside the Soviet, Chinese, and Yugoslav delegations was Heidemarie Wieczorek-Zeul of the SPD leadership.[50]

<hr>

45. Urban, *Moscow and the Italian Communist Party,* 313 (see note 1).
46. See Giulietto Chiesa's report from Moscow in *l'Unità,* March 2, 1986, 5.
47. See Rubbi, *Incontri,* 118–25.
48. See Chapter 1 herein.
49. *L'Unità,* November 7, 1987, 9.
50. For details, see Joan Barth Urban, "The PCI's 17th Congress: A Triumph of the

Moscow bent over backwards to show respect for the Italian Communists on this occasion. Lev Zaikov, newly appointed Politburo member and CPSU secretary in charge of the USSR's military-industrial complex, headed the Soviet delegation. His presence stood in sharp contrast to the low-level representation at the PCI's 1983 congress, where the Kremlin's highest ranking member was the editor of *Pravda*. Zaikov was accompanied by Zagladin, who, despite his record as ideological watchdog during the Brezhnev years, now surprisingly remarked to an Italian reporter that he had no problem whatsoever with the PCI's international posture: "We Soviets also consider ourselves an integral part of the European left."[51] The official Soviet greeting to the congress added to the sense of Moscow's eagerness to please. Echoing Gorbachev's report to the 27th CPSU Congress, it affirmed that the "unity of communists has nothing to do with uniformity and hierarchy."[52]

On the other hand, Gorbachev's simultaneous insistence at his own congress in February that the communists were ideologically and historically superior to social democrats could hardly be reconciled with Zagladin's casual statement in April. And in fact *Pravda*'s coverage of the PCI congress was selective and sparse. Whereas in February 1985 it had devoted an entire page on two successive days to the proceedings of the French Communist Party's congress, it limited its reporting on the 1986 PCI congress to three half-page columns on Natta's opening speech.[53] Plainly the ideas advanced by the Italian Communists were still deemed unsafe for dissemination to a Soviet mass audience.

Over a year later, moreover, Gorbachev continued to equivocate on the desirability of holding a world communist conference, during an interview with the editors and Moscow correspondent of *l'Unità*. In a written reply to one question, he said, "Frankly speaking, I do not understand the circumspection that exists in some parts of our move-

---

'New Internationalism,'" in Raffaella Nanetti, Robert Leonardi, and Piergiorgio Corbetta, eds., *Italian Politics: A Review*, vol. 2 (London: Pinter, 1988), 41–52.

51. See Paolo Garimberti's interview with Zagladin in *la Repubblica*, April 12, 1986, 5.

52. Text in *Pravda*, April 9, 1986, 3, and *l'Unità*, April 11, 1986, 9.

53. *Pravda*, April 10, 1986, 4; cf. *Pravda*, February 8, 1985, 4.

ment toward proposals for multilateral meetings of the world's communists."[54] But in a more informal question-and-answer conversation, he suggested a gathering of "not only communists but also representatives of other parties" during the forthcoming seventieth anniversary festivities of the October Revolution. In reply, one of the Italian editors specified that such a meeting should include socialists and social democrats, and Gorbachev agreed.[55] Very possibly the written opinion reflected a long-held conviction while the oral exchange prompted him to broach a project only then being formulated within his circle of reform-minded advisers. As Heinz Timmermann has persuasively argued in Chapter 1, by the late 1980s Soviet reformers had actually come to regard social democracy as the CPSU's "preferred partner" in Western Europe.[56] This idea was apparently beginning to take shape in mid-1987.

Once the PCI became convinced that Moscow was serious about holding an open-ended dialogue among a broad spectrum of left and center-left forces, it gladly cooperated.[57] Natta, leading a delegation composed of Rubbi, Napolitano, and Renato Sandri, was one of the first of some two dozen foreign communist leaders to speak at the formal seventieth anniversary ceremony on November 3, the day after Gorbachev's seminal address on the need for historical *glasnost* and a "second revolution" in the USSR. The Italian general secretary hailed the October Revolution as "one of the decisive events of our century"; but he then hastened to add that "as you have recognized, a new transformation has become indispensable today . . . to revive the ideals of the October Revolution."[58]

During the lunch break on the first day of the informal talks, Gorbachev met privately with the PCI delegation for forty minutes. In response to Natta's praise of the roundtable idea, the Soviet leader quipped, "We have done as you wished." He then continued, "Joking aside, for us this meeting is a first-time experience of great value. We must acknowledge that the PCI has maintained for some time that this

54. Text in *l'Unità*, May 20, 1987, 13–16.
55. Ibid., 13.
56. See Chapter 1 herein.
57. Rubbi, *Incontri*, 128.
58. Text in *l'Unità*, November 4, 1987, 7.

is the path to follow, and it seems to us that it produces good results."[59] Gorbachev concluded the conversation with the suggestion that the two leaders soon hold another meeting like the January 1986 one, "with as much time as necessary" to discuss the issues that had arisen in the meantime.[60]

The Eurocommunist Critique, Gorbachev's Reforms, and the Soviet-PCI Dialogue

With Gorbachev's acknowledgment that Moscow had heeded the Italian Communists' advice in convening the November 1987 roundtable talks, Soviet-PCI relations began to acquire the character of an entente among like-minded reformers. Up until then the Soviet leader's bid for a reconciliation with the Italian party was part of an overall policy of outreach in the international arena, of relaxing tensions abroad in order to attend to problems at home. To be sure, a rapprochement with the PCI emerged for the particular reasons already noted: the impression Berlinguer's funeral made on Gorbachev, the wish to cultivate ties with European social democracy, the opportunity to gain insight into center-left thinking in the West. But these considerations merely gave impetus to actions that were part of a broader move toward détente with the United States, Western Europe, and China.

In November 1987, however, as the reforms undertaken by the Kremlin began to resemble ever more closely the Eurocommunist agenda articulated in the late 1970s and early 1980s, the Soviet-PCI relationship took on an added dimension: Gorbachev turned to the PCI as a sounding board for his contemplated European initiatives and as a source of encouragement and policy guidance. While there is no reason to suppose that the Italian party had any role in his basic decision to push for radical reform of Soviet domestic and foreign policy, once Gorbachev chose this course he sought to exchange ideas with interlocutors who were both sympathetic to his reforms and knowledgeable about a key focus of his concern, Western Europe.

59. Quoted in Rubbi, *Incontri*, 145.
60. Ibid., 145–46.

Gorbachev's November 1987 suggestion of another Soviet-PCI summit was therefore quickly acted upon. In March 1988 he and Natta engaged in a full day of talks. And in February 1989 the Soviet leader met for a day with Achille Occhetto, who succeeded Natta as PCI general secretary following the party's poor showing in Italy's June 1988 municipal elections.[61]

The Eurocommunist Agenda and Gorbachev's Early Policies

Before turning to what occurred during these talks, a brief overview of the parallels between the PCI's pre-1985 criticisms of Moscow and the reforms adumbrated by Gorbachev during his first three years in power is in order to illustrate the extent to which the two leaderships' outlooks had already converged.[62] Such parallels can be discerned in their respective views on the structure and strategy of the international communist movement, on the necessity of systemic reform within the Soviet Union, and on the need for a transformation of the USSR's international role as well.

Issues relating to Soviet conduct in the international communist movement were the most vital to the PCI and thus the first it subjected to criticism. With the public outbreak of the Sino-Soviet conflict in 1963, the Italians began to urge respect for autonomy and equality in relations among communist parties, and to call for a dialogue among equals in place of ostracism or orchestrated browbeating of one's opponents. The Warsaw Pact invasion of Czechoslovakia in 1968 prompted the Italian party to denounce the CPSU's "general laws" for the construction of socialism (which the Dubček reformers were accused of violating) and to insist upon the nonbinding nature of decisions reached at multilateral conferences of communist parties. At this juncture the PCI also began to advocate a constitutional and pluralist form of socialism in Western Europe. This was the crux of the Eurocommunist vision it propagated during the second half of the

---

61. For details, see Joan Barth Urban, "Italy," in Richard F. Starr, ed., *1989 Yearbook on International Communist Affairs* (Stanford, Calif.: Hoover Institution, 1989), 590–98.

62. For the PCI's criticisms, see Urban, *Moscow and the Italian Communist Party*, part four (see note 1).

1970s. After the 1982 *strappo,* as we have seen, the Italian party rejected the very idea of an international communist movement and opted to identify itself with the Western "Euroleft."

If the structure and strategy of the international communist movement were the most important issues for the PCI, they were also the ones that Gorbachev probably found it easiest to accommodate. This was because Soviet relations with foreign communist parties had been since the late 1920s the exclusive province of the CPSU general secretary and his closest associates rather than of the party apparatus as a whole. Accordingly, Gorbachev had no difficulty in turning his January 1986 meeting with Natta into a freewheeling dialogue between equals. In so doing, moreover, he signaled his acceptance of diversity rather than uniformity within the world communist movement, of national paths rather than "general laws"—even if he himself still yearned for multilateral consultations among communists. In line with this tolerance of diversity, the rapprochement with the PCI was accompanied by the Soviet leader's appeal for the full normalization of relations with China, which Harry Gelman recounts in Chapter 3. Finally, the November 1987 roundtable gathering in Moscow heralded the start of Gorbachev's ideological opening to Western social democracy.

With regard to the domestic Soviet scene, in the mid-1970s the PCI began to systematically denounce the repressiveness of the Soviet political system and Moscow's violations of human rights in particular. The catalyst for this shift from implied to direct criticism was the CPSU's crushing of the small Soviet dissident movement that had gathered momentum after the signing of the Helsinki Accords in August 1975. The high point of the Italians' systemic criticism of the Soviet Union was, of course, Berlinguer's assertion in the early 1980s that the October Revolution had "exhausted its propulsive force," but that moment was preceded by PCI sponsorship of detached scholarly research on some of the most sensitive questions of CPSU history.[63] Meanwhile, Italian Communist publicists also lamented the USSR's cultural vacuousness, monolithic press, and economic hypercentral-

---

63. See Robert V. Daniels, "Eurocommunist Views of the Development of the Soviet System: The PCI and Stalinism," *Slavic Review* 49, no. 1 (Spring 1990):109–15.

ization. And after the *strappo,* PCI leaders and official documents alike began to exhort the Soviet Union to undertake broad and deep systemic reforms. Perhaps out of deference to its own insistence on the principle of absolute autonomy, however, the Italian Communist leadership refrained from spelling out exactly what shape such reforms should take.

Whatever the reasons for Gorbachev's decision to embark upon a radical reform of Soviet society, he began along the path of least resistance: the introduction of *glasnost,* or openness, into the creative arts and mass media. By the close of 1987 he was also prepared to champion the cause of *glasnost* in Soviet history.[64] On the other hand, although he spoke of the need for radical political and economic reforms during 1987, the period of actual revolutionary transformation of the USSR still lay ahead. This was a topic that would figure prominently in the Soviet-PCI talks of 1988 and 1989.

As for Soviet foreign policy, the PCI's criticisms in this regard were the most intolerable to the Brezhnev leadership and largely responsible for the *strappo.* In a nutshell, the Italians accused the Kremlin of playing "great power" politics, of competing with the United States to divide the world into spheres of influence and hegemonic blocs. The USSR's support of repressive rule in Eastern Europe, beginning with the intervention in Czechoslovakia and culminating in the crushing of Solidarity, was the foremost target of PCI reprobation. But as a result of the Soviet invasion of Afghanistan, which the Italian Communists sharply and repeatedly condemned as an unacceptable violation of national sovereignty, they also took aim at the "logic of bloc politics" which drove the Soviet Union (as well as the United States) to expand beyond its natural sphere of influence. A more muted but equally cutting complaint had to do with the Soviet buildup of SS-20s targeted on Western Europe. From late 1979 onward the PCI repeatedly called for Soviet-American negotiations to achieve parity in intermediate-range nuclear forces at the lowest possible level.

Gorbachev was quick to move toward the elimination of all intermediate-range nuclear forces—initialing in December 1987 a Soviet-

---

64. R. W. Davies, *Soviet History in the Gorbachev Revolution* (London: Macmillan, 1989), chapter 10.

American INF treaty that included Moscow's unprecedented acquiescence to on-site verification—but he was less able to rapidly withdraw Soviet forces from Afghanistan and was plainly hesitant to champion change in Eastern Europe. At the same time, the conclusion of the INF Treaty was accompanied by a heightened Soviet interest in Western Europe and a fixation on the appealing if incoherent notion of a "common European home." These latter issues as well as Gorbachev's preoccupation with understanding the process of European integration were among the topics discussed at the Soviet-PCI talks in March 1988.

The Gorbachev-Natta Talks of March 1988

Both delegations to the 1988 meeting were well suited to discuss Soviet policy toward the West. Gorbachev was accompanied by Dobrynin, then head of the CPSU's International Department, and Aleksandr Yakovlev, soon to become chairman of the CPSU Commission on International Affairs, as well as by his frequent aides Chernyaev and Zagladin. In addition to Rubbi and Natta's personal assistant Sandri, the Italian side included Giorgio Napolitano,[65] who for over a decade at least had been engaged in developing PCI ties with European socialist and labor parties and cultivating contacts with American academic and political circles.

As previously, Gorbachev's candid conversational manner set the tone of the talks, but on this occasion he seemed even more eager than in 1986 to sound out the Italians on European issues. A clue as to why may be found in a remark he made at the outset of the discussion on domestic Soviet reforms. In trying to explain why his leadership group had not realized back in 1985 the need for a "revolutionary renewal" of the Soviet system rather than simply "partial reforms," he made this startling disclosure: *"The truth is that we did not know our society well."*[66] How much less, then, must they have understood the outside world.

The talks began with Gorbachev pressing the Italians for informa-

---

65. Rubbi, *Incontri*, 163–64.
66. Quoted in ibid., 187; emphasis added.

tion on two themes that seemed uppermost in his mind: the prosperity of the increasingly integrated European Community and the PCI's conception of what an eventual socialist alternative in Western Europe might look like. With regard to the first, he wanted to understand where capitalism got its dynamism, its ability to turn the internationalization of the economy to its advantage. By the same token, he wanted to know why Italy had a higher rate of growth than Great Britain or France and how exactly the Italian economy functioned, including the relationship between public and private enterprise and the role of small and medium-sized industrial firms. With regard to the second theme, Gorbachev was especially interested in hearing the PCI's view on how the European left might build a socialist alternative because he was scheduled to meet soon with Willy Brandt, chairman of the Socialist International and "a person worthy of great consideration and respect."

In response to this last line of inquiry, Natta and Napolitano expounded on the need to find a new conceptual and programmatic basis for unity on the left. Eurocommunism had been an initial step in this direction, they explained, but it had failed because of the political-cultural backwardness of most West European communist parties and also because of the CPSU's open polemics against the idea right from the start. Now, they continued, the diverse components of the "Euroleft" had to join forces in order to strengthen and democratize the institutions of the European Community, above all the European Parliament, and in order to endow the forthcoming creation of a unified European market with social welfare norms and goals.[67]

For its part, the PCI delegation raised the subjects of conventional force reductions in Europe and the war in Afghanistan. On both these points the discussion was more one-sided, with the Italians reiterating their long-standing opposition to Moscow's policies and the Soviets listening in an attentive but noncommittal fashion. In order to promote the reduction rather than the buildup of West European conventional forces in response to Soviet-American strategic arms cuts, Natta insisted, the existing asymmetrical relationship in conventional weapons which favored the East had to be eliminated. To this end he

---

67. Ibid., 166–70.

bluntly urged the USSR and the Warsaw Pact to undertake "concrete initiatives, even of a unilateral character."[68]

As for Afghanistan, Natta reiterated the PCI's judgment that the USSR's intervention had been "a tremendous error" and called for the complete withdrawal of Soviet troops. Gorbachev refrained from any explicit reference to the military intervention. Still, he spoke sadly of the "pseudo-revolutionary extremism" that had gripped the Kabul regime after the April 1978 insurrection: "One tried to skip over stages in a tremendously backward society."[69]

If Gorbachev was cautious on Afghanistan, he was downright contradictory on the question of how to reconcile his pet idea of a "common European home" with the continuation of opposing political systems on the European continent. On the one hand, he maintained that the USSR had embraced the vision of a "common European home" because it saw itself as above all "a European country." On the other hand, he hastened a bit later to declare that the "diversity between the two present Europes" could not be overlooked or eliminated.[70] This comment turned out to be rather revealing in light of his reserve in response to Natta's queries about Eastern Europe. When asked about the impact of *perestroika* on the socialist countries and on Czechoslovakia in particular, Gorbachev replied in effect that this was none of Moscow's business, that those countries' relationships with the USSR were now less binding and more autonomous than in the past.[71] In short, Gorbachev seemed to be using the principle of noninterference in the affairs of his allies to conceal an inclination toward the status quo in Eastern Europe.

The PCI leadership's uneasiness over Gorbachev's ambiguous vision of a "common European home," as well as its wish to project a public image of critical detachment from Moscow, found echoes in the media treatment of the March 1988 summit. The Soviet press, first of all, corrected its initial coverage of the meeting by replacing its use of the loaded term "comrade" with the word "friendly" to characterize relations between the CPSU and the PCI. It also deleted a passage

68. Ibid., 172; cf. 184–85.
69. Quoted in ibid., 195.
70. Ibid., 181, 186.
71. Ibid., 191–92.

in the original TASS report on the talks claiming that both Gorbachev and Natta advocated more active cooperation "in setting out the common tasks which can be resolved in the 'common European home' by joint efforts."[72]

Plainly these corrections were made at the insistence of the Italians, for *l'Unità*'s report on the meeting made no reference whatsoever to the idea of a "common European home."[73] Furthermore, *l'Unità*'s account of the Natta-Napolitano postsummit press conference in Moscow underscored the distinction between the Soviet and Italian Communists' definitions of democracy. As Natta put it, "We are for a pluralist political system. . . . [O]urs are the choices of a party that functions in a Western reality." Napolitano added that the PCI's differences with the CPSU in the interpretation of democracy were very pronounced.[74] Upon returning to Italy, moreover, he gave a long interview to the center-left daily, *la Repubblica,* in which he flatly declared that the PCI's criticisms of the USSR at the time of the *strappo* had been vindicated by the Kremlin's efforts under Gorbachev to correct the Soviet Union's systemic flaws.[75]

The Gorbachev-Occhetto Talks of February 1989

By the time of the next Soviet-PCI summit in late February 1989, both parties had experienced considerable upheaval. In the May 1988 municipal elections, the Italian Communists won only 21.9 percent of the votes cast, their poorest showing in decades. Natta, seventy years old and ailing, promptly resigned in favor of his fifty-two-year-old deputy, Achille Occhetto. And as the PCI prepared for its 18th Congress scheduled for March 1989, there was widespread talk of the need to chart a "new course" and to redefine the very identity of the party. Gorbachev, meanwhile, had unveiled his plans for the democratization of the Soviet political system at the 19th CPSU Conference in the early summer of 1988. By February 1989 preparations were under way for the partially competitive elections to the new Congress of People's Deputies in the spring.

72. Urban, "Italy," *1989 Yearbook,* 596 (see note 61).
73. See the report by Renza Foa in *l'Unità,* March 30, 1988, 9.
74. Urban, "Italy," *1989 Yearbook,* 596.
75. Ibid.

Moreover, several of the international issues discussed at the March 1988 Natta-Gorbachev meeting were now moot. In June 1988 the Eastern bloc's Council for Mutual Economic Assistance (Comecon) established relations with the European Community on the EC's terms. The following December Gorbachev announced from the podium of the UN General Assembly Moscow's intention to reduce its armed forces by 500,000, including withdrawal of some 50,000 troops and six tank divisions from Eastern Europe. In a related development, negotiations between NATO and the Warsaw Pact for a broad-based reduction of conventional forces in Europe were slated to begin in March 1989. Above all, in mid-February 1989 the last Soviet troops withdrew from Afghanistan, a matter of cardinal importance to the PCI.

The two general secretaries thus sat down to an agenda that was at once more limited and more portentous than before. Gorbachev, who was joined by Yakovlev, Chernyaev, and Valentin Falin, head of the International Department since October 1988, was now evidently prepared to forge a new relationship with Western social democracy. For his part, Occhetto, accompanied by Rubbi, Boffa, and a personal aide, was bent upon affirming the reformability of the East European communist regimes and ascertaining Gorbachev's intentions in this regard.

Gorbachev's interest in establishing a political entente with the leading forces of European social democracy was, on the face of it, a logical corollary of the USSR's incipient democratic transformation. But it also suggested a search for new doctrinal moorings as the Soviet polity shed the dogmatic incrustations of its Marxist-Leninist past. Thus the Soviet leader spoke not only of the CPSU's desire to establish closer ties with social democratic parties and their international organizations but also of the fact that many things written by Lenin were no longer valid. "Today it is not only you but also we who are being accused of revisionism!" he remarked.[76] And when Occhetto suggested on behalf of Willy Brandt several areas of possible collaboration between the Socialist International and Moscow, Gorbachev was plainly receptive.[77] As Occhetto pointed out at a postsummit press

76. Quoted in Rubbi, *Incontri*, 240; cf. 251.
77. Ibid., 225, 248.

conference, the Soviet president expressed the desire to establish the same kind of relations with social democratic parties that he had with the PCI.[78] Meanwhile, as Timmermann describes in Chapter 1, the ground for building such a relationship was being prepared by the CPSU reformers' reevaluation of European social democracy as the preferred political and doctrinal partner of the CPSU.[79]

Occhetto, on the other hand, was eager for information on Gorbachev's attitude toward reform in Eastern Europe because for the PCI the ultimate test of Gorbachev's reformism was whether he was willing to countenance autonomy and liberalization in the Soviet Union's East European empire. The Italian party had made this clear at the time of Alexander Dubček's visit to Italy in November 1988 (his first trip abroad since his purge in 1969) to receive an honorary degree from the University of Bologna on the occasion of its ninth centennial celebration.

Prior to Dubček's arrival, the Italian Communists had begun a campaign to pressure Moscow into acknowledging that the Warsaw Pact invasion of Czechoslovakia in 1968 had been an unacceptable violation of national sovereignty. To this end, in early January 1988 *l'Unità* published a lengthy interview with Dubček which signaled his reentry into political life. Seven months later, on the eve of the twentieth anniversary of the invasion, Napolitano published a lead article in *l'Unità* entitled "Rehabilitate Dubček." In it he argued that the current Soviet reform process demonstrated "the validity and vitality of the ideas that flourished in Prague in 1968." Two days later a *l'Unità* editorial deplored a recent TASS dispatch defending the military intervention in 1968 and asked, pointedly: "What is the credibility of a Soviet renewal that does not come to terms . . . with Czechoslovakia 1968?"

In November, while Dubček was a guest of the PCI in Rome, he had a meeting with Occhetto which was announced on the front page of the party daily with the headline, "Occhetto to Gorbachev: 'Rehabilitate Dubček'." During their talk Occhetto dismissed the idea (voiced by Gorbachev at the previous Soviet-PCI summit) that one should not interfere in the internal affairs of Czechoslovakia, bluntly stating that

78. See the report by Fabrizio Rondolino in *l'Unità*, March 2, 1989, 5.
79. See Chapter 1 herein.

the "suffocation of the [Prague] Spring was in fact imposed from outside." He then insisted that "the success of *perestroika* is tied to a positive evaluation, on the part of *all,* of the Czechoslovak experience." By *"all"* Occhetto meant "the Soviets," as the journalist describing the encounter explained editorially.[80]

In his February 1989 meeting with Gorbachev, Occhetto pleaded the case of Dubček and the Prague Spring with force and conviction. The PCI was concerned, of course, about the prospects for reform movements elsewhere in the region, but Czechoslovakia was obviously closest to their hearts. Occhetto spoke of his unforgettable meeting with Dubček the previous November, remarking emphatically: "I had the unequivocal impression of finding myself in the presence of a true communist and an authentic combatant for socialism."[81]

Gorbachev, along with Yakovlev and Falin, listened attentively and indicated substantial agreement with Occhetto. But the gist of the Soviet leader's response was to equivocate and temporize. He reiterated Moscow's determination not to interfere in the internal affairs of those countries, yet moments later he explained Soviet restraint solely in terms of a preoccupation with avoiding the destabilization of Eastern Europe. He maintained that reform and democratization should "mature naturally," yet he thereupon affirmed the urgency of change: "I tell everyone I meet that the depth of the crisis is such that he who wastes time will know serious defeats."[82] On balance, Gorbachev seemed once again, as in March 1988, to be using the principle of noninterference to justify ambivalence and inaction. He did not explain what he meant by the "destabilization" of Eastern Europe, but his comportment suggested a premonition that, should reform really come to that part of the world, the Soviet Union would reap the whirlwind.

Eight months later, as democratic revolutions swept away the Soviet-installed communist regimes in East-Central Europe and the two Germanys began their rush to reunification, Gorbachev finally

80. For the above discussion, and quotations, see Urban, "Italy," *1989 Yearbook,* 597 (see note 61).
81. Quoted in Rubbi, *Incontri,* 246.
82. Quoted in ibid., 247–48; cf. 236.

conceded the error of the USSR's ways with regard to the Prague Spring. By then Dubček was back in the public eye, embracing the democratic revolutionaries in Prague as Gorbachev embarked upon a state visit to Rome and the Vatican. It was to the Soviet president's credit that he chose Italy as the place to admit, on December 1, 1989, that in 1968 the Kremlin "did not make full use of all the political methods at its disposal to respond correctly to the Czechoslovak situation."[83]

The earlier inability of Gorbachev and the PCI leaders to find a common language on reform in Eastern Europe did not, however, diminish the esteem in which the Soviet president held the PCI. The monthly chronicle of international exchanges of visitors and delegations published in the CPSU Central Committee's new information bulletin from December 1988 through September 1990 made this quite clear. While the Kremlin's other foreign contacts were listed without editorial comment, meetings with Occhetto were described in glowing terms: the mid-February 1989 talks in Rome between the first deputy head of the CPSU International Department, Karen Brutents, and Occhetto were said to have taken place "in a warm, friendly atmosphere;" Occhetto's subsequent meeting with Gorbachev (recounted in the preceding pages) was called "a further step in the development of CPSU-PCI relations, whose contents and dynamic in recent years reflect the novelty of the processes occurring in their countries, in Europe, and in the world."[84] No other bilateral exchange, whether with communists or social democrats, party heads or government leaders, was singled out for this kind of favorable editorializing.

The Revolutions of 1989 and the PCI's Search for a Postcommunist Identity

The Italian Communists' fixation on the Prague Spring, their unrelenting opposition since 1968 to Soviet domination of its Warsaw Pact

83. *Corriere della sera*, December 2, 1989, 5; *Pravda*, December 3, 1989, 2.

84. "Peregovory, vstrechi, besedy (Khronika za yanvar—fevral 1989 g.), *Izvestiya TsK KPSS*, no. 3 (March 1989):78.

allies, had complex roots. The demand for the rehabilitation of the Dubček reform movement on the ground that this constituted the true measure of Gorbachev's reformism was doubtless sincere. It also played well in the domestic Italian political arena. But that was hardly the whole story. The crux of the matter was that for many PCI members their own political identity, their self-perception as communists, was inextricably linked to the cause and fate of communist reformism in Eastern Europe.

For the Italian Communists the Prague Spring had held out the promise of reconciling their socialist goals with their democratic political culture. The Warsaw Pact invasion of Czechoslovakia was a wrenching betrayal of that promise and the fundamental catalyst for the emergence of the Eurocommunist phenomenon in the 1970s. Indeed, the Prague Spring formed the legitimizing matrix of the PCI's Eurocommunist vision. It stood as proof that the fusion of democracy and socialism was not simply the distant hope of nonruling communists in the West but could be the operational plan of communists in power as well.

By the mid-1980s the PCI's Eurocommunist vision had been discarded in favor of the prospect of an integrated European left. There were a number of reasons for this, among them the "backwardness" of most Western communist parties and Soviet hostility toward the concept, as Natta explained to Gorbachev in March 1988. The mounting repressiveness and adventurism of the Brezhnev Politburo, culminating in the invasion of Afghanistan and the instigation of martial law in Poland, were additional considerations. They led the PCI to reject the very notion of a world communist movement. The transition from Eurocommunism to "Euroleft" was also facilitated by the death of Berlinguer, who had come to personify the former, as well as by the growing influence on party policy of activists from the radical but nonpartisan youth movements of the late 1960s.

All the same, in deciding to proclaim itself "an integral part of the European left" in 1986, the PCI had embarked upon a path filled with uncertainty and ambivalence. The choice of the "Euroleft" option signified in fact the start of the PCI's transition to a postcommunist identity even if at the time this was not spelled out nor probably even perceived by most of those involved in the decision. Indeed, the extent of ambivalence and conflicting perceptions as to what exactly the new course meant was to become clear only at a stormy meeting of the Central Committee during November 20–24, 1989, when Occhetto proposed to discard the very name and symbols of the communist heritage and transform the PCI into a "new political formation."[85] This initiative quickly split the party into warring factions. Of the 326 Central Committee members present, seventy-three—including Alessandro Natta—voted against this call for radical change and another thirty-four abstained.[86]

In retrospect, the stage reached by the Gorbachev revolution as of late 1988–early 1989, with its heartening transformation of the Soviet polity and its portent of communist reform in Eastern Europe as well, gave a much-needed boost to the Italian Communists. Their call for Moscow's rehabilitation of Dubček and the Prague Spring was symbolic of their hopes, calculations, expectations that communists in power would finally create an order with which they could be proud to identify. In short, the illusion of the reformability of the communist regimes in the East gave the PCI a brief respite from its own mounting crisis of identity.

By the same token, the nature of the revolutions that subsequently occurred in Poland, Hungary, East Germany, and ultimately Czechoslovakia, the unqualified rejection of the communist idea even in Hungary where communist reformers were prepared to move far beyond the measures then advocated by Gorbachev, represented for the Italian Communists a singular moment of truth. Not only was communist rule as hitherto experienced not the way to build a better society, but reform communism turned out to be simply a transitional stage on the path to a democratic political order in which the people's choice was overwhelmingly anticommunist. This, then, was the backdrop against which Achille Occhetto proposed on November 12, 1989, three days after the opening of the Berlin Wall, the fundamental restructuring of the Italian Communist Party.

Occhetto's decision to break with the communist tradition was not,

---

85. For the text of Occhetto's speech, see Guido Moltedo and Norma Rangeri, *PCI: La grande svolta* (Rome: Edizioni Associate, 1989), 36–59.
86. Ibid., 27.

however, a bolt from the blue. The path to the *"superstrappo"*[87] of November 1989 had been paved by two related developments. The first was the delegitimization from early 1988 onward of the PCI's historic leader, Palmiro Togliatti, triggered by Moscow's rehabilitation of the CPSU's Old Bolsheviks, whose execution at Stalin's bidding Togliatti had publicly applauded in the late 1930s.[88] The second was the Occhetto leadership's acknowledgment that the reform communism of Imre Nagy in 1956 Hungary had been as worthy of support and emulation as that of Alexander Dubček in 1968 Czechoslovakia.

If the Warsaw Pact's invasion of Czechoslovakia gave rise to Eurocommunism, and the imposition of martial law in Poland prompted Berlinguer to reject the very concept of an international communist movement, public admission of the Togliatti leadership's moral complicity in the crushing of the Hungarian Revolution signaled the Occhetto group's readiness to move beyond reform communism, with which Togliatti's name had long been associated. The Italian Communists' official reassessment of the 1956 events in Hungary had been heralded, to be sure, by the publication of critical scholarly accounts of what had actually occurred by their own revisionist historians.[89] But the first official PCI break with its long-standing position that Dubček was good, and Nagy bad, came only in June 1988 when Secretariat member Piero Fassino attended the dedication in Paris of a symbolic tomb to Nagy.[90]

One year later, on June 16, 1989, Occhetto himself was present at the posthumous funeral and reinterment of Nagy in Budapest. On that occasion the Italian leader declared not only that Nagy had been

87. The term *superstrappo* was coined by Federigo Argentieri, one of the contributors to this volume.

88. The debate within the PCI's own ranks over how to evaluate Togliatti's legacy was plainly more important than sallies from anticommunist quarters; see in particular Occhetto's speech at Civitavecchia in which he acknowledged that Togliatti was "co-responsible for the choices, the acts of the Stalinist era," in *l'Unità*, July 9, 1988, 4.

89. See Federigo Argentieri and Lorenzo Gianotti, *L'Ottobre ungherese* (Rome: Valerio Levi, 1986); Adriano Guerra, *Il giorno che Chruščëv parlò: Dal XX Congresso alla rivolta ungherese* (Rome: Riuniti, 1986). Cf. Federigo Argentieri, *Miklos Vásárhelyi: La rivoluzione ungherese Imre Nagy e la sinistra* (Rome: Valerio Levi, 1988).

90. Urban, "Italy," *1989 Yearbook*, 598; I am indebted to Federigo Argentieri for this interpretation and the documentation that follows.

right in 1956 but that Togliatti had been wrong in backing the Soviet suppression of the Hungarian Revolution.[91] Shortly thereafter, in August 1989, a prominent PCI intellectual created an uproar by publishing an article bluntly identifying Togliatti (on the 25th anniversary of his death, no less) not just with the Stalin era but with the entire historically bankrupt communist system.[92] Finally, in mid-October 1989, Occhetto and Napolitano traveled to Budapest to congratulate the Hungarian reform communists on their decommunization—their creation of the new Hungarian Socialist Party in juxtaposition to the orthodox Hungarian Socialist Workers' Party.[93]

This sequence of events contributed, in short, to the partial delegitimization of the older generation of PCI leaders who had risen to prominence during the late Togliatti era, especially at the 8th Congress of the PCI in 1956, and who had declined to challenge Togliatti on the question of Hungary.[94] This, then, helps to explain the support by two-thirds of the PCI membership for the transformation of their own party into a noncommunist political force.

The Path to the PCI's Superstrappo

A brief account of the PCI's congresses of 1986, 1989, and 1990 may serve to illustrate the convoluted course by which the Italian party arrived at this historic juncture.[95]

Natta's speeches to the 17th Congress (Florence, April 9–13, 1986) already projected a theoretical profile that went, as it were, beyond Marxism.[96] There was a world of difference between his 1986 addresses and the tenor of Berlinguer's speeches to the party's 16th Congress in 1983. Gone was the vision of a global march toward

91. *L'Unità*, June 17, 1989, 3.

92. Biagio De Giovanni, "C'erano una volta Togliatti e il comunismo reale," *l'Unità*, August 20, 1989, 1.

93. *L'Unità*, October 17, 1989, 5. On that occasion the PCI general secretary is reported to have said, "Here everything is collapsing"; cf. note 90.

94. As secretary of the PCI's university section in Milan in 1956, Occhetto had opposed the *Direzione*'s position on the Hungarian Revolution; see *l'Unità*, June 17, 1989, 3.

95. The author was present as an academic observer at all three congresses, as well as the last PCI congress in early 1991.

96. Urban, "The PCI's 17th Congress," passim (see note 50).

socialism that pervaded Berlinguer's discourses. Gone, too, were the doctrinal moorings of a "working class" identity and "Marxist matrix" for the PCI. Indeed, Natta did not mention Marx at all in his congress report. And he referred to him only once in his concluding address when, after warning against "any form of dogmatic crystallization of thought," he hailed the critical heritage of Western culture to which, he added, "Marx also belongs."[97]

In his opening report Natta also declared that the PCI had long since liberated itself from "any sort of philosophy of history that considers implicit in it the socialist end of which we speak."[98] And in speaking of contemporary capitalism, he employed language suggesting that it was not inherently unworkable but merely mismanaged at present in the name of neoliberal orthodoxy. This kind of ideological laicization provided the context for the rallying cry of the 17th Congress: the convergence of the PCI with European social democracy, and its designation as "an integral part of the European left."

The setting and atmosphere of the 17th Congress were also suggestive of the shift from Marxist messianism to European reformism. The sports arena was decorated in muted rainbow shades of blue, pink, and white with only a few splashes of red depicting the PCI symbol and congress slogan. The prelude to the opening session was Vivaldi's "Four Seasons," and the prelude to the closing ceremony Beethoven's Violin Concerto in D (a gesture of esteem for the SPD delegation?). Foreign communist delegations and noncommunist observers alike sat together in a section at one end of the rectangular hall, cut off from the tribune of PCI dignitaries which spanned the front and faced the delegates seated in rows of desks on the floor of the arena. The numerous delegates who rose to speak debated many issues, but in a dignified and, for the most part, unexceptional manner. And in the end there was a high degree of consensus, the only contentious issue having to do with civilian nuclear energy usage.

As already mentioned, CPSU Politburo member Lev Zaikov headed the Soviet delegation. He could be observed arriving early and sitting, often quite alone, in the front row of the seats reserved for foreigners

97. Ibid., 42.
98. Ibid.

during the daily rounds of speeches. While the other non-Italians mixed freely with one another, few paid any attention to Zaikov. Nor was there much mention of the Soviet Union during the congress proceedings. Natta did praise the USSR's "new international course" and wished the CPSU success in its proposed "radical reforms." But he also alluded to "many harsh and unresolved questions, beginning with that of democracy," and he expressed the hope that Moscow would end its occupation of Afghanistan. Above all he reaffirmed Berlinguer's policy of refusing "any choice of camp."[99]

The 18th Congress (Rome, March 18–22, 1989) was significant not because of any change in the PCI's basic alignment with the "Euroleft," but because of the air of triumphalism the party projected—a curious note in view of its electoral decline during the 1980s. The policy statement prepared for approval at the congress as well as Occhetto's opening report enthusiastically endorsed Gorbachev's "battle for democracy," hailed the prospects for reform in Hungary and Poland, and called again for the restoration of political honor to Dubček and the Prague Spring.[100] All the while, the congress documents did not hesitate to say that the PCI had "anticipated and championed" these struggles for years. Indeed, the party's central theme on this occasion was that "democracy is not *a* path to socialism but is *the* path to socialism."[101]

In contrast to the 17th Congress, moreover, the staging of the 18th Congress conveyed mixed signals. On the one hand, the official foreign delegations included a spectrum of views from the Palestine Liberation Organization (PLO) on the radical left to the SPD, represented by Karsten Voigt, on the center left. On the other hand, the setting and atmosphere recalled an earlier era of internationalist fervor. The décor was once again predominantly red. The foreign delegations were seated in a tribune of honor directly adjoining the area reserved for the members of the PCI Directorate and Central Committee, while unofficial observers were relegated to seats distant from the

99. Ibid., 44.

100. See the text of Occhetto's report distributed to the congress, *Il nuovo Pci in Italia e in Europa: È il tempo dell'alternativa*, 12. See also Urban, "Italy," *1989 Yearbook*, 595.

101. See Urban, "Italy," *1989 Yearbook*, 595; emphasis added.

dignitaries and high up in the grandstand. The Soviet delegation was headed by Gorbachev's close adviser, Yakovlev, and the Hungarian one by Imre Pozsgay, leader of his party's reform faction and widely viewed as the next president of Hungary. Both were much sought after by admiring crowds. And the high points of the proceedings were a videotaped message from Gorbachev, shown on two large and prominent screens, and a letter of greetings from Dubček, read from the podium shortly before Occhetto's concluding address.[102] Plainly, little thought was given to the possibility that 1989 would see not the regeneration of communism but its widespread collapse.

Just one year later the 19th Congress (Bologna, March 7–10, 1990) was convened for the express purpose of debating Occhetto's November 1989 proposal to replace the PCI with an entirely new political entity. As such it marked a dramatic break with the past. Gone were the slogans, festive bunting, visitors' loges, and simultaneous translation facilities of previous congresses. Gone, too, were the delegations of leftist parties from around the world. Unofficial foreign observers numbered fewer than one hundred and included a mixture of ex-communists (the Spaniard Manuel Azcárate), erstwhile communist dissidents (the Russian Roy Medvedev), and nonpartisan scholars. It goes without saying that there were also no gala receptions for foreign guests.

Occhetto minced no words in his opening report. "If an entire cycle of struggle for socialism has been exhausted" due to the sufferings produced by "real socialism," he declared, this did not mean that the problems that gave rise to the socialist movement were not still present in acute form. Moreover, "if in the USSR, Gorbachev himself . . . is opening the path to pluralism," thereby placing in question the leading role of the Communist Party, there was no reason why the Italian Communists should not have the courage to create a "new political formation," one that could aggregate and reorganize the Italian left by appealing not only to important sectors of the working class but also to intellectuals, liberal Catholics, environmentalists, and other reform-minded groupings. This "new political formation"—hopefully as part of the Socialist International—would, moreover, partici-

---

102. Texts in *l'Unità*, March 22, 1989, 6, 18. Also shown were videotaped greetings by Karsten Voigt and representatives of the PLO and Brazilian left.

pate in the creation of a "Euroleft" capable of embracing the new reformist forces maturing in Eastern Europe. The PCI's goal was, above all, to unite "for the first time in the history of humanity" the ideals of liberty and equality.[103]

Occhetto opened the 19th Congress with a technical victory assured. On the basis of the prior consultations of the one-hundred-odd local PCI federations, he enjoyed the support of 65.8 percent of the party, with the major opposition led by Natta and Pietro Ingrao backed by 30.8 percent and the doctrinaire maverick Armando Cossutta by only 3.3 percent.[104] The ensuing debate was nonetheless intensely acrimonious. The gist of the opposition argument was that since the PCI had been right for so long, opposing "real, existing socialism" and championing the universal value of democracy, why should *it* now have to change? As Natta put it, the party should have the courage once again "to go against the current" in order to preserve its very special identity as an innovative force.[105] After Occhetto's concluding address a momentary release of tension occurred. The elder statesmen from the opposition, first Ingrao, then Natta and Pajetta, came one by one to embrace the younger general secretary, whereupon Occhetto buried his face in his arms and burst into tears. Meanwhile the applauding throng of spectators burst into singing the "Internationale" and the PCI anthem, "Bandiera rossa." This explosion of emotion had, however, no impact on the final vote. A full two-thirds of the delegates endorsed the majority resolution[106] to begin forthwith the process of devising the character, name, and symbol of *la cosa* ("the thing"), the popular designation of the entity that would soon replace the PCI.

The Rimini Congress: From PCI to PDS

At the 20th PCI Congress (Rimini, January 31–February 3, 1991), the Italian Communist Party transformed itself into the Democratic

103. See the text of Occhetto's report distributed to the congress, *Un nuovo inizio: La fase costituente di una nuova formazione politica*, 3–18.

104. Francesco Merlo, "Il Pci: Cos'era, che Cosa sarà," *Corriere della sera*, March 4, 1990, 9.

105. *L'Unità*, March 10, 1990, 19.

106. *L'Unità*, March 11, 1990, 3.

Party of the Left (*Partito democratico della Sinistra*—PDS) with the assent of 807 of the 1259 delegates and 86.6 percent of those voting.[107] Taking as its emblem a large green oak tree, at the roots of which stood a diminutive replica of the PCI's traditional hammer and sickle, the new party hoped to become the fulcrum of a center-left coalition capable of competing with the Italian center-right in the formation of alternating parliamentary majorities. In line with this aspiration, foreign guests included representatives of the "Euroleft," of traditional communist movements, and of newly formed democratic parties from Eastern Europe and the USSR. In the Soviet delegation, for example, were not only functionaries from the CPSU and the Russian Communist Party but also organizers of the new social democratic force, the Republican Party of Russia. The staging of the congress was attuned to this expansive vision, conveying the image of an Italian piazza rather than a formal auditorium. The red-draped leadership tribune was much reduced in size compared to previous years, and it merged into the rows of green-covered desks and green-carpeted pathways of the delegates' central arena. The outreach to the Italian environmental movements was clear.

Yet the political outlook projected by the proceedings of the formative congress of the PDS was clouded from the start. Profound opposition to the war in the Persian Gulf was voiced by most speakers, starting with Occhetto in his opening report,[108] with old-style anti-imperialist rhetoric frequently being invoked in support of this position. With public opinion in Italy shifting in favor of the U.S.-led coalition's attack on Iraq,[109] the Rimini congress took as its theme song John Lennon's "Give Peace a Chance" in a throwback to the peace movement of the Vietnam era—and in a clear outreach to

107. While only seventy-five delegates voted no and forty-nine abstained on the motion to create the PDS, 328 others chose not to vote at all, including Aldo Tortorella, spokesman for the main faction opposing the transformation, and Alessandro Natta. A group of about ninety delegates backed Armando Cossutta in refusing to join the new party. *L'Unità*, February 4, 1991, 1.

108. Text in *l'Unità*, February 1, 1991, 15–18. About one-half of the two-hour-and-twenty-minute speech was devoted to issues relating to the war.

109. According to one survey, support for the war effort had risen from 32 to 48 percent between January 4 and February 1, while opposition had declined from 61.9 to 42.9 percent; see *l'Unità*, February 4, 1991, 1, 11.

Italian youth by a party whose members under the age of twenty-five had slipped from 11.2 percent in 1977 to 2.1 percent in 1988.[110]

At the same time, the PCI's traditional left, center, and right tendencies reemerged with regard to the Gulf War. While the center and right had been united on the need to create the PDS, the center now effectively joined the left in its call for a unilateral cease-fire in the Gulf and the withdrawal of Italian forces from the anti-Iraqi coalition.[111] And opposition to the rightward swing of the central Soviet government, sharply voiced at the time of Moscow's military crackdown in Lithuania the night of January 12–13, 1991,[112] was all but drowned out by the condemnation of U.S. conduct in the war.

The resulting crosscurrents of animosity and resentment among the delegates contributed to the inability of the newly created 547-member National Council of the PDS to elect Occhetto as party leader in the first round of voting on February 4, 1991. With 132 absentees, forty-one abstentions, eight blank ballots, and 102 nays, Occhetto fell ten votes short of the absolute majority required by the new party statutes for election to general secretary.[113] Four days later, 72 percent of the National Council finally confirmed Occhetto as PDS head at a meeting convened in Rome.[114] But the spectacle of internal disarray combined with ideologically conditioned pacifism had already alienated the party's would-be allies within the Italian center left, and damaged from the start the public image of the "new political formation."[115]

In the Soviet Union, meanwhile, the fate of democratization and economic reform hung in the balance as a counterrevolutionary offensive by chauvinistic circles in the military and security forces and

110. See the demographic analysis of the PCI's membership by Marco Ruffolo in *la Repubblica*, January 31, 1991, 14–15.

111. Stefano Marroni, "Le 'correnti' nel Golfo," *la Repubblica*, February 5, 1991, 6; cf. *l'Unità*, February 4, 1991, 5.

112. *L'Unità*, January 14, 1991, 8; cf. the front-page article by Adriano Guerra in the same issue, 1–2, and Federigo Argentieri's interview with the Lithuanian envoy to the Vatican in *l'Unità*, January 13, 1991, 2.

113. *L'Unità*, February 5, 1991, 1, 3–4; cf. *la Stampa*, February 5, 1991, 1–3.

114. *L'Unità*, February 9, 1991, 1, 3–5.

115. See the commentary by editor-in-chief Eugenio Scalfari, "La farfalla che aveva paura di volare," *la Repubblica*, February 5, 1991, 1, 4.

reactionary CPSU apparatchiks gained momentum in a process that foreshadowed the abortive coup attempt of August 1991.[116]

The Last Hurrah of the Internationalist Mystique

By the winter of 1991 the camaraderie and consensus that had characterized Gorbachev's relations with the PCI leadership in the second half of the 1980s looked like the last genuine manifestation of the ethos of internationalist solidarity that had been integral to the experience of the world communist movement in the twentieth century. Communist parties around the world had claimed to be the vanguard of the global march to socialism because of their presumed insight into the universal laws of historical development. In fact, however, the history of both the Comintern and the communist movement after Stalin's death was one of constant squabbling over how exactly to fulfill that vanguard role, how best to proceed toward the common goal of world socialism.

The glue that actually held the international communist movement together was thus not some shared understanding of how to make revolution and build socialism; rather, it was an emotive spirit of internationalism and the political self-confidence that each party gained from being part of a worldwide movement. This internationalist mystique was, to be sure, more important to nonruling communist parties than to the ruling ones that merely sought legitimacy for their domestic dictatorships by boasting of a worldwide constituency. Whatever other purposes international communist gatherings served over the years, they were invariably ritualistic pep rallies for the faithful, especially for those nonruling communist militants who needed psychological reinforcement in their seemingly endless struggles for a socialist future. This function was performed not only by the formal international communist meetings of the Stalin-Khrushchev-Brezhnev eras but also by the individual congresses of East and West European communist parties in recent decades, attended as they were by fraternal delegations from around the world.

116. See the ultrareactionary declaration by the plenum of the CPSU Central Committee held at the beginning of February in *Pravda,* February 4, 1991, 1.

The intensity of the CPSU-PCI entente during the Gorbachev revolution, particularly from 1986 through early 1989, can be best understood in the light of this tradition. Gorbachev, in addition to the motives discussed earlier in this chapter, seemed to derive reassurance of the defensibility of his reformist path from his close association with the Italian Communists. Beyond that, he was also able to buttress the ideological legitimacy of his policies in the eyes of his hardline opponents in the Soviet political-military establishment by cultivating the support of the largest ruling and nonruling communist parties in the world, those of China and Italy. Indeed, these communist movements beyond the empire seemed more important to Gorbachev the reformer than the communist regimes of Eastern Europe. And until the tragedy of Tienanmen Square in June 1989 and the *superstrappo* of the PCI the following November (on top of the collapse of communism in East-Central Europe), this policy seemed to have had a certain payoff.

As for the PCI, on the other hand, the enthusiasm with which its leaders greeted Gorbachev's overtures was a bit ironic, given their disavowal of a separate and distinct international communist movement at the time of the *strappo*. Upon closer reflection, however, it is clear that the PCI never rejected the idea of internationalism as such. Rather, under the banner of a "new internationalism" which emphasized political convergence rather than ideological uniformity, it set out to forge a coalition of left-oriented reformist parties that included the Eurocommunists in the 1970s, the "Euroleft" and the Chinese Communists in the early to mid-1980s, and the reform communists of the Soviet bloc in the second half of the 1980s. The continuing lure of the internationalist mystique was underscored by Occhetto's personal invitation to Gorbachev to address via videotape the 18th PCI Congress.[117]

In the final analysis, since the late 1960s the PCI had sought to advance its domestic political position by championing the cause of democratic reform in Eastern Europe, in the Soviet Union, and in the world communist movement at large. Nowhere was this stated more candidly than at the Rimini congress. In the words of Massimo D'Alema, widely viewed as Occhetto's second-in-command, the funda-

---

117. Gorbachev disclosed this invitation in his videotaped message; see note 102.

mental reason for the PCI's transformation into the PDS lay not simply in the "exhaustion of the historical function of the communist movement," the failure of communist parties to create a more just order, and the "ruinous collapse" of the communist regimes. It was also due to "the defeat of that hope, of that political purpose, of democratic evolution, of reform and regeneration of the communist experience *that was our political purpose, which made us different and which characterized our identity and which gave us a global function.*"[118]

In other words, the conviction that the PCI was endowed with a special internationalist role and character had been as vital to its reformist leaders as to the more traditional cadres and militants who still constituted important pockets of the party's membership and who rallied to the anti-imperialist slogans and rationales that pervaded the Rimini congress. Indeed, it would appear that the outbreak of the Gulf War enabled the body politic of the PCI to avoid the real transformation that most members knew in their minds was needed but evidently rejected with their hearts.

In the winter of 1990–91, both the PCI and the CPSU were thus confronted, paradoxically, with a common challenge. The utopian visions, rationalizations, and escape valves associated with the internationalist mystique of "world communism" were gone forever. Shorn of an international vocation, each was called upon once and for all to come to terms with its national setting. If the new PDS was to muster electoral support, it had to devise a platform responsive to the concrete political and economic concerns of its potential constituency within Italy. By the same token, if the CPSU was to retain a modicum of legitimacy, of ability to garner votes in multiparty competitive elections, of authority to govern without recourse to raw force, it had to reach a modus vivendi with the volatile nationalist and populist sentiments unleashed by the promises and failures of *perestroika.*

Gorbachev gave evidence of understanding the urgency of this challenge when he reached the nine-plus-one compromise agreement of April 1991 with Boris Yeltsin to intensify the process of the democ-

---

118. The quotations from D'Alema's speech are taken from the text transcribed from the taped version and distributed at the Rimini Congress; cf. *l'Unità*, February 3, 1991, 17. Emphasis added.

ratization, economic reform, and federalization of the USSR. The CPSU's hard-line plotters of the August 1991 coup plainly did not. With their bid to turn back the wheel of history to the centralized, authoritarian bureaucratic party-state of yesteryear, they deprived the CPSU of any lingering claim to credibility and legitimacy. Whether the PDS faced brighter prospects in Italy remained to be seen.

[3]

Gorbachev and Sino-Soviet Normalization

Harry Gelman

During the tumultuous years after Gorbachev came to power, both the Soviet and the Chinese elites gradually came to see the changing relationship between their two societies in more complex terms than they anticipated back in 1985. The direction of change has not altered. The overall trend has been and remains one of fairly steady, incremental improvement. But both capitals are now acutely aware that there are offsetting considerations at play, and that although some factors argue for an acceleration of the normalization process, others argue for slowing it down, or even pushing it back. By the start of the 1990s both sides had rejected the last alternative, and on balance both Moscow and Beijing were likely to continue to see an overriding self-interest in pressing forward. However, both were now also aware of new reasons for prudence that were not on the horizon a few years ago.

What were these opposing considerations?

First on the positive side, and most important, both Gorbachev and Deng Xiaoping had welcomed the progressive reduction of Sino-Soviet tensions as an essential backdrop for economic development and modernization. Each saw continuation of the normalization process as one of the prerequisites for minimizing his military burden. The Soviets in particular now knew that without massive reductions in that burden they had little hope of economic stability, let alone modernization.

Second, both the Soviet and the Chinese leaders had come to believe that many, if not all of the assumptions that produced confrontation between them over the years were gradually becoming anachronistic. Both now interpreted the fears and lurid antagonism of the past as having been somewhat excessive, driven as much by the personal obsessions of Stalin, Khrushchev, Brezhnev, and Mao as by the underlying conflicts of national interest. Although these conflicts of interest did indeed exist and to some extent still do, both sides saw them as having been significantly reduced by the changing circumstances that will be discussed below.

And third, both sides tended to value an improvement in their bilateral relations as adding some leverage to their relations with other states. Gorbachev viewed the effort to bolster relations with China as the centerpiece of his campaign to reconstruct the very poor Soviet position in the Far East that he inherited from his predecessors. He endeavored to use the improvement of Sino-Soviet relations as an instrument of pressure on Japan,[1] while the Chinese attempted to use that same improvement as an instrument of pressure against Vietnam. Meanwhile, the American aspect of Sino-Soviet dealings, so important in past decades, did not completely disappear, although it was modified. The drastic weakening of the Soviet position as superpower competitor to the United States had enhanced the attractions of Sino-Soviet rapprochement in both Moscow and Beijing. Both Gorbachev and his Chinese interlocutors had always assumed that a visible improvement in their relationship might be useful to each in dealings with the United States, provided that it was employed with due discretion.[2] And contrariwise, the Chinese in particular were impelled

---

1. That is, Soviet representatives constantly suggested to the Japanese that they were being left behind by Sino-Soviet rapprochement and Soviet-American détente and ran the risk of becoming isolated if they did not accept détente with the USSR on Soviet terms—that is, without obtaining those concessions they sought regarding the Northern Territories.

2. Both Moscow and Beijing walked a tightrope in handling this question, wishing the United States to be a bit concerned about Sino-Soviet rapprochement and to take into account the improved geopolitical position this rapprochement is supposed to bring. But neither the Soviet Union nor China wanted the United States to be very

by concern over President Reagan's developing relationship with Gorbachev to accelerate their own movement toward normalization with the Soviet Union.

Today, all three of these central motives for persevering with rapprochement appear to remain valid, but a fourth key factor has been greatly affected by changing realities. Until the spring of 1989 both Gorbachev and Deng tended to see their internal reform processes as, on the whole, mutually encouraging and reinforcing. They saw each other as legitimizing a common exploration of new forms of socialism that had previously been ruled out in both capitals as ideologically unacceptable.[3] This sense of mutual reinforcement has now vanished.[4] It has become clear that, since the end of the 1980s, the two countries have taken sharply divergent paths in their responses to the political dilemmas presented by reform. Moreover, not only have those paths diverged, but as will be seen below, the domestic realities that have emerged in Moscow and Beijing have each come to represent something of a political threat to the other. This threat is particularly acute in the minds of the Chinese leadership. Three decades after the Chinese first accused a Soviet leader of betraying socialism, the so-called ideological dispute has thus been resurrected in a new and peculiar form.

Neither leadership at present appears to wish to return to the formalized public polemics of the past,[5] or to allow the emergence of

---

concerned, since each had an important stake in its bilateral relationship with America, and had something to lose from excessive American alarm. This was particularly true of the Soviet side.

3. It is true that some Chinese leaders had had reservations about the pace and direction of Soviet political reforms long before the time of the Tienanmen events. Deng Xiaoping is alleged to have remarked in 1988 that he thought Gorbachev was moving "too fast." But until the Chinese crisis emerged in 1989, these qualms were secondary in importance.

4. On the economic front the Soviet Union and China do still confront many of the same problems—for example, in dealing with issues of price reform, the market, central planning, inflation, and so on. But each of these matters has now become intertwined with political issues about which the two societies have thus far made significantly different choices.

5. That is to say, polemical onslaughts unambiguously identified with one leadership and clearly directed at the other. However, there has been considerable mutual criticism between Moscow and Beijing since the Tienanmen events at a somewhat more subdued or less authoritative level. The radical Soviet press has been fairly outspoken in expressing its dislike for Beijing's behavior, while many Chinese articles have made

dramatic differences over internal policy to halt the expansion of official interaction, the growth of trade and business contacts, and the further reduction of military confrontation. But the reform process, rather than becoming the unifying factor it promised to be in the initial years of Gorbachev's regime, has now become a limiting, constraining factor, and a source of considerable ongoing distrust.

The discussion to follow will review how the process of rapprochement between Moscow and Beijing evolved under Gorbachev to produce this paradoxical result. As will be seen, the outcome was heavily influenced by the fact that this rapprochement was not simply a bilateral process, but was continuously affected by each society's interaction with the West.

The Normalization Process before Gorbachev

When Gorbachev became general secretary in March 1985, the People's Republic of China (PRC) was hoping for significant shifts in Soviet policy toward China that might radically alter the pattern that Chinese dealings with the Soviets had followed up to that point. In the six years before Gorbachev's arrival the normalization process had made some progress, but still was moving on two widely divergent tracks.

On the one hand, since early in the decade the Soviets and the Chinese had both seen it in their interests to pursue a series of slow, step-by-step improvements in certain aspects of their state-to-state relations, particularly in the economic and cultural spheres. The Brezhnev regime had sought major improvements in the immediate aftermath of Mao's death in 1976, but had been rebuffed at the time. In 1979, however, when Mao's successors decided to serve notice of formal abrogation of the long-defunct Sino-Soviet treaty of alliance, they also decided to take the occasion to propose talks with the Soviets about the future of the relationship. Although these talks were broken off by the Chinese after the Soviet invasion of Afghanistan,

---

scarcely veiled allusions to the disastrous consequences of Gorbachev's policies, reflecting the more explicit denunciations that authorities have circulated privately within China.

they were revived in modified form in 1982 at the deputy foreign minister level, and continued twice a year thereafter. From the fall of 1984 on, these periodic contacts were supplemented by encounters between the two foreign ministers at the UN.

These contacts served at first mainly to ventilate the long list of mutual grievances, but their existence legitimized the growth of contacts at other levels, and particularly the gradual expansion of economic intercourse. Although there were many ups and downs in the accompanying atmospherics during the first half of the 1980s, the process as a whole served to reduce tension between the two powers and cumulatively to impart a certain civility and normality to the relationship. This was a considerable change from the situation under Mao.

Meanwhile, however, on the second track an inherited geopolitical conflict was continuing between Moscow and Beijing. This conflict centered on Soviet military policies in the Far East which the Chinese had long regarded as attacks on their interests or threats to their security. This Soviet behavior to which Beijing objected was summed up in typically encapsulated form by the Chinese as their famous "three obstacles" to normalization. Throughout the 1980s, PRC representatives recited the Chinese formula about these obstacles on many occasions. The formula specified that the Soviets must drastically and unilaterally reduce their military force confronting China in Asia,[6] that the Soviets must withdraw their forces from Afghanistan; and that the Soviets must induce Vietnam to withdraw from Cambodia. In the absence of these enormous changes, so the Chinese contended, there could be no Sino-Soviet "normalization." As will be seen, the Chinese soon modified the essence of this position, although they did not acknowledge that fact.

The Elusive Quest for "Normalization"

Meanwhile, throughout these pre-Gorbachev years, the Chinese carefully refrained from defining precisely what they meant by "nor-

---

6. In its most explicit, pristine form, as enunciated at the start of the 1980s, this was a demand that the Soviet Union reduce its total force posture east of the Urals to the level that had existed in Khrushchev's day—that is, from fifty-odd divisions to between

malization." This ambiguity was cultivated deliberately, partly so they would be free to revise the promised reward as they saw fit if Soviet concessions materialized, and partly, on the other hand, so they would be free to belittle the extent of the change represented by normalization if American anxieties should exceed what was desired and should seem to need soothing. Nevertheless, Beijing's behavior in the first half of the 1980s tended to suggest that it did have in mind certain practical distinctions among the desiderata which the Soviet Union had sought from the Chinese since the mid-1960s.

Rewards Never to Be Expected

In the first place, the PRC indicated that although some of the Soviet desires might be satisfied under some circumstances, there were some the USSR could never obtain under any circumstances. It was made clear, for example, that no matter what the Soviets conceded to China, they could not hope to return to the alliance relationship of the 1950s. The Soviet elite absorbed the fact of this restriction long before Gorbachev took office, although not all Soviet leaders seemed reconciled to it.

Rewards Awaiting "Normalization"

On the other hand, the Chinese also indicated to Moscow that two specific requests the USSR had been advancing for many years could be satisfied, but only as rewards at the end of the rainbow, as adjuncts to normalization. One of these was the Soviet demand for a summit meeting, which the USSR had been particularly anxious to obtain ever since high-level Sino-American contacts began in the early 1970s. As will be seen, this issue came up six months after Gorbachev took power, and remained a matter of contention and bargaining until the Gorbachev summit visit to China finally materialized in the spring of 1989.

The other was a long-standing Soviet request for the restoration of

---

seventeen and twenty. This formula was thus not a request for a mere local pullback from the vicinity of the Sino-Soviet border, but a demand that the Soviet troop buildup in Asia conducted by Brezhnev against China be totally undone.

party-to-party relations which Beijing had broken off in 1966. The Soviets had sought such a restoration ever since the rupture, largely because they saw the party-to-party tie as an aspect of the relationship which was intrinsically impossible for the United States to match in its own dealings with China. The Chinese were well aware of the Soviet feelings on this score, and from 1983 on, the Chinese Communist Party began in effect to dangle before Moscow the possibility of restoring the party relationship as one of the rewards to be expected if normalization were ever achieved. Beijing held out this inducement to Soviet concessions by ostentatiously restoring party relations with a number of communist parties associated with Moscow while denying this favor to the Soviets themselves. The suggestion intended was that the CPSU could obtain a similar honor, but only after paying the appropriate price.[7]

Improvements That Could Come Earlier

Still other Soviet requests were treated in a third way. In order to encourage Soviet concessions, the Chinese proved willing—even in advance of what they deemed to be the official entry into "normalization"—to take two steps sought by Moscow and previously resisted in Beijing. One was the signing of a long-term trade agreement, which the Soviet Union had been proposing, and China refusing, ever since the last one was abrogated in Khrushchev's day. The USSR had traditionally sought such a new agreement as a symbolic step back toward what was remembered as the glorious era of the 1950s, when the two economies were intermeshed. Precisely because these agreements had previously been associated with an era of political intimacy and dependence, the PRC had traditionally declined to revive them;

7. As it turned out, the Soviets also eventually obtained satisfaction of a third specific request as a concomitant of normalization. This was their proposal for Sino-Soviet military talks on mutual force reduction and confidence-building measures. The Soviets had urged such negotiations since the early 1970s, and Brezhnev in March 1982 explicitly renewed the offer to discuss confidence-building measures in the Sino-Soviet border region. Over the years the PRC consistently declined these proposals, however, since it was the traditional Chinese position that any force reduction must be unilateral on the Soviet side. As will be seen below, the Chinese finally consented to begin such discussions as a result of Gorbachev's 1989 visit to China, but the PRC continues to show great sensitivity on the subject of reciprocity.

but by the year before Gorbachev's accession Beijing's viewpoint had changed sufficiently for the Chinese to agree.

The other early Chinese concession was agreement to resume the border negotiations with the Soviet Union which the PRC had broken off in 1978. The Chinese treated this agreement to talk as a concession—despite the fact that they were the ones seeking territory from the Soviets in these negotiations—simply because they had refused to resume the border talks earlier. As the Soviets later revealed, Brezhnev had formally asked for resumption of the border talks in an unpublicized proposal to China in December 1981, but Beijing temporized, claiming a need to prepare thoroughly. The Soviets have claimed that in February 1982 they repeated the proposal, but as we shall see, it was not until 1986 that the Chinese consented, evidently as a reward for Gorbachev's new, more conciliatory posture.[8]

Opposing Policy Goals

In the years leading up to Gorbachev's arrival on the scene, the two sides pursued this two-track interaction from opposing points of view. The Chinese were testing whether the Soviet leaders could be induced to make significant concessions regarding the three obstacles as a result of Beijing's consent to expand bilateral contacts and trade. For their part, Brezhnev, Andropov, and Chernenko sought to discover how far China could be induced to improve the bilateral relationship without such concessions.

On the whole, China did not yield very much in this contest, and the relationship was still quite cool and limited by the time of Chernenko's death in March 1985. The Soviet leaders, however, yielded even less. Although Beijing periodically implied that it would accept a gradual approach to removing the obstacles, calling on the Soviets at least to do "one or two things" so that progress could be made,[9] the

8. Mao Zedong had of course allowed border negotiations to proceed with the Soviet Union throughout much of the 1970s, without depicting the fact of these negotiations as a major concession to Moscow. Deng Xiaoping's success in positioning China so that resumption of these talks could be portrayed as such a concession was remarkable.

9. Hu Yaobang said this in his September 1, 1982, report to the 12th Chinese Party Congress (Xinhua news agency, Beijing, September 4, 1982). In January 1984 Defense Minister Geng Piao was similarly cited in the journal *Liaowang* as calling on Moscow to do "one or two concrete things to show its sincerity."

Soviet leadership in the first half of the decade showed no propensity to begin any of the geopolitical retreats which the Chinese were, in effect, demanding. This was not particularly surprising, as such intransigence was also generally characteristic of Soviet behavior toward the West in the pre-Gorbachev period.

The Chinese, then as later, were particularly eager to see the start of a Soviet retreat regarding Indochina, and in this regard they remained unsuccessful. Despite understandable disquiet in Hanoi over the Sino-Soviet contacts, and well-founded Vietnamese suspicions that the Soviets would eventually betray them, these suspicions were still premature. The Soviets publicly insisted that they would not discuss the affairs of "third countries"—that is, the Vietnamese—in their conversations with the Chinese. This posture, which persisted through the first two years of the Gorbachev regime, the Chinese found quite frustrating and irritating.

The pre-Gorbachev obstinacy in Moscow regarding the three obstacles in turn gave the Chinese leaders cause to hold on to their ambiguous American security connection as a hedge against a Soviet security threat which appeared increasingly hypothetical but which had not yet fully dissipated. Although the Chinese repeatedly spoke of their determination to remain free of alliances with either superpower, their conduct demonstrated that this did not mean equidistant relations, and throughout the first half of the 1980s they continued in many ways to "lean to one side" toward the United States, particularly after a Sino-American compromise over the Taiwan issue was reached early in the Reagan administration.

This Chinese behavior in turn fed the arguments of those in the Soviet elite and leadership who remained bitterly opposed to important concessions to Beijing, and who tended to exaggerate the extent and significance of Sino-American security cooperation in order to justify their position.[10] This attitude was made particularly visible

10. In the elite immediately surrounding the leadership, this sentiment was espoused at the time particularly by Oleg Rakhmanin, then a deputy chief of the Socialist Countries Department of the Central Committee, by Mikhail Kapitsa, then the deputy foreign minister concerned with China policy, and by the leaders of the Institute of the Far East of the Academy of Sciences whom they supported and encouraged. Marshal Nikolay Ogarkov, chief of the General Staff until mid-1984, was also inclined to emphasize the dire significance of the alleged Sino-U.S.-Japan military alliance. It is

during the interregnum of the weak Chernenko leadership in 1984, and in the spring of that year the aging Soviet oligarchs responded to President Reagan's visit to China by deferring the visit of Deputy Premier Ivan Arkhipov to China to arrange a long-term trade agreement which the USSR had long desired.[11] The Chinese bitterly complained that the stiffer policy of the Chernenko regime was a step back from the modest hopes that had been raised under Andropov.

By the fall of 1984, however, the Chinese leadership could apparently see better days on the horizon, in the person of Gorbachev. This Andropov protégé was now the ranking Soviet party secretary after the ailing and aged Chernenko, and was widely considered to be the heir apparent. We now know that in this period, behind the cautious public front obligatory for all Soviet leaders, Gorbachev was intensely occupied in private discussions of internal reform. Moreover, it is clear from Joan Urban's discussion in Chapter 2 that by the summer of 1984 Gorbachev was conducting groundbreaking private conversations with the Italian Communist leaders while attending the funeral of Enrico Berlinguer in Rome. It is plausible to suppose that during the last half of 1984 he or members of his entourage were similarly in private communication with the Chinese, and that he indicated his intention to promote decisive improvements in this relationship. Indeed, such conversations may conceivably have taken place during the Berlinguer funeral, which was also attended by the Chinese premier, Zhao Ziyang.

Over the last six months of Chernenko's life the Soviet leadership ceased direct criticism of China and repeatedly professed a desire for better relations. Certainly Chinese behavior in these last months before Gorbachev's accession suggested that Beijing was anticipating and encouraging change on the Soviet side. The PRC welcomed the rescheduling of the visit by Arkhipov to negotiate the five-year trade agreement, which Chernenko had postponed in May. When Arkhi-

---

interesting to note that the cessation of Soviet polemics with China in the fall of 1984 and the rescheduling of the cancelled Arkhipov visit occurred not long after Ogarkov's removal.

11. During the previous fall the divided Soviet leadership had made the even more counterproductive decision to walk out of the INF negotiations after NATO decided to proceed with INF deployment.

pov arrived in late December, the Chinese duly welcomed him as an "old friend of China,"[12] and sent an ostentatious signal to Moscow by referring to Arkhipov as "comrade"—the first time the Chinese had identified any Soviet leader in this way since the Cultural Revolution. But although the Chinese hailed the occasion as signifying an "upgrading in exchanges and contacts," they also made it clear they continued to demand a price for comradeship, and throughout Arkhipov's visit seldom failed to advertise the three obstacles which they were waiting for Moscow to remove.

Gorbachev's Accession and the Focus on Indochina

When three months later Chernenko died and Gorbachev took power, the signals professing good intent were amplified on both sides. Beijing at this point acknowledged, for the first time in two decades, that the Soviet Union and China were neighboring "socialist" countries. The PRC now also improved on its representation at recent funerals of Soviet general secretaries by sending Vice Premier Li Peng to Chernenko's ceremony, and Gorbachev responded by receiving Li. This was the first meeting between a senior Chinese official and a Soviet general secretary in twenty years.[13] For his part, Gorbachev on March 11 called for a "serious improvement" in relations, provided that the USSR met with "reciprocity" from the PRC. And at a Central Committee plenum in April, the new Soviet leader singled out China, saying that the Soviet Union would work "persistently and with a sense of purpose" to strengthen ties with "other socialist countries, including the PRC."

The Chinese now began to test what concessions Gorbachev was in fact prepared to make. At the Chernenko funeral Li Peng for the first time in many years alluded to the possibility of improving "political"

---

12. Arkhipov had played a prominent role in Soviet assistance to Chinese industry in the 1950s, and apparently got along well with the Chinese. He was therefore understood by both sides to be an appropriate choice as icebreaker thirty years later.

13. As Joan Urban notes in Chapter 2 herein, Gorbachev similarly used the occasion of Chernenko's funeral to receive the Italian Communists and to signal his desire to improve relations with them.

relations between the two states, and the following month, at the conclusion of the sixth round of the ongoing series of bilateral talks between deputy foreign ministers, the Chinese for the first time agreed to a joint statement expressing readiness to expand dealings in the political sphere as well as in the economic, scientific, and cultural areas mentioned in previous communiqués. It turned out, however, that the Chinese had a specific object in mind when they agreed to this: they wanted Gorbachev to begin "political" talks about getting the Vietnamese out of Cambodia.

To this end, Beijing now began to intensify the spotlight on Indochina as the most important of the three obstacles.[14] In mid-April, while the semiannual deputy foreign minister talks were going on in Moscow, Deng Xiaoping in Beijing took the occasion to remark publicly that although all three of the "obstacles" were of "equal gravity" because each was a "threat to China," nevertheless "the easiest one for the Soviet Union to start with would be to encourage Vietnam to withdraw its troops from Cambodia."[15] A few days later in Moscow, Deputy Foreign Minister Qian told Gromyko bluntly that "China waits for the Soviet Union to make a move in this regard."

Five months later, in a move of their own behind the scenes, the Chinese leadership for the first time offered Gorbachev a concrete inducement to abandon Vietnam. In the fall of 1985, during a visit by Romanian president Nicolae Ceauşescu to China, Deng Xiaoping privately asked Ceauşescu—who had acted as an intermediary between China and the United States early in the Nixon administration—to play a similar role with the Soviet Union. Ceauşescu was requested to tell Gorbachev that if the Cambodian obstacle were

14. Over the previous few years the Chinese had been hinting that they would accept a gradual approach in removing the obstacles, and since 1983 they had been intimating that the Soviet Union should begin with the Indochina obstacle. It was now, however, that they became vigorous and explicit on the subject.

15. Beijing television, April 17, 1985 (Foreign Broadcast Information Service Daily Report—China [FBIS-CHI], April 18, 1985, G-1). Deng also went on to say that it would be all right with him if the Soviets kept their bases in Vietnam under these circumstances. Although this remark was treated by some Western observers with great solemnity, it was almost certainly an ironic Chinese joke at Soviet expense. Both Beijing and Moscow were well aware that the political basis for a Soviet military presence in Vietnam would be eroded to the degree that Moscow pressed Vietnam to give up its hold over Cambodia.

removed, either Deng or Chinese party secretary general Hu Yaobang would go to Moscow to meet with Gorbachev.[16] A year later, after the Soviets had begun publicly probing for a summit without such a precondition, the Chinese revealed Deng's private 1985 proposal and the Soviets' failure to reply.[17]

Meanwhile the new Gorbachev leadership, while continuing to stall the Chinese on the Indochina issue, concentrated on exploiting the openings with China already created. In July 1985 two economic agreements completed after the Arkhipov visit to China in December were signed in Moscow. One was a five-year trade pact aiming at a doubling of bilateral trade by 1990. The other was a cooperative agreement for the Soviets to help build or refurbish twenty-four industrial enterprises in the PRC.

The latter agreement was of considerable symbolic importance on the path to rapprochement, for it involved the first Chinese acceptance of the return of Soviet economic advisory personnel to the PRC since Khrushchev's punitive action in the summer of 1960, when he suddenly withdrew thousands of Soviet economic advisers from China and thereby inflicted a heavy blow on the Chinese economy. Gorbachev could take satisfaction from the demonstration that after twenty-five years, Mao's heirs were finally willing to put aside the memory of this event. In the spring of 1986, during a second Arkhipov visit to China, the two sides followed up these agreements by establishing a bilateral commission on economic, trade, scientific, and technological cooperation.

At the same time, in the semiannual political talks conducted in the fall of 1985 and the spring of 1986, the two sides now acknowledged that they had discussed "certain international issues."[18] The Chinese apparently discovered, however, that Gorbachev was not yet prepared—or not yet in a position—to move on any of the three obstacles, and the PRC gradually began to display more impatience.

16. *Ta Kung Pao* (Hong Kong), September 9, 1986. *Tai Kung Pao* is the most authoritative Chinese Communist newspaper in Hong Kong.

17. It would appear that the PRC maintained silence about Deng's summit proposal for an entire year to avoid unduly alarming the United States until more progress had been made with Gorbachev.

18. Previously they had described themselves as having discussed only bilateral issues.

In December 1985, when Deputy Foreign Minister Kapitsa visited China to arrange for an exchange of foreign minister visits the next year, the PRC showed considerable irritation (not for the first time) with Kapitsa's rather crude and transparent efforts to exaggerate improvements in the bilateral political relationship, in the absence of major Soviet concessions on Indochina.[19] Chinese commentaries in January 1986 sharply reasserted the importance of the three obstacles, and asserted that the Soviets seemed to have a misconception that they could avoid them.

In February the Chinese complained that they could see no concrete change toward themselves in Gorbachev's speech to the 27th CPSU Party Congress. Beijing's Xinhua News Agency lamented that he had "again sidestepped the three obstacles . . . and instead emphasized the so-called issue of harming third countries."[20] (In other words, he had dodged concessions on the Indochina question by once again stressing the need to avoid injuring the interests of third countries—that is, of the Vietnamese.) In March, when "old friend" Arkhipov returned to Beijing, he repeated Gorbachev's formula of professing eagerness to improve relations with Beijing while not jeopardizing the interests of any third country. In response the Chinese ceased to call him "comrade," and were blunt in recapitulating their demands on the Soviets. In April, when Vice Foreign Minister Qian Qichen visited Moscow, Foreign Minister Eduard Shevardnadze took the occasion to call for a summit meeting without preconditions—that is, without Soviet satisfaction of China's precondition regarding Indochina.[21] A Chinese foreign ministry spokesman publicly replied that such a meeting would be "unrealistic" while the obstacles remained.[22] In June, discussing the eighth round of political talks held in the spring, the Chinese

19. When Kapista implied that the agreement for the exchange of foreign minister visits was settled, the Chinese immediately said it was not quite settled. On the day after meeting with Kapitsa, Foreign Minister Wu Xueqian took the occasion to say that "to our regret there has been no fundamental improvement," despite the fact that there had been "increased exchanges to a certain extent" (Xinhua, December 8, 1985). The Chinese had long found Kapitsa personally obnoxious, and this was one of the reasons Gorbachev decided to retire him the following spring.

20. Xinhau, February 26, 1986 (FBIS-CHI, February 27, 1986, C-2).

21. TASS, April 14, 1986 (FBIS-SOV, April 15, 1986, B-1).

22. Xinhua, April 16, 1986.

decried what they said was a general lack of progress, and ascribed this to the fact that Moscow would "neither acknowledge nor discuss" the three obstacles.

Through the summer of 1986 the Chinese generally sought to portray their relationship with Gorbachev as stable and expanding in certain areas which were nevertheless walled off by certain key political differences that remained of great and enduring importance. The Soviets sought to minimize the importance of the differences and to imply that the relationship was expanding in all directions.

Watershed: The Vladivostok Speech

After the February 1986 Soviet party congress, however, pressure to change this pattern dominated by inertia began to grow in the Soviet elite. The influential forces around Gorbachev became increasingly convinced that the Soviet Union would make little progress in improving its weak position in East Asia unless it registered a breakthrough with China, and that some concessions to China were sooner or later unavoidable. Deng's offer of a Sino-Soviet summit as a reward for changes in Soviet policy is indeed likely to have played a role in these deliberations. After lengthy internal discussion, a document presenting a platform for a new Soviet policy in the Far East— centering on the conciliation of China—was prepared in the foreign ministry, coordinated in the Soviet leadership, and finally delivered by Gorbachev as a speech in Vladivostok in midsummer.[23]

This Vladivostok address was a watershed for Gorbachev not only because it sought for the first time to lay out what purported to be a new, vigorous, integrated Soviet policy for Asia, but more important because it offered concrete geopolitical concessions that at last touched on Chinese security interests. Though in themselves fairly modest and largely symbolic in nature, they proved sufficient to engage the Chinese in a process of interaction and mutual concessions that eventually led to the Sino-Soviet summit three years later.

First, by stating that the USSR had been "discussing" with Mongo-

23. *Pravda,* July 28, 1986.

lia the withdrawal of a "considerable" part of the Soviet troops there, Gorbachev finally took up an option long available to the Soviets to offer a relatively inexpensive military concession to Beijing. The Chinese for many years had been demanding a complete withdrawal of the five Soviet divisions in Mongolia, which were particularly resented because the Soviet tanks directly threatened the North China plain leading to the Chinese capital. Gorbachev did not yet say how many troops he would remove, or where he would move them to in the Soviet Union. But by raising for the first time the prospect of a Soviet pullback, he finally offered a concession relevant to the first of Beijing's three obstacles to normalization. He clearly intended to suggest to the PRC that conciliation of the Soviet Union might bring more important concessions.

Second, Gorbachev proposed to begin negotiations with the PRC about "balanced" reductions in conventional ground force levels in the Far East. This gesture touched on another aspect of the first obstacle, the Chinese demand that Soviet forces east of the Urals be reduced to the level of Khrushchev's day. In contrast to the notion of a pullback from Mongolia, however, this proposal was apparently not envisioned as leading to unilateral Soviet action. Instead, Gorbachev evidently desired to draw the Chinese into conventional force negotiations analogous to what were then the Mutual and Balanced Force Reduction talks in Europe, and to exact a still unspecified price for any Soviet force reductions in Siberia. In 1989, in the wake of the Sino-Soviet summit, these talks did in fact finally materialize.

Because of the great asymmetries in the nature and dispositions of the forces deployed on the two sides, the Chinese had never been enthusiastic about negotiating balanced conventional reductions in Asia. Their position, like that of NATO, had traditionally been that the Soviet Union should unilaterally abandon the regional military advantage it had unilaterally created. Yet the Chinese could hope that in the fullness of time such negotiations would eventually produce heavily asymmetrical Soviet cuts with only token Chinese reductions sufficient to save Gorbachev's face—as has indeed been the case in Europe.

The third subject Gorbachev addressed was the Sino-Soviet border dispute. For many years this dispute had been a focal point of Sino-

Soviet animosity. One issue had been the Chinese claim that the tsarist treaties with imperial China which defined the border were "unequal"—that is, signed when China was too weak to defend its interests. More concretely, Beijing had claimed that the Soviet Union illegally occupied some Chinese territory that was not given the USSR even by those "unequal treaties." In practice, this was a claim for some thousands of square kilometers in the Pamir Mountains, at the western end of the border, and some hundreds of disputed islands on the Chinese side of the central channel of the Amur and Ussuri rivers, which form the eastern border. Throughout most of the 1970s, Brezhnev had conducted unsuccessful negotiations with the Chinese on these issues.

Now, in his Vladivostok speech, Gorbachev announced that the Amur river boundary "could pass along the main channel." This was the first time any Soviet leader had publicly conceded this point, although it appears that during the Sino-Soviet border negotiations of 1969–78 the Soviets may have already indicated to the Chinese that they would accept such a main channel rule in most cases. The biggest sticking point in past border talks, however, had always been not Soviet acceptance of the main channel doctrine in principle, but rather the exceptions to the rule which the Soviets had always insisted on—notably their demand that they retain, in violation of the rule, Bear Island (called Heixiazu by Beijing), the large island near the Chinese side of the river at the junction of the Amur and Ussuri opposite Khabarovsk.

Gorbachev gave no hint in July 1986 as to whether he was now ready to yield on this matter, the real heart of the problem. Indeed, four years later, by the end of 1990, the status of this island was still unresolved in the new Sino-Soviet border talks. Nevertheless, Gorbachev's general attitude toward settling the border, when taken in conjunction with his more forthcoming demeanor on other issues, was sufficiently encouraging to give the Chinese reason to test his intentions in practice.

Regarding the other two Chinese obstacles—Afghanistan and Indochina—Gorbachev's changes were much more marginal, although in hindsight they proved to be harbingers of more significant Soviet shifts to come in the next two years.

On Afghanistan, he claimed that he was withdrawing six Soviet regiments. The significance of this assertion was regarded with skepticism by both the United States and China, as it brought to mind previous efforts by Brezhnev to use alleged withdrawals as deceptive gestures intended to weaken Western and Muslim support for the Afghan resistance and to help promote a settlement that would preserve the essence of Soviet domination while embellishing the form. The Soviets reacted with anger when the PRC refused to accept this claim about partial withdrawal at face value. Nevertheless, it seems likely that the very failure of this Brezhnevite gambit reinforced the factors that were nudging the Soviet leadership toward more meaningful action—that is, toward the decision taken privately late in 1987 and publicly formalized in 1988 to withdraw all Soviet forces from Afghanistan.

On Indochina, Gorbachev adopted a bland posture of urging the PRC and Vietnam to settle their differences. This position did represent something of a shift from the standard Soviet statement about refusing to prejudice the interests of third countries, and it surely irritated the Vietnamese because of its weak display of solidarity with them. Yet it stopped far short of what the Chinese were demanding, which was the direct application of Soviet pressure on Hanoi sufficient to force the Vietnamese to leave Cambodia. Subsequently Beijing vigorously reiterated its unhappiness with what it described as Gorbachev's continued recalcitrance on the most important issue between the two countries. But again, this small gesture by Gorbachev eventually proved to have been an opening step toward much more substantial change later.

The Chinese Response

On the whole, the Chinese reaction to the Vladivostok speech was one of cautious interest. They acknowledged that Gorbachev had made "new remarks on Sino-Soviet relations that had not been heard before,"[24] and they said they "attached importance" to and welcomed

24. Chinese Foreign Ministry statement reported by Agence France-Presse, August 7, 1986 (FBIS-CHI, August 8, 1986, C-1).

what he had said. But they stressed that he was still a long way from removing the three obstacles, especially getting Vietnam out of Cambodia, "and the Chinese side is not satisfied with this."[25]

Meanwhile the PRC sought private elaboration of what Gorbachev had said publicly. In early August, a few days after the speech, "old friend" Arkhipov, whom Gorbachev obviously considered a useful message-carrier, visited Beijing, ostensibly for medical treatment, and conferred with Chinese leaders. Soon thereafter a Chinese vice foreign minister journeyed to Mongolia, evidently to discuss and learn more about the promised troop withdrawal.

Apparently these soundings were sufficiently encouraging for the Chinese to take two steps in response. First, Deng Xiaoping decided to announce publicly the conditional summit offer he had made privately to Gorbachev in 1985. In a September interview on American television that was widely covered in the Chinese media, he said he would "go any place in the Soviet Union to meet with Gorbachev"— if the Soviets ended their support for the Vietnamese occupation of Cambodia. Indochina, said Deng, was a "hot spot" and an arena of direct "confrontation" between the two countries. It was the "main obstacle in Sino-Soviet relations." Gorbachev, Deng declared, had evaded the issue in his Vladivostok speech, and therefore, according to Deng, Gorbachev had "not taken a big step."[26]

By using American television to voice this complaint—but simultaneously publicizing for the first time his terms for a Sino-Soviet summit—Deng killed two birds with one stone: he applied public pressure on Gorbachev to move further on Indochina, and he also began the long process of conditioning American opinion for an eventual Sino-Soviet summit.

The New Border Talks

The second step was taken two weeks later when the Chinese foreign minister met with Shevardnadze at the UN and agreed to resume Sino-Soviet border talks at the vice foreign minister level early

25. Statement attributed to Foreign Minister Wu Xueqian by foreign ministry spokesman, *China Daily,* August 13, 1986 (FBIS-CHI, August 15, 1986, C-1).
26. Xinhua, September 6, 1986 (FBIS-CHI, September 8, 1986, B1-B2).

the next year. With this shift, the PRC at last became engaged once more with the Soviet Union in bilateral negotiations affecting a concrete security issue. Since this new series of talks began in February 1987, the border dispute has still not been fully resolved; on the other hand, the negotiations have evidently made some progress, and the atmosphere has been vastly better than that of the previous border talks in the 1970s.

To be sure, the Chinese had by now changed their own public posture regarding the border issues, though without acknowledging it. When the new discussions began, Vice Foreign Minister Qian made a public statement calling for a "comprehensive and equitable" overall settlement, but he conspicuously omitted two demands invariably heard in Mao's time. One, already mentioned, had been that the Soviets acknowledge that many of their holdings in the Far East were acquired through "unjust treaties" imposed on China by the tsars.[27] The other was that prior to a new adjudication of the border the USSR agree to a preliminary withdrawal of the armed forces of both sides from all those regions that China chose to identify as being in dispute. The jettisoning of these propaganda demands—which Mao had known would never be accepted by the Soviet Union—was a reflection of the new Chinese belief that a deal with Gorbachev on the border was not only possible but now desirable for Chinese interests.[28]

Whereas Mao had thought it advantageous to keep the border issue alive and unresolved as a political instrument to use against the Soviet Union, during the ten years since his death his successors had revised this view. From the Chinese perspective, the decisive new element that made an eventual border settlement seem more desirable was the military bait now held out to China by Gorbachev with his announce-

---

27. Since 1969 the Chinese have always made it clear that they do not claim any of the territory gained by the USSR through these "unjust treaties," but only those additional areas which they say were illegally occupied by tsarist Russia and the USSR in violation of the treaties. Nevertheless, the traditional Chinese demand that the Soviet Union acknowledge that the treaties were in fact unjust—as an added prerequisite for any border settlement—had imposed a political precondition that effectively blocked movement toward a settlement.

28. The PRC had evidently been preparing for this change in negotiating position for some time. Since well before Gorbachev's coming to power, the Chinese had ceased alluding publicly to either of these demands.

ment of the first withdrawals from Mongolia. This offer raised the prospect that a border settlement, in conjunction with a further improvement in the overall atmosphere of the relationship, might facilitate significant unilateral reductions in the Soviet forces facing China.

In August 1987 the two sides announced agreement to resolve the eastern sector of the border on the basis of the "relevant existing" treaties and the principle of the main channel in the border rivers. They announced that "working groups of experts" would be formed to examine the practical issues involved. In January 1988 these experts held their first session, and in early November, during the runup to the Sino-Soviet summit the next year, Moscow and Beijing stated that they had reached a "common understanding" regarding "most" of the eastern sector. The two sides said that although disputed areas still remained in the eastern sector, they had nevertheless agreed to form working groups to discuss the western sector and to conduct joint aerial surveys there. Most significant, both sides termed the talks beneficial and said that both had shown a "willingness to make progress."

Gorbachev Begins Deployment Retreats

Since long-existing disputes about specific areas along the border nevertheless remained—apparently including the vexed problem of Heixiazu island—it would appear that after two years of negotiations both sides were displaying an optimism about the talks that transcended their concrete results so far.[29] But there was reason for such optimism. By late 1988, the Chinese attitude regarding the future of the border talks was conditioned by newly accumulating evidence that Gorbachev had indeed begun to retreat from some of the military deployments around the Soviet periphery that had been undertaken by Brezhnev and long objected to by the Soviet Union's neighbors.

In the late summer of 1987 the USSR had agreed to the double-zero intermediate-range nuclear force (INF) agreement, yielding to the

---

29. Most of the eastern sector of the border had in fact been tacitly agreed to long before, during the negotiations in the 1970s. The statements of both sides in the late 1980s were remarkably ambiguous regarding what had been resolved now that had been unresolved before.

last-minute demand of the United States that all the Soviet theater nuclear missiles deployed in Asia be removed as well as all those deployed against Europe. Gorbachev thus relieved the concern of Japan and China—voiced with increasing vigor in 1986 and 1987[30]—that an agreement might be signed that removed this threat from Europe but left them still vulnerable to some or all of the SS-20s in Asia.

Gorbachev yielded on this point primarily because he found it unavoidable if he were to obtain an INF agreement in Europe, which was his central concern at the moment. This did not prevent him, however, from citing his agreement to remove the missiles from Asia as an immense concession to Asian opinion.[31] And indeed the Chinese, while knowing full well why Gorbachev had taken this decision, nevertheless had reason to welcome the result, which signified a partial reduction in the Soviet nuclear threat about which they had been complaining.

Next, in early 1988, the Soviet Union announced its decision to withdraw its forces from Afghanistan. Again, this decision was driven by a variety of motives besides a desire to please the Chinese,[32] but it did nevertheless represent a move toward overcoming the second of the three obstacles to normalization. And although the Soviet presence in Afghanistan had always been the least important of the three obstacles to Beijing, the Soviet decision to depart certainly had a major influence on the Chinese attitude toward Gorbachev. Here was concrete evidence that the Soviet claims about "new thinking" in foreign policy could indeed have a major effect on Soviet military behavior.

Finally, at the end of 1988, Gorbachev went on to announce significant unilateral reductions in the Soviet armed forces and important

30. After the United States in the spring of 1987 had initially prepared and circulated to its friends a proposal to present to the Soviet Union that would have settled for a 50 percent reduction in the Asian SS-20s, the protests of Japan and China induced Washington to toughen this proposal and present Gorbachev with an ultimatum for total elimination of those missiles as the price of an agreement.

31. Notably, in his interview with the Indonesian newspaper *Merdeka* in the summer of 1987, reported in *Pravda,* July 23, 1987 (FBIS-SOV, July 23, 1987, CC-1).

32. Externally, the benefits to be derived from this step in the West and in the Muslim world were probably more important to Gorbachev than the Chinese reaction. But the internal factor was probably most important: the felt need to heal a wound that was increasingly damaging Gorbachev's hope to revitalize the Soviet Union.

unilateral withdrawals from Eastern Europe. From the Chinese perspective, the implications of this announcement for their own security were not entirely clear. Although the Soviets asserted that some 200,000 of the half-million men scheduled to be removed from the armed forces would come from the forces in Asia, they were (and, as of this writing, still are) far more reticent about the specifics of the Asian reductions than they were about those in Europe. Even after they specified that the Asian reductions would involve some twelve combat divisions, they were far more ambiguous about the location and nature of the units involved than about the units being withdrawn from Europe.[33] And again in contrast to their statements about the stocks of tanks and artillery to be destroyed west of the Urals, the Soviets said virtually nothing about weapons reduction in the ground forces of the Far East. Finally, the Soviet Union remained far more reticent about the nature of the reorganization being planned for its forces in Asia than about the reorganization claimed to have begun in Eastern Europe and European Russia.

All these calculated ambiguities signified to the Chinese that the process of force reduction and reorganization that Gorbachev had initiated would probably take place much more deliberately in Asia than in Europe, where the incentives for Soviet action were far more pressing. Yet the Chinese could hardly fail to be impressed by the fresh evidence—superimposed on the Afghan announcement—that the Soviet General Staff, despite its obvious reluctance, was being compelled to agree to a succession of major force withdrawals and force cuts. The cumulative impression left by these events was that powerful internal economic pressures as well as new foreign policy priorities were driving Soviet strategic policies toward overall retrenchment. If this was the case—and if the Soviet military leadership no longer called the tune in Moscow—there was good reason to hope that

33. By the time of Gorbachev's visit to China in the spring of 1989, the Soviets did make it clear that there would be further reductions in the five Soviet divisions originally deployed in Mongolia, culminating in their complete withdrawal by 1992. This presumably was part of the twelve-division reduction promised for the Far East. The units comprising the remainder of that reduction, however, have never been identified by Moscow. See, in this connection, the disingenuous statement by Defense Minister Dmitrii Yazov addressing the issue of Soviet deployments in Asia in the spring of 1989, in *Pravda*, May 28, 1989 (FBIS-SOV, May 30, 1989, 9).

further Chinese conciliation of Gorbachev might indeed produce a gradual reduction of the military presence that Brezhnev had assembled on the PRC's northern frontiers.

The Erosion of the Indochina Prerequisite

These growing hopes and gradually shifting perceptions were duly reflected in the changing bilateral atmospherics. In October 1986 the Soviets ceased jamming Beijing's Russian-language broadcasts to the USSR, and in December Gorbachev permanently removed from the air Radio Ba Yi, the clandestine radio which the USSR had directed at China for seven years, purporting to represent dissident sentiment within the Chinese armed forces. In August 1987, in the first such case since 1967, Defense Minister Dmitrii Yazov sent personal greetings on the People's Liberation Army anniversary to his counterpart "comrade Zhang Aiping." Then in November the Chinese sent a delegation to Moscow for the October Revolution anniversary for the first time in twenty-three years. And in January 1988 the Chinese unbent sufficiently to publish a Gorbachev interview in a PRC publication.[34] This step in particular was quite significant as a public signal to the world—and to the Chinese elite—that the Chinese leadership believed Gorbachev indeed represented a new trend in Soviet policy.

But the issue of Indochina remained a fly in the ointment. Throughout 1987 and 1988, even as the Chinese incrementally eased their posture toward Gorbachev, they continued to complain that he had not done enough to change Hanoi's attitude. In November and December 1987 Deng and Gorbachev engaged in low-key personal polemics on whether the satisfaction of China's demand for a Vietnamese withdrawal should be a prerequisite for a Sino-Soviet summit meeting, as the Chinese insisted. Gorbachev contended that summit

---

34. Gorbachev interview of December 28, 1987, published simultaneously in the Chinese weekly *Liaowang* and the Soviet *Izvestiya* on January 11, 1988. (FBIS-SOV, January 11, 1988, 23–25.) Gorbachev took the occasion to renew his plea for a Sino-Soviet summit, to comment optimistically about the prospects for a renewal of Sino-Soviet party relations, to portray the two countries as becoming ever more intimate, and to assert that the Soviet Union advocated a "just settlement" of all regional conflicts.

meetings were held "precisely to discuss and solve complex issues," and he noted that the Soviet-U.S. summits had been held despite "far more disputable problems." Deng professed to continue to find this unacceptable, insisting that without Soviet aid "Vietnam could not fight a single day in Cambodia," and that Gorbachev had "actually refused my aspirations" by not compelling Vietnam to cease.[35]

One gets the impression, however, that China's determination to make complete satisfaction of its demands regarding Indochina a prerequisite for a summit was continuously eroding throughout 1987 and 1988. In March 1987 Chinese commentaries credited Shevardnadze as showing "great enthusiasm" for a resolution of the issue and as having visited Indochina to try "to find a way for a political settlement." The following October, Deputy Foreign Minister Qian, after discussions with his counterpart Igor Rogachev in Beijing, hinted that the Soviets were showing a bit of flexibility, and said that they had "expressed willingness to make their own efforts for a political settlement," though he added that "what will happen remains to be seen."

Having acknowledged that the Soviets were trying to satisfy Beijing on Vietnam, the PRC then began to move toward a summit before the Soviets had produced results. In the fall of 1988 both sides began to suggest that preparations for such a meeting were already underway. After a visit by the Chinese foreign minister to Moscow in December, a return visit to Beijing by Shevardnadze in early February 1989 resulted in mutual confirmation that summit dates had been fixed for May 15–18. There were intimations of disagreement within the Chinese elite about this announcement,[36] and Deng Xiaoping continued to make statements indicating unhappiness that the Indochina obstacle had not been removed.[37]

35. *People's Daily*, December 5, 1987. It should be noted that despite these words, Deng three weeks later allowed Gorbachev to be interviewed by a Chinese publication.

36. At the conclusion of his February visit Shevardnadze told reporters that he and the Chinese had agreed upon a date of mid-May for the Gorbachev visit. He then boarded his plane, and immediately after it took off, Chinese vice foreign minister Tian contradicted him, saying that Shevardnadze had proposed that date, but that this had not yet been decided, and that the Chinese side still wished to study the matter; reported in the *Los Angeles Times*, February 5, 1989. The next day, however, *People's Daily* confirmed the dates of May 15–18 for the summit. The sequence of events suggested considerable disarray in the Chinese Politburo. See also Kyodo news service, Tokyo, February 11, 1989 (FBIS-CHI, February 13, 1989, 6).

37. During the Shevardnadze visit Deng rather comically asserted that Gorbachev's visit would only mark the "formal start" of normalization, intimating that even after

But having at last agreed to and announced a summit date before the final resolution of the Cambodia issue, the Chinese in fact had sacrificed a good deal of their leverage on Moscow. Although in early April Vietnam and Pnom Penh announced that Vietnamese troops would indeed be withdrawn by the end of September 1989, Hanoi warned that this withdrawal might only prove temporary if the Pnom Penh government were threatened.[38] Beijing exhibited great unhappiness with this caveat, and so the Indochina issue, the third obstacle, would continue to cloud the Sino-Soviet summit when it materialized. But the PRC went ahead with Gorbachev's visit nonetheless.

In retrospect, the erosion of China's long insistence on an Indochinese prerequisite to this visit can be attributed to two factors. One has already been indicated: the accumulation of evidence, increasingly persuasive to the Chinese leaders, that Gorbachev was gradually retrenching the Soviet military position all around the Soviet periphery, which gave the PRC reason to encourage him.[39]

The second factor was almost certainly the Chinese reaction to Gorbachev's growing American connection. The PRC had observed that the USSR's concessions to the United States and to the West—which were considerably more dramatic than its concessions to China—had radically transformed the Western and American attitude toward the Soviet Union. In June 1988 Chinese comment on President Reagan's final summit with Gorbachev had concluded that "the two superpowers are changing the nature of their rivalry, with an easing of tensions and the formulation of new rules for the rivalry." The momentum for détente, noted Beijing, "may last for quite a long time."[40] In this situation the Chinese leadership sensed increasing

---

entry into normalization, it could be interpreted as having many further degrees and stages with incremental rewards; reported in *People's Daily,* February 5, 1989 (FBIS-CHI, February 9, 1989, 3). There were many indications of disagreement during the Shevardnadze visit, and the Chinese (but not the Soviets) described the atmosphere as "frank." The Soviet radio on February 5 claimed that a joint communiqué had been issued, but this was not the case, and *Pravda* published a unilateral account of the visit which read like the unsuccessful Soviet draft of such a communiqué; *Pravda,* February 5, 1989.

38. In fact, Hanoi did subsequently send forces back temporarily some months later, to help the Hun Sen government beat back a Khmer Rouge offensive.

39. It was during the Sino-Soviet summit that Li Peng indicated to Soviet reporters that Gorbachev had told him the Soviets intended eventually to withdraw all troops from Mongolia. TASS, May 16, 1989; *People's Daily,* May 17, 1989.

40. *People's Daily,* June 5, 1988 (FBIS-CHI, June 6, 1988, 10–11).

pressure to improve its own position in the triangular relationship by consenting to normalization with Gorbachev.

The Summit and the Chinese Crisis

But when the long-awaited, long-negotiated summit meeting finally materialized in May 1989, it was overshadowed by a series of extraordinary events that neither leadership had anticipated. First, Gorbachev's visit served as a catalyst, a fresh stimulant to the Chinese domestic storm that was already developing. His presence—dramatizing the hopes for liberalization that he symbolized—encouraged an escalation of the massive protests against the regime, and thus helped to bring to a climax the long-building crisis within the leadership.[41] The popular tumult forced major revisions in Gorbachev's schedule that were humiliating to the Chinese leaders, and soon after his departure the crisis moved rapidly to its bloody resolution, with the fall of Zhao and his supporters and Deng Xiaoping's use of the army to massacre student protesters in Tienanmen Square.

In the aftermath, despite Gorbachev's studied declarations of neutrality concerning the Tienanmen events, the new hard-line leadership was angry at him. Although the Chinese leaders continued to welcome Gorbachev's relaxation of the Soviet military posture toward China,[42] they now saw concrete reason to dread the subversive effects of his domestic behavior. Gorbachev had not troubled to disguise his sympathies for Zhao Ziyang during the summit visit to China. The Soviet leader's policies of radical political reform and *glasnost* were, after all, the conduit, the intermediary, through which the dread menace of Western pluralism had come to consolidate its presence in Chinese society. If the United States was the source of the infection, Gorbachev was Typhoid Mary. And if America became the special

41. Among other things, certain statements made to Gorbachev by Secretary General Zhao Ziyang about Deng Xiaoping's role in the Chinese leadership were used against Zhao by Li Peng as the leadership struggle intensified.

42. In an address during the summit visit Gorbachev revealed that of the 200,000 men to be removed from the Soviet forces in Asia, 120,000 would come from the forces in the Far East, and that these would include twelve ground force divisions. *Pravda,* May 17, 1989.

bête noire of leaders such as Li Peng who blamed foreign interference for the Chinese leadership's difficulties, Gorbachev's Soviet Union was henceforth a second object of suspicion.

The Consequences of the Fall of Eastern Europe

Even more striking was the reaction of the hard-line Chinese leadership to the series of democratic revolutions that took place in Eastern Europe soon thereafter, in the last few months of 1989. The Chinese leaders were embittered at Gorbachev's acquiescence in the rapid unraveling of communist rule in the East European states, and they were frightened at the precedent set by the violent demise of their ally Ceauşescu after he had carried out a massacre similar to their own.[43] These sentiments were then visibly reinforced by Gorbachev's agreement, at the watershed February 1990 plenum of the CPSU Central Committee, to legitimize political competition for the Soviet Communist Party.

The initial Chinese reaction to these events was to denounce Gorbachev and his policies in a series of unpublicized documents circulated widely throughout the Chinese Communist Party in the winter of 1989–90. Beginning in late December, the cadres were told that the changes in Eastern Europe were a subversion of socialism for which Gorbachev was directly responsible.[44] In an unpublished speech after the Soviet February party plenum, the new Chinese party secretary general Jiang Zemin is said to have called Gorbachev a "traitor" to communism who had "rejected" the socialist system.[45] The Chinese party leaders are alleged to have directed that all party members be "thoroughly educated" on the perfidious nature of Gorbachev's re-

---

43. Interestingly, the Chinese leadership's horror at what Gorbachev had permitted to happen to the communist parties in Eastern Europe was loudly shared by the Stalinist leaders of Vietnam and North Korea, two other states in the Far East whose parties had long been independent of Soviet control. The spectacle of this Far Eastern phalanx of socialist states denouncing the European democratic revolutions of late 1989 and vehemently rejecting "bourgeois" political reform has been cited by some observers as evidence for Karl Wittfogel's contention that there is an "Asiatic mode of production" predisposing regimes toward "Oriental despotism." See Karl A. Wittfogel, *Oriental Despotism* (New Haven: Yale University Press, 1957).

44. *The New York Times*, December 28, 1989.

45. *The Economist*, March 3, 1990.

forms, and that to this end they be set to studying old party documents—presumably, from the era of Mao's polemics with Khrushchev—denouncing Soviet revisionism.[46]

PRC publications commented on the chorus of denunciations Gorbachev was encountering at home and took comfort from the increasing gloom in Western appraisals of his prospects. In December 1989
one Chinese leader, Li Ruihuan, observed that China believed that
Soviet socialism, with its long history, would not be changed "by the
will of one man."[47] In January a Chinese commentary said that
Gorbachev was in "a serious situation of being attacked front and
rear,"[48] and Deng Xiaoping in an address to a party gathering is
reported to have predicted Gorbachev's eventual downfall at the
hands of the conservatives.[49] In February a Chinese party internal
directive is said to have emphasized Gorbachev's internal isolation,
and to have noted that the West was not optimistic about his future.[50]
And in early April Deng Xiaoping is said to have told another party
meeting that "we should place our hopes on the Soviet people and the
broad ranks of genuine Bolsheviks."[51]

Nor did the Chinese leadership entirely limit itself to the private
expression of such hopes. In an unusual act of effrontery, the Chinese
government in March is said to have privately informed the Soviet
Union through diplomatic channels that it would support any military action the USSR might take to deal with the problem of secession-
ism.[52] As we shall see, the PRC had good practical reasons of its own
to want Gorbachev to curb the influence of Soviet separatist dissi-
dence. Although the March message was ostensibly a statement of
support for Gorbachev opposing Western pressure on him to refrain
from using force in Lithuania, it was in fact an initiative intended to
reinforce the internal demands Gorbachev was already receiving from
the military and party conservatives that he take forceful action

46. *South China Morning Post* (Hong Kong), February 17, 1990.
47. Kyodo, December 9, 1989 (FBIS-CHI, December 12, 1989, 5).
48. *Ta Kung Pao* (Hong Kong), January 20, 1990 (FBIS-CHI, January 22, 1990, 4–5).
49. *South China Morning Post*, January 25, 1990.
50. *Cheng Ming* (Hong Kong), May 1, 1990.
51. Ibid.
52. *South China Morning Post*, March 30, 1990.

against the Lithuanian separatists. Thus the Chinese diplomatic initiative was, in effect, an act of intervention in the internal Soviet political struggle. In general, conservative Soviet comment suggests that Chinese appeals to Soviet ideologues have not been totally without effect.[53]

Gorbachev and Minority Subversion

The indignation of the Chinese Communist leadership early in 1990 was reinforced by the fact that the unrest and centrifugal tendencies Gorbachev had allowed to emerge in Central Asia were affecting the Chinese regime's relations with its own minority nationalities. Beijing had particularly well-founded fears about the effects on Xinjiang of the instability that *glasnost* had begun to foster in Kirghizia and Tadzhikistan. In addition, the PRC saw the vigorous tendencies toward political reform which Gorbachev's example was producing in Soviet-oriented Mongolia as a menace to stability in the Chinese province of Inner Mongolia.[54]

In early 1990 Li Peng publicly warned against "separatist" tendencies which he said had arisen among minority nationalities.[55] Subsequently, at a meeting of the Chinese Central Military Commission in

53. Thus, in April 1990, a report published in the leading publication of the reactionary wing of the Soviet party went so far as to allude approvingly to the Tienanmen massacre, asserting that "many [Chinese] deputies believe that the 'decisive measures' to stop the mass demonstrations and hunger strikes staged right there, under the windows of the House of People's Assembly, were the decisive factor in the country's continued progression along the path of socialism." *Sovetskaya Rossiya*, April 6, 1990. Clearly, there are many in Moscow who are still thirsting for a "Chinese solution."

54. In late March 1990 an Inner Mongolian official told a Hong Kong newspaper that separatists were spreading "rumors" in Inner Mongolia, and that unidentified hostile foreign forces were trying to promote a "peaceful subversion" of the established order through economic activity. He then admitted that "the recent political changes in Mongolia have had some impact on people's thinking" in Inner Mongolia. "Our people," he said, "are able to listen to radio broadcasts from Mongolia which mainly report news about the political reforms there." *Hongkong Standard*, March 23, 1990 (FBIS-CHI, March 23, 1990, 1–3). Beijing is aware that East Germany's loss of its propaganda monopoly over the local population's information—because of the proximity of West Germany and the impossibility of preventing reception of West German radio and television—had been one of the factors contributing, over the long term, to Erich Honecker's loss of control.

55. *The New York Times*, February 20, 1990.

March, President Yang Shangkun is said to have called on three military regions to step up surveillance of "splittist" activities in border areas with heavy minority concentrations.[56] In late March a Xinjiang official publicly alluded to what he said was the subversive and separatist local activities of a "handful of people." He revealed that some had spread "reactionary leaflets and slogans," but that "many" had been arrested, and that although "there have been some reactionary organizations, . . . they were banned."[57] Two weeks later, bloody clashes took place between Chinese troops and the Kirghiz population in the vicinity of Kashgar and in two other places in western Xinjiang.[58] There were subsequent reports that tens of thousands of troops had been transferred to western Xinjiang, and that additional forces were also deployed to Inner Mongolia.[59]

Deng's Decision to Exercise Public Restraint

But despite these various reasons for resentment at Gorbachev, by the spring of 1990 the Chinese leadership had turned another corner in its behavior toward him. After extensive debate, Deng Xiaoping persuaded his colleagues to avoid public polemics with Moscow and to proceed with the dealings with the Soviets that were already in train since the summit. There were at least four reasons why the PRC leadership decided to impose these limits on its reaction to Gorbachev's behavior.

First, the question of whether or not to attack the Soviets publicly was intertwined, as in past decades, with the question of future Chinese domestic policy and the ongoing Chinese leadership struggle. While some indignant Chinese leaders wanted to expand the attack on Gorbachev to the public domain,[60] Deng Xiaoping was reluctant to do so in part because he believed that this would play into the

---

56. *South China Morning Post,* April 18, 1990 (FBIS-CHI, April 18, 1990, 33–34).

57. *Ta Kung Pao* (Hong Kong), March 25, 1990 (FBIS-CHI, March 26, 1990, 49–50). As a result of these punitive measures, the official said, the situation in Xinjiang was "very stable."

58. *Los Angeles Times,* April 11, 1990; *The Economist,* April 14, 1990; *Far Eastern Economic Review,* April 19, 1990.

59. *South China Morning Post,* April 18, 1990.

60. *South China Morning Post,* January 6, 1990.

hands of those colleagues who wanted to impose a tougher—and, incidentally, more anti-Western—domestic policy than he thought advisable. Deng prevailed.

Second, the powerful military reasons for continuing to deal with Gorbachev had not gone away. A stable relationship with him and the expansion of the multiple contacts and negotiations already begun still offered the prospect of major security benefits to China over the long term—both in terms of an eventual border agreement and in terms of a possible further reduction in the Soviet force posture. These inducements were not to be tossed away lightly.

Third, the PRC was now in a poor international position to break publicly with Gorbachev. Angry Western reaction to the Tienanmen events gave the Chinese leadership cause to feel that its position in the Sino-Soviet-U.S. triangle had suddenly deteriorated, and that its new difficulties with the United States and the overall improvement of Soviet-American relations had together weakened Chinese leverage in dealing with both the Soviet Union and the United States.[61] Indeed, the PRC had reason to fear that in view of the spectacular multiplication of centrifugal forces in the USSR, the sudden and astonishing disintegration of the Warsaw Pact, and the rapid erosion of the Soviet geopolitical position in Europe, public sentiment in the United States might become less inclined to place a high value on propitiating China as a strategic buffer against the Soviet Union. Fearing isolation, then, the PRC had reason to hesitate in picking a new quarrel.

And finally, as already suggested, the Chinese had been given some encouragement by the increased conservative pressure on Gorbachev in 1990, fed by the angry reaction of many in the Soviet party, military, and KGB to the shocking loss of Eastern Europe and the decay of Moscow's control over the republics. The Chinese leaders, although still exasperated by Gorbachev's behavior, pinned their hopes on his domestic enemies—if not to remove him, than to compel him to

---

61. Thus an article in the foreign affairs weekly *Liaowang* on January 8, 1990, expressed open anxiety about the "major changes" in U.S.-Soviet relations that it attributed to Gorbachev's "new thinking," and indicated concern that U.S-Soviet cooperation might harm China's interests. (FBIS-CHI, January 9, 1990, 1–2.) Ironically, it was just two years earlier that the same journal had published an interview with Gorbachev, signaling an important step forward at the time for Sino-Soviet relations.

change course sharply. Indeed, as a result of Gorbachev's retreat before this pressure the future of the Soviet reform process was becoming increasingly problematical. As Heinz Timmermann observes at the conclusion of Chapter 1, whether the "social-democratization" of the Soviet party would ever be completed had become highly uncertain; and while the West continued to hope that this would eventually happen, the Chinese Communist leaders retained a vested interest in assuming that it would not.

The Li Peng Visit and the Emergence of Military Contacts

Against this background, the Chinese leadership from the spring of 1990 resumed its policy of vigorously pursuing contacts with Moscow. In April 1990, Premier Li Peng, after much preliminary negotiation, came to the Soviet Union and, in effect, offered to live and let live. Li said that every socialist country has "its own path to development," and that China's path was different from the USSR's, but that after talking to the Soviet leaders he had decided that "*perestroika* has a socialist direction" after all.[62] But the atmosphere remained constrained, and no formal communiqués were issued. Six governmental agreements were signed, including provision for each side to provide credits to the other to facilitate moving away from the barter system and to provide more flexibility for trade. The potentially most important agreement, however, was as yet only an empty shell. This was one dealing with principles for reduction of forces along the border and military confidence-building measures (CBMs). The resulting document did not (as some in the West suggested) provide for any specific force reductions or CBMs, but rather only agreed on general guidelines for future negotiations on these matters.

The most important consequence of the Li Peng visit was not anything accomplished during the visit itself, but rather the impetus it provided for a significant expansion of Sino-Soviet party and military contacts along lines that had been anticipated by the two sides at the time of the Gorbachev summit,[63] but not yet implemented. The mili-

---

62. *Pravda*, April 26, 1990.

63. At that time, one Soviet officer had publicly asked why, "if the Soviet Union can have all kinds of contacts such as exchanges of military delegations, reciprocal visits by

tary contacts were more important in their implications than those on the party side. Two weeks before Li Peng's arrival, a delegation of the Foreign Affairs Bureau of the Chinese Ministry of Defense visited Moscow, in the first such formal official visit in nearly three decades. The Soviets made a reciprocal visit to Beijing at this level in early June; but more important, another Chinese delegation led by General Liu Huaqing, vice chairman of the Central Military Commission, simultaneously went to Moscow for consultations on a variety of subjects, notably including military technology. The Chinese described Liu's discussion with Vice Premier Yegor Belousov—overseer of Soviet military industry—as "significant and fruitful."[64]

Soviet chief of staff Mikhail Moiseyev said that the first few rounds of these talks were intended to be merely preliminary, to formulate the "principles" needed to establish "relations in the military economic fields."[65] Eventually, however, they could well presage resumption of some Sino-Soviet cooperation regarding military technology and some weapons trade between the two countries. Under Gorbachev, the Soviets in recent years had developed military-industrial contacts and exchanges with the United States as part of "military détente," and the Soviets had sought analogous contacts with China for some time. The Soviet Union in the Gorbachev era had also considerably relaxed constraints on the sale of weaponry such as military aircraft in the West (partly because of the more pressing need for hard currency); and since 1989 the USSR had publicly offered to begin such sales to China.[66]

In sum, this aspect of Gorbachev's policy toward Beijing now appeared to have started to pay off. The Chinese seemed to have begun the process of shifting, if not to an equidistant policy, then at least toward a somewhat less unbalanced policy, in an area—foreign military procurement—where they had been totally oriented toward the West for many years because of Sino-Soviet mutual hostility.

---

warships, and so forth with NATO countries, it should not have them in relations with the PRC too?" *Krasnaya Zvezda,* May 19, 1989 (FBIS-SOV, May 19, 1989, 26–27).

64. Xinhua, June 1, 1990 (FBIS-CHI, June 4, 1990).

65. *People's Daily,* June 7, 1990.

66. At the time of the Gorbachev summit visit, one of the editors of *Red Star* had told a Japanese newspaper that "if the Chinese side wants, there will be no political obstacles to the Soviet Union selling its most sophisticated weapons, such as MIG-29 fighters, to China." *Tokyo Shimbun,* May 15, 1989.

Conclusions

On balance, Gorbachev by late 1990 had cause for satisfaction over the results of his handling of the Chinese since 1985. Although some aspects of the new world of Sino-Soviet normalization had proved less than idyllic, the most important goal of Gorbachev's policy was now within sight: a visible improvement sufficient in scope to convince his own military that there really had been a radical diminution of the "Chinese threat," and therefore to justify the future force reductions in Asia desperately needed by the Soviet economy.

In addition, the General Staff seemed likely over time to become less and less concerned about Chinese-American security cooperation. The symbolic aspect of these strategic dealings—which since the early 1970s had implied the existence of a U.S. counterweight to the Soviet Union in the Sino-Soviet-American triangle—had been eroded on one side by the crisis in Sino-American relations since the Tienanmen massacre, and on both sides by the steady, continued decline in perception of a Soviet threat. This shadowy part of the Sino-American relationship had already become an anomalous and vestigial remnant, very much like the former Sino-Soviet treaty of alliance in the years after 1960. This change seemed unlikely to be explicitly acknowledged, however, until a settlement for the entire Sino-Soviet border was eventually concluded and sizeable, highly assymetrical Soviet force reductions were carried out in Asia in addition to those already announced. Meanwhile the Chinese were likely to delay explicit public disavowal of those increasingly anachronistic security arrangements with America put in place a decade earlier.

In addition to defusing the sense of a Soviet threat in Beijing and the sense of a Chinese threat in the Soviet defense ministry, Gorbachev had accomplished the considerable feat of overcoming Soviet fear of Chinese geopolitical rivalry as an impediment to radical changes in Soviet policy elsewhere in East Asia. This was most evident in Soviet policy toward the Korean states, where Gorbachev had been able to pursue further and further Soviet economic interest in a relationship with South Korea in defiance of the growing fury of Kim Il-sung.

In previous decades the Soviet Union would have been inhibited from going nearly this far by, among other things, concern over the prospect of Chinese political gains at Soviet expense, not only in Korea but among the world left generally. The change was facilitated by the fact that the PRC—despite its indignation about Eastern Europe, its overtures to Castro, and its retreat toward domestic orthodoxy since 1989—was still not much more oriented toward traditional Marxist-Leninist priorities in its foreign policy than was Gorbachev himself. While Sino-Soviet competition for influence still endured in some places—notably Indochina—the global scope and ideological cast of that competition had long since disappeared. Despite all the defensive ideological rhetoric generated in Beijing in the aftermath of the 1989 crisis in the communist world, the pragmatic concerns shared by Gorbachev and Deng continued to produce huge areas of overlap in foreign policy.

One of these areas of common ground was the concern of both leaders to retain a political and economic connection with the major industrialized states of the West, and particularly with the United States. As suggested earlier, both Moscow and Beijing had reason to regret the global imbalance created by the collapse of the Soviet Union as a competitive superpower; yet both also had geopolitical incentives to strive to minimize difficulties with the United States. Although both the Soviet Union and the PRC derived benefits from their expanding bilateral economic ties, both remained well aware that their hopes for modernization were far more dependent on their dealings with the capitalist industrialized world. Both therefore retained an interest in ensuring that Sino-Soviet rapprochement did not have an adverse affect on their relationships with the West and Japan. In particular, once Sino-Soviet relations had reached the stage of military-industrial contacts, both leaderships became somewhat more alert to the need to avoid alarming the United States. This concern, however, was felt considerably more by Moscow than by Deng, who had ongoing friction with America over human rights and other issues. In the last analysis, the Soviets felt a more profound need than did Deng for good relations with the Americans not only because they were more deeply engaged in negotiations with Washington on a multitude of fronts, but also because the Soviets' economic and political position was more grave than Deng's.

Finally, the chief threat to further progress in Sino-Soviet rapprochement continued to be the uncertainties of the domestic political process in both countries.[67] Deep policy divisions remained in the Chinese leadership, and the calming of Beijing's behavior toward both the Soviet Union and the United States since the spring of 1990 could once again prove ephemeral, particularly after the death of Deng Xiaoping. The Soviet political future, of course, remained even more uncertain. Having at one time expressed a desire for the political demise of the "traitor" Gorbachev, the Chinese leadership could be unpleasantly surprised if it ever got its wish. On the one hand, the removal of Gorbachev by the chauvinistic hard-line forces of the Soviet Communist Party and the Soviet military industrial complex could jeopardize those concrete geopolitical concessions that the PRC still awaited from the Soviet Union—in the Sino-Soviet border negotiations and in force withdrawals from Asia. And on the other hand, the defeat of Gorbachev by the separatist forces of the Soviet republics and the democratic forces led by Boris Yeltsin would threaten the Chinese leaders in a more profound way, by multiplying the danger that the subversive infection Gorbachev had already unleashed would eventually spread to China.

67. In addition, some differences over Indochina endured, but the PRC, after the Sino-Soviet summit, seems to have abandoned its long effort to hold improvements in Sino-Soviet relations hostage to the changes it seeks in Vietnamese behavior.

[4]

Moscow's "New Thinking" on Third World Liberationism

S. Neil MacFarlane

The struggle for liberation in the Third World has perhaps contributed more than any other factor to the alteration of the political map of the globe since 1945. The ostensibly anti-imperialist focus of this process greatly facilitated Soviet entry into much of the Third World and the establishment of the status of the USSR as a global power. The USSR and the Third World found themselves to be "objective allies" in a common struggle against the hegemonic Western powers.

Yet much has changed in this relationship since 1980. The USSR appears to place much less emphasis than previously on political, social, and economic trends in the Third World. In its analysis of and practice toward Third World politics, the focus on radical forces purportedly committed to revolutionary transformation of their societies and of their societies' links to the North has weakened, with state-to-state and economic relations taking precedence instead.

It is my purpose to describe and to explain this change. I begin with

The author's understanding of recent Soviet perspectives on national liberation in the Third World has been substantially enhanced by participation in the American Council of Learned Societies/USSR Academy of Sciences exchange in international relations and security, sponsored by the International Research and Exchanges Board. He is also grateful for the support of this research by the University of Virginia and the National Council for Soviet and East European Research.

a brief account of the place of Third World liberationism in pre-Gorbachev Soviet theory and practice. I then analyze how the role of liberation forces has been transformed in Soviet policy under Gorbachev and conclude with an effort to explain these changes and situate them within the broader context of Soviet perspectives on the "global left."

Several clarifications are useful at the outset. First, this chapter does not purport to provide a comprehensive analysis of the development of Soviet foreign policy in the Third World since 1985, but is rather about the evolving Soviet relationship with the liberationist left. Other aspects of Soviet policy—such as economic assistance, arms transfers, and the Soviet diplomacy of conflict resolution—are touched on only when they clarify the principal focus of this analysis.

The focus on the "left" necessarily gives an ideological emphasis to this analysis. Some comment on the role of ideology is appropriate, particularly since many Soviets currently deemphasize the role played by ideology in defining Soviet objectives in the Third World during the previous era.[1] The ideologically derived objective of world revolution has not been a determining factor in Soviet policy in the Third World (or elsewhere) since the earliest days of the Bolshevik regime. It is unlikely, however, that Soviet policymakers were uniformly dismissive of or scornful toward ideological prescriptions. Indeed, those dominating Soviet policy toward liberation movements under the Brezhnev regime (for example, Boris Ponomarev) are now referred to as "dogmatists" in part because of their fidelity to such prescriptions. Nonetheless, policy in the Third World appears to have been dominated largely by the quest for global influence and status and by the desire to weaken the United States and its Western allies in areas that had traditionally been their preserve.

Ideology in general, and the Marxist-Leninist interpretation of politics in the Third World in particular have not, however, been irrelevant to policy. The call of Gorbachev and others for "freeing international relations from ideology"[2] suggests that, in their view,

---

1. This was evident in panel discussions at the International Congress of Soviet and East European Studies meetings in Harrogate, England, in July 1990, at which this paper was initially presented.

2. Mikhail Gorbachev, "Address to the United Nations" (December 7, 1988), as reprinted in *Soviet Life*, no. 2 (1989).

ideology was an important constraint on policy in the previous era. Prescription of objectives, moreover, is only one function of ideology. Others include the provision of a cognitive structure to order one's interpretation of events and one's response to them, the definition of tactics in pursuit of objectives that may or may not be derived from ideology, and the legitimation of the regime, both internally and externally.

Marxism-Leninism provided the basic concepts (including class struggle, national liberation, anti-imperialism, noncapitalist path of development, socialist orientation, the vanguard party) dominating the discourse, structuring the interpretations, and defining the tactics of Soviet analysts and policymakers prior to the arrival of Gorbachev, and it continues to vie with the less dogmatic formulations of "new thinking" since then. The concept of global class struggle strongly influenced Soviet conceptions of interest and threat in international relations in the Third World.[3] Those of socialist orientation, noncapitalist development, and the vanguard party strongly affected the manner in which the USSR pursued influence. Soviet policymakers and advisers propagated these orientations in policy because they believed that relations with and influence over regimes accepting them would be more durable. In turn, Soviet allocation of resources in the Third World focused to a considerable extent on regimes espousing these concepts, particularly in areas such as Africa where no immediate vital interests of the USSR were at stake.[4]

Finally, ideology provided a basis for the legitimation of the Soviet regime and its foreign policy. To the extent that Soviet citizens could be convinced that the Communist Party (CPSU) and the USSR were the leading forces in a revolutionary movement of world historical significance, they might more easily accept the privations visited upon them by the communist elite. To the extent that outsiders sharing the purported revolutionary objectives of the USSR took Soviet commitments seriously, they might be predisposed to cooperation with the Soviets and hence be more useful as instruments of Soviet foreign policy.

3. Eduard Shevardnadze, address at a conference in the Ministry of Foreign Affairs, reprinted in *Vestnik Ministerstva Inostrannykh Del SSSR,* no. 15 (August, 1988):35–6.

4. There are of course exceptions where strategic and power political considerations dictated the pursuit of close relations with Third World states in spite of their orientation. India is an obvious example.

On the other hand, such strategies of legitimation had constraining effects. If Soviet leaders believed their domestic legitimacy was tied to the "expansion of the positions of socialism," failure and loss of position had potentially serious domestic consequences in that they undermined the prevailing view of history. Retreat from the promotion of socialism abroad risked raising nagging questions about the wisdom of the party's approach to socialism and governance at home. Failure to promote the advance of the "forces of progress" and to protect them against those of "reaction" also gave the lie to Soviet claims to leadership of a "world revolutionary process," diminishing Soviet prestige and influence over like-minded movements and regimes elsewhere.

In sum, the proposition that Soviet policy toward the Third World was dominated by a traditional power political rationale hardly negates the significance of ideology and ideological commitments in Soviet policy.

Definitions and Dimensions of Analysis

National liberation means different things to different people. Although there may be a common core meaning, one encounters important divergences once one moves beyond it. Indeed, these definitional discrepancies are among the several important factors limiting the Soviet capacity to draw durable advantage from involvement in struggles for national liberation.[5]

Since this chapter is about Soviet policy, I concentrate on national liberation as the Soviets have defined it. As traditionally conceived, the process of national liberation involves three struggles: for political independence, for economic liberation (independence from exploitative economic relations with the imperialist economies), and for social revolution (the elimination of mutual human exploitation).[6]

---

5. For a more complete discussion, see S. Neil MacFarlane, *Superpower Rivalry and Third World Radicalism* (Baltimore: Johns Hopkins University Press, 1985), chap. 5.

6. A representative comment from the 1961 CPSU Program, for example: "A national liberation revolution does not end with the winning of political independence.

The struggle for national liberation takes place not just against colonialism or neocolonialism, but also against "internal reaction" and for the achievement of socialism.

Such struggles can be either peaceful or violent. The principal strategy chosen may vary across the history of the struggle, depending upon the immediate situation. This chapter focuses on Soviet views of movements involved in armed struggle for political independence or for social revolution, although it must of necessity also deal with the overall phenomenon of liberation and with Soviet views on states created out of national liberation revolutions.

In assessing the change in Soviet perspectives on the significance of liberationism in world politics and in Soviet foreign policy, we must address the following questions:

(1) what is the content of the national liberation revolution?

(2) what form does this revolution take?

(3) what is the role of the national liberation revolution in the struggle against imperialism and for socialism?

(4) what is the responsibility of the USSR with respect to the national liberation revolution?

(5) how does the liberation struggle in the Third World and the involvement of the Soviet Union and the United States in it relate to the central questions of their relations?

Answers to these questions, in that they justify greater or lesser activism in Soviet policy, serve as indicators of trends in Soviet behavior in the Third World.

The first question measures the relative importance of particular revolutions. If the national liberation revolution is recognized as socialist or as leading more or less rapidly to socialism, then it is a matter of importance to those socialist states accepting internationalist responsibilities. If the revolution is seen as essentially international (or transnational) in character, then it has global significance. If, by

---

This independence will be unstable and turn into a fiction if the revolution does not lead to profound changes in social and economic life." "Programma KPSS," *Pravda,* November 2, 1961, 4.

contrast, it is seen as a phenomenon whose sources are local in character and whose basic significance is parochial, the opposite is true. The second question refers principally to the choice of tactics (armed versus peaceful struggle and narrow versus broad alliances) and is a measure of Soviet enthusiasm for more or less radical approaches to the problem. The third provides an additional measure of the significance of national liberation in world politics. If the movement is considered to be one of the leading forces in global class struggle, then one might expect enhanced Soviet involvement in support of it. The fourth question is a more direct indicator of Soviet willingness to become involved in revolutionary struggle in the Third World. The same is true of the fifth. If Soviet commentary displays sensitivity to the potential for escalation from revolutionary conflict in the Third World or stresses the potentially significant costs in the central political/diplomatic relationship emanating from involvement in such conflict, it follows that the Soviets would be reluctant to become involved. If these constraints are not recognized or are played down, by contrast, one might expect involvement.

The Historical Inheritance

Soviet perspectives on the question of liberation have varied considerably over time in response to an array of domestic and international factors. This section focuses principally on Soviet thinking about national liberation in the mid and late 1970s, since this is the inheritance that has by and large informed the reconsideration of the subject under Gorbachev. Moreover, from a policy perspective this period evoked particular concern in the West, since it was one of unabashed and substantial Soviet support of a variety of liberation movements and new states in conscious challenge to the perceived interests of the United States and other Western countries.

On many of the issues to be covered here, a strong consensus of views did not exist, either in the party leadership or in the academic and analytical communities during the late Brezhnev era. Opinion in the party ranged from the conspicuously enthusiastic (namely, party leaders and officials associated with the International Department of the CPSU Central Committee, such as Mikhail Suslov, Boris Ponomarev and Rostislav Ulyanovsky)[7] to the quietly skeptical (domestic economic specialists such as Aleksei Kosygin). Nonetheless, the rather consistent support of revolutionary liberation movements and their successor socialist and socialist-oriented states in the late 1970s suggests that what one might call the "Suslov line" was preponderant.[8] The following discussion is based on this more radical perspective on Third World liberation.

According to this view, the national liberation revolution, though it might not be socialist in itself, led in the direction of socialism when directed by groups espousing some variant of scientific socialism. The seizure of power was to be followed by the reasonably rapid implantation of quasi-socialist economic structures (socialization of agriculture, nationalization of basic industry, close government control over if not nationalization of the retail sector of the economy) and the adoption of a Leninist political model based on the transformation of the national liberation movement into a vanguard party organized along principles of democratic centralism, fully controlling the political life of the country while mobilizing the population for political action within channels created and supervised by the party.[9] This noncapitalist path of development, which allowed the new societies to bypass the capitalist stage, achieving a reasonably painless and rapid

7. Even among these analysts opinion was not uniform. Karen Brutents, for example, broke with the majority in holding that Soviet policy should emphasize relations with major Third World states independently of ideological orientation, on grounds of strategic and economic significance. On Brutents's perspectives, see Francis Fukuyama, *Moscow's Post-Brezhnev Reassessment of the Third World* (Santa Monica: RAND Corporation, 1986), 9.

8. In conversation, Soviet scholars have spoken of the existence during the mid and late 1970s of a "Suslov Doctrine" of military support for national liberation movements and new states committed to the transformation along "scientific socialist" lines. Soviet involvement with national liberation movements during this period is exhaustively detailed in Galia Golan, *The Soviet Union and National Liberation Movements in the Third World* (Boston: Unwin Hyman, 1989), chap. 6.

9. Leonid Brezhnev, "Report of the CPSU Central Committee to the 23rd Congress of the Communist Party of the Soviet Union," in *23rd Congress of the CPSU* (Moscow: Novosti, 1966):38–41; A. Kiva, "Sotsialisticheskaya Orientatsia: Nekotorye Problemy Teorii i Praktiki," *Mirovaya Ekonomika i Mezhdunarodnye Otnoshenia*, no. 10 (1976):26; Rostislav Ulyanovsky, *National Liberation: Essays on Theory and Practice* (Moscow: Progress, 1978); Yuriy Irkhin, "Avangardnye Revolyutsionnye Partii Trudyashchikhsya Osvoboditelnykh Stran," *Voprosy Istorii*, no. 4 (1982).

transition to socialist construction, was the only approach to real development available to less developed Third World societies. The pursuit of capitalist development strategies, by contrast, was a recipe for underdevelopment and dependence.[10] In terms of external relations, the corollary was that dissociation from the exploitative structures of the imperialist world economy was necessary if independent development were to occur.[11]

It is difficult to generalize about the form of the national liberation revolution which the Soviets favored during this period. They never abjured entirely, for instance, the possibility of peaceful transition to independence and socialist orientation.[12] Their support of movements committed to armed struggle was never total, but displayed sensitivity both to the objectives of the movement in question (they were reluctant to involve themselves in national liberation struggles of ethnic minorities in independent states), and to the probable response of the imperialist powers to such struggle (only slowly did the Soviets come to embrace armed struggle in Central America). However, Soviet theory and practice across a wide array of instances—the "liberation" of South Vietnam in 1975, the support of the Popular Movement for the Liberation of Angola's (MPLA's) first and second wars of liberation in Angola, endorsement of and support for the African National Congress's (ANC's) armed struggle against the South African government and of the Zimbabwe African People's Union's (ZAPU's) war on the white regime in Rhodesia, similar support for the Palestine Liberation Organization's (PLO's) armed struggle against the Israelis for the liberation of the occupied territories, and ultimately, their embrace of armed struggle as a means of social and anti-imperialist revolution in Nicaragua and El Salvador—all suggest that the USSR was more sanguine about the armed approach to revolutionary praxis in this period than they had been previously or—as we shall see—

10. Ulyanovsky, *National Liberation*, 226–33 (see note 9).

11. The Soviets rather tentatively offered a menu of alternatives (apparently not agreeing on their comparative merits): (1) national self-reliance; (2) collective self-reliance; (3) cooperation with the socialist camp. They were, in other words, far less clear on what should replace participation in the world capitalist economy than they were on the undesirability of such participation.

12. Leonid Brezhnev, "Otchot TsK KPSS i Ocherednye Zadachi v Oblasti Vnutrennei i Vneshnei Politiki," *Pravda*, February 25, 1976, 4.

than they have been since. This conclusion is supported by the evolution of their perspective on local war and escalation, as discussed below.

With regard to the global significance of the national liberation movement, the first factor to note is that world politics was generally conceived in the USSR to be dominated by the struggle between socialism and capitalism.[13] In theory, at least, the essence of international relations was class and not nationality. According to authoritative Soviet statements, there were three principal component forces in this struggle between the forces of progress and those of reaction: the world socialist system, the proletariat of the advanced capitalist countries, and the national liberation movement.[14]

The place of Third World liberation in the struggle between socialism and capitalism had been a subject of occasional debate since the Second Comintern Congress in 1920. There, M. N. Roy argued that, given the reliance of the major capitalist states on revenue from the colonial world to stabilize their own social orders during the imperialist era, revolution in the metropolitan countries could be stimulated only by revolution in the colonial and semicolonial world. This would deny the bourgeoisie the huge profits with which it bought social stability. This was of course not a popular perspective among socialists from the advanced capitalist states. They had trouble accepting the proposition that their own fate lay in the hands of the colonial peoples on the "periphery" of world civilization.

The general perspective of the Brezhnev era was that the world socialist community and by extension the CPSU constituted the leading force in the world revolutionary process.[15] Their view of this struggle in the mid-1970s was reasonably optimistic. They saw the era as one in which the "correlation of forces" was shifting significantly in the direction of world socialism. As Brezhnev put it at the 25th Congress, "The world is changing before our eyes, and it is

13. Ibid., 2–4; Leonid Brezhnev, "Otchot TsK KPSS XXVI Sezdu KPSS i Ocherednye Zadachi v Oblasti Vnutrennei i Vneshnei Politiki: Doklad Generalnogo Sekretarya TsK KPSS tov. L. I. Brezhneva," *Pravda,* February 24, 1981, 2.

14. Leonid Brezhnev, "Report to the 23rd Congress," 41 (see note 9); Karen Brutents, *National Liberation Revolutions Today,* vol. 1 (Moscow: Progress, 1977), 52.

15. Brutents, *National Liberation,* I, 15, 58–68.

changing for the better."[16] The struggles for national liberation in Vietnam, Southern Africa, the Horn of Africa, and later Central America—and the defeats inflicted on imperialism in these areas— were a significant contributor to this shift in the correlation of forces.[17] The historical conditions were such that it was in the Third World that important gains could be made. The European center of the struggle remained frozen in its post–World War II mode, largely because of the risks associated with nuclear war.

This appraisal had important implications for the Soviet perception of their own relationship with national liberation movements. In the late 1960s and early 1970s the intensity and number of statements of Soviet support for such movements gradually increased.[18] These in- cluded advocacy of military support, though not of direct military participation by Soviet forces in ground combat.[19]

The extension of Soviet support for the national liberation move- ment included relations with states formed from national liberation revolutions, as is evident from the series of treaties with states such as Angola and Mozambique after independence and Ethiopia after its military coup. These treaties generally included clauses covering con- sultation and mutual assistance in the event of threats to the security of either party.

Soviet practice suggested that their public commentary on this subject was, if anything, rather circumspect. The USSR provided logistical, financial, and technical support for Cuban intervention in the final stages of Angola's "war of liberation," and massive training and weapons assistance to ZAPU in the years prior to Zimbabwe's negotiated transition to majority rule in 1979. In the aftermath of the MPLA's victory in Angola, the USSR significantly upgraded military assistance to units of the South West African People's Organization

16. Brezhnev, "Otchot TsK KPSS," 2 (see note 12).

17. Ibid.; Brutents, *National Liberation,* I, 65 (see note 14); Brezhnev, "Otchot TsK KPSS XXVI," 2 (see note 13).

18. Leonid Brezhnev, "Speech at the International Meeting of Communist and Workers' Parties," in *International Meeting of Communist and Workers' Parties* (Mos- cow: 1969); Brezhnev, "Otchot TsK KPSS," 2–3 (see note 12); Ulyanovsky, *National Liberation,* 235–36 (see note 9).

19. For a detailed analysis of Soviet views on the utility of force in the Third World during the relevant period, see Mark Katz, *The Third World in Soviet Military Thought* (Baltimore: Johns Hopkins University Press, 1982).

(SWAPO) and the ANC operating in and from bases in Angola (and, in the latter case, from Mozambique until the early 1980s).

Although the Soviets were generally careful about military involvement in areas where significant American interests were clearly in play, by the end of the 1970s they had come to the point of proffering arms indirectly to the Faribundo Marti Front for National Liberation (FMLN) in El Salvador, and building substantial arms transfer relationships with the newly established governments of Nicaragua and Grenada.[20] This activity suggested a broadening over time of the Soviet willingness to support the process of liberation even in areas where the risk of alienating the United States was high.

This point brings us to the connection between the national liberation process and the relationship between the USSR and the United States and between East and West. This subject has two important aspects: the military and the political. The nub of the military aspect was the Soviets' assessment of the danger of escalation from local to general conflict associated with their involvement in the process of liberation. In the 1970s, with the exception of Middle Eastern disputes, this was judged to be slight by contrast with the 1960s. What little comment there was seemed to focus on the insignificance of such danger, the growing might of the USSR serving to deter imperialism from attempts to suppress the process of liberation.[21]

The political aspect concerns linkage: the possibility either that the United States would hold the evolution of détente hostage to Soviet behavior in the Third World, or that the success of Soviet-supported "left-wing radical" movements in the Third World might poison the political atmosphere of relations between the superpowers, making it impossible for American policymakers to proceed with détente (whatever they might rationally desire). The USSR repeatedly rejected the notion of linkage as policy. Brezhnev noted in 1976, for example, that détente in interstate relations did not and could not mean a cessation of class struggle by the USSR.[22] And when the Soviets were warned

---

20. The transfers to Grenada were hardly substantial in an absolute sense, but were significant in the context of the military balance of the Eastern Caribbean states.

21. On this point, see S. Neil MacFarlane, "The Soviet Conception of Regional Security," *World Politics*, 37, no. 3 (April, 1985).

22. Brezhnev, "Otchot TsK KPSS," 4 (see note 12); Ulyanovsky, *National Liberation*, 196 (see note 9).

that their actions in Ethiopia were affecting American politics in such a way as to make it difficult for the Carter administration to pursue détente, the Soviets dismissed this objection out of hand.[23] To them the matter was clear. Détente was based on concrete mutual state interests in areas such as arms control, trade, and the territorial stabilization of Europe. These interests persisted whatever was going on elsewhere. As such, linkage was an absurdity or a political trick.[24]

In sum, aside from questions of ideological commitment, Soviet commentary suggested a belief that the struggle for national liberation was an important aspect of the global struggle between East and West and of considerable utility in the Soviet Union's effort to establish itself as a global power. Prospects for the liberation struggles themselves were judged to be promising, as was the likelihood that the process of national liberation, supported by the world socialist system, would substantially undermine the position of the West in the Third World.

This comparatively enthusiastic assessment of the national liberation process and increasingly ambitious definition of the Soviet role therein were products of a number of factors:

(1) the increasing Soviet military power and ability to project it;

(2) the reemergence of China, since the Cultural Revolution, as a competitor for influence among left-wing forces in the Third World;

(3) the evolution of détente with the United States and the effect of this relationship on the Soviet self-image as a revolutionary actor in world politics;

(4) evidence of a weakened U.S. ability, since Vietnam and Watergate, to act in the Third World;

(5) an increasing awareness that the USSR was constrained by resource shortages from the use of economic instruments alone to pursue its objectives in the Third World. The asymmetries of Soviet power encouraged a reliance on military instrumentalities and a focus on situations where these might be useful.

23. Georgii Arbatov, "Vremya Otvetstvennykh Reshenii," *Pravda*, March 28, 1978, 4.

24. V. Osipov, "Razryadka i ego Protivniki," *Izvestiya*, May 22, 1975, 4.

The Reassessment under Gorbachev

Soviet perspectives on the process of national liberation have undergone a substantial qualitative transformation since the heyday of Soviet enthusiasm in the mid-1970s.[25] This shift was already evident by 1980 in certain venues (Africa) and with regard to certain aspects of the process (the advocacy of armed struggle in Southern Africa), and it became increasingly explicit under Yurii Andropov. Under Gorbachev the redefinition of Soviet theory and practice regarding Third World liberationism consolidated trends already well established before he took office.[26]

The reassessment covered all the dimensions enumerated earlier. With regard to the content of national liberation revolutions, the new Soviet position seemed to be that much of the Third World was in the early phase of capitalist development. National liberation revolutions, rather than laying the basis for a transition to socialism, set the stage for capitalism, which appeared to be the dominant economic system at this stage of socioeconomic development in the Third World.[27] In these conditions, attempts to socialize the means of production were premature and damaging to the local economy, given that the principal means of capital accumulation was the expansion of indigenous and foreign private investment and entrepreneurship.[28]

25. It is worth reiterating that unanimity does not exist on many of the questions to be discussed below. For example, the concepts of socialist orientation and noncapitalist development clearly have defenders and critics, both given ample play in Soviet media. But it is evident that there are far more critics than defenders, and the latter have greatly moderated their substance.

26. For discussion of this evolution, see Elizabeth K. Valkenier, *The USSR and the Third World: An Economic Bind* (New York: Praeger, 1983); Jerry F. Hough, *The Struggle for the Third World: Soviet Debates and American Options* (Washington: Brookings Institution, 1986); Golan, *The Soviet Union* (see note 8).

27. See Gleb Starushenko, "Obshchee i Osobennoe v Razvitii Stran Afriki," *Narody Azii i Afriki*, no. 2 (1980):104; Georgii Mirsky, "Newly Independent States: Ways of Development," *Asia and Africa Today*, no. 5 (1987):53; I. A. Zevelev and A. A. Kara-Murza, "The Destiny of Socialism and the Afro-Asian World," *Asia and Africa Today*, no. 3 (1989):5.

28. These propositions extend to a critique of Soviet assistance policy as well, since historically aid has been guided by Soviet postulates concerning the state sector and noncapitalist development. A recent comment by a Soviet scholar is worth reproducing in detail here: "The African states that received the most Soviet assistance became the least successful in economic terms. This assistance was originally intended to help

Uncritical attempts to replicate the Soviet model of economic development were particularly misguided.[29]

The issue, therefore, was not one of bypassing the capitalist stage of development, but at best regulating and guiding it in such a way as to maximize return to the society in question.[30] The building of socialism was something for the distant future. For example, Viktor Goncharev, a deputy director of the USSR's *Institut Afriki,* averred that he was an optimist on the prospects for socialism in South Africa, and opined that the country would be socialist in a century.[31] In the meantime, however, the preferred recipe was that of the mixed economy, with a substantial role for domestic and foreign private capital.[32] This is of course what South Africa has already. Goncharev's view on South Africa is particularly telling, as the country has a relatively advanced industrial base and a large urban proletariat, two of the basic prerequisites for socialist development; it has traditionally been seen by Soviet commentators as the area of the continent where prospects for socialism are brightest. Soviet reassessment of the desirability of accelerated noncapitalist development was also related to the reevaluation of the nature of capitalist systems, with a new focus on their capacity to reform (as Heinz Timmermann explains in Chapter 1).

Soviet analysts became far less sanguine about the capacity of the

---

countries that had recently achieved political independence to become economically independent as well. The former colonies were regarded as the natural allies of world socialism and their economic independence was seen as a means of weakening capitalism, but efficiency and common sense were casualties of the process. The African protégés established economically dubious import substitution industries while the competitiveness of their exports was declining. In sum, Moscow exported to the developing world the worst principles of its administrative economic system." Sergei Shatalov, "Soviet Assistance to Africa: The New Realities," *CSIS Africa Notes,* no. 112 (Washington: Center for Strategic and International Studies, 1990):2.

29. G. A. Krylova, "Natsionalno-demokraticheskaya Revolyutsia v Svete Novogo Politicheskogo Myshlenia," *Narody Azii i Afriki,* no. 1 (1989):43–44; O. V. Martyshin, "K Polemike vokrug Nekapitalisticheskogo puti Razvitia," *Narody Azii i Afriki,* no. 3 (1989); M. A. Olimov, "Etalon Nekapitalisticheskogo Razvitia," *Narody Azii i Afriki,* no. 4 (1989):18.

30. Krylova, "Natsionalno-demokraticheskaya," 53 (see note 29).

31. "Soviet Policy in Southern Africa: An Interview with Viktor Goncharev by Howard Barrell," *Work in Progress,* no. 4 (1987):7.

32. Gleb Starushenko, *Problems of Struggle against Racism, Apartheid, and Colonialism in South Africa* (Moscow: ANSSSR Institut Afriki, 1986), 7, 11.

developing states to exit the international capitalist economy, and less certain of the desirability of so doing.[33] Participation in the Western-dominated world economy was seen as necessary in an era of interdependence. Moreover, North-South economic relations were recast in such a way as to emphasize not their necessarily exploitative character, but the possibility of benefit to Third World societies emanating from these unavoidable relations. Indeed, the overarching issue for much of the Third World was not so much economic liberation, but the avoidance (by whatever means) of what Anatolii Gromyko once referred to as "irreversible deterioration."[34] The USSR could contribute to the avoidance of this fate only "to the extent of its abilities."[35]

Just as doubt regarding the prospects for socialism was increasing, so too was unhappiness with the vanguard party model embraced by many Third World proponents of liberation. Successful implementation of the model required numbers of conscious party cadres which were simply not available throughout much of the Third World. The consequence was a tendency toward isolation of the party and exclusion of significant portions of the population from participation in politics, with resulting fragmentation and civil unrest.[36] The leaders of socialist-oriented states meanwhile displayed little genuine commitment to socialist concepts, focusing instead on Marxist-Leninist forms of political organization to retain power. In foreign policy their principal loyalties and preoccupations were nationalist rather than internationalist. Their étatist approach to political and economic development fostered inefficient state sectors presided over by artificially large, inefficient, and exploitative bureaucracies.[37] Where their efforts extended into the economic sphere, they were frequently characterized by a utopian desire to skip stages of development, to

33. V. F. Vasiliev, "Nekotorye Voprosy Sotsialisticheskoi Orientatsii," *Narody Azii i Afriki,* no. 5 (1986):20–21; Nikolai Kosukhin and I. Belikov, "Kommunisticheskoe Dvizhenie v Afrike," *Azia i Afrika Sevodnya,* no. 5 (1988):8; Krylova, "Natsionalno-demokraticheskaya," 43–44 (see note 29); M. Kapitsa, in "Developing Countries and Today's World," *Asia and Africa Today,* no. 2 (1990):5; Evgenii Tarabrin, "In the Grip of Contradictions," *Asia and Africa Today,* no. 3 (1990):9–10.

34. Anatolii Gromyko, "Sudba Kontinenta," *Narody Azii i Afriki,* no. 1 (1989):22.

35. "Programma KPSS," *Pravda,* March 7, 1986, 7.

36. Krylova, "Natsionalno-demokraticheskaya," 47–53, (see note 29).

37. V. Sakharov, "Socialist Orientation in Word and Deed," *Asia and Africa Today,* no. 3 (1990):4.

the considerable detriment of their own societies—and, occasionally, their Soviet allies. As Joan Urban notes in Chapter 2, Gorbachev himself lamented this tendency in his comments on Afghanistan.

The ethnic and cultural heterogeneity of many Third World societies favored instead deliberate efforts to integrate broad sectors into the political process, even if this meant dismantling important components of the vanguard system. This view had the additional instrumental advantage of justifying the development of wide-ranging ties with other political movements and figures in the Third World that had considerable influence in local politics. One sees this, for example, in Soviet acquiescence to the inclusion of the National Union for the Total Independence of Angola (UNITA) in the political system of Angola, and for that matter in the Soviet attitude toward the Nicaraguan elections.[38] Eduard Shevardnadze's remarks subsequent to his visit to Managua in 1989 suggested comparative indifference to the risks run by the Sandinistas in allowing free elections.[39] Similar perspectives were evident in Soviet comment on the Ethiopian revolution.[40] This reevaluation suggested an awareness that at the stage of political development faced by many Third World liberation movements once they come to power, stability was more important than ideological purity. Stability required strategies of inclusion, even if this threatened the movement's hold on power. This broadening of the spectrum of potentially fruitful cooperation and the consequent reevaluation of the historical nature and role of forces other than the vanguard parties corresponded to the wider redefinition of Soviet perspectives on the noncommunist left, and to criticism of past Soviet sectarianism described in Chapters 1 and 2 herein.[41] This broadening

38. See Jill Jolliffe, "Russia 'in Favour of Deal with UNITA'," *The Manchester Guardian*, March 25, 1988, 12; Michael Parks, "Soviets Urge Angolan Allies to Talk to Rebels," *Los Angeles Times*, August 11, 1988, 4, 8. Before his resignation Eduard Shevardnadze met with Jonas Savimbi in Washington to discuss an Angolan internal settlement. See "Guerrillas Report Pact with Angola," *The New York Times*, December 15, 1990, 6.

39. Eduard Shevardnadze, "Vneshnaya Politika i Perestroika," *Pravda*, October 24, 1989, 2.

40. Krylova, "Natsionalno-demokraticheskaya," passim (see note 29); Eduard Shevardnadze, comments in "Priem Poslov," *Pravda*, November 12, 1989, 4.

41. This reevaluation of ties with other elements of the left and center was particularly well developed in Soviet discussions of Latin America. The journal *Latinskaya*

was also part and parcel of the Soviet communist reconsideration of the vanguard role at home.

These shifts reflected doubt as to the applicability of Marxist theory derived from European experience to conditions in the Third World.[42] As Georgii Kim, a former director of the USSR's Institute of Oriental Studies, put it:

> For a long time our historians considered it their major methodological task to prove that the Orient obeyed the general laws of historical development, elaborated by Marx and Engels upon a study of European life, first and foremost. The result was a considerable discrepancy between this universal theory and the actual laws operating at a lower specific historical level. Thus, distinctive features of Oriental history were treated as secondary in importance or, sometimes, completely ignored.[43]

With regard to the form of liberation struggles, the following discussion refers to those struggles toward which the USSR has historically had positive views, and notably the Namibian and South African cases. In these instances sufficient commentary and practice existed to draw reasonably confident conclusions about Soviet perspectives.[44] In all these cases the focus of Soviet commentary lay very much on the side of negotiation leading to peaceful settlement, rather than armed conflict. Such negotiations would include a large array of groups including the liberation movements' direct opponents. This inclusive approach implicitly devalued the status previously accorded the liberation movements as the sole legitimate representatives of their peoples.

This Soviet perspective caused significant friction with the liberation movements whose commitment to waging the armed struggle

---

Amerika for the years 1987–89 contains an extremely interesting and prolonged polemic on the nature of other left and moderate forces and on the appropriate posture of the communist parties towards them.

42. See Georgii Mirsky, "K Voprosu o Vybore Puti i orientatsii Razvivayushchikhsya Stran," *Mirovaya Ekonomika i Mezhdunarodnye Otnoshenia*, no. 5 (1987), 71.

43. Georgii Kim, "Soviet Oriental Studies in Time of Perestroika," *Asia and Africa Today*, no. 1 (1989): 3.

44. The Namibian case is now resolved, but was ongoing for the first three and one half years of Gorbachev's tenure in office.

seemed relatively unambiguous. SWAPO, for example, was greatly irritated that the USSR moved to resolve the Namibian independence question in negotiations which excluded the liberation movement but included its principal adversary, the South African government. The settlement that was achieved in 1988 potentially limited SWAPO's capacity to control the political evolution of Namibia by providing for free elections under UN supervision, with a two-thirds majority in the constituent assembly necessary to define the country's constitutional future. There was no guarantee that a free election would deliver such a pro-SWAPO majority, and indeed it did not. That the USSR actively participated in this negotiation suggested that a settlement of the conflict was preferable to unambiguous victory for the Soviet client.

The SWAPO leadership's unhappiness with the outcome was evident in their decision to violate the terms of the cease-fire agreement by infiltrating armed units across the border from Angola in April 1989. South African forces intercepted these units with the acquiescence of UN authorities and inflicted significant casualties before the cease-fire was patched together again. After an initial burst of anti–South African rhetoric, Soviet commentators began to criticize SWAPO for its role in this affair, while the USSR as a guarantor of the settlement strongly supported a compromise whereby surviving SWAPO units were withdrawn to southern Angola. Such a stance hardly suggested Soviet enthusiasm for a continuation of armed struggle.[45]

In South Africa, ANC and South African Communist Party (SACP) statements in 1988–89 displayed considerable irritation toward unnamed parties that were pressing for negotiation at any price. The target of these barbs was not difficult to discover, given the insistence in Soviet commentary since 1987–88 that the South African issue should be resolved at the negotiating table. Some Soviet commentators even openly advocated the abandonment of armed struggle, well before the ANC itself was ready for this step.[46] In addition, Soviet

45. See V. Korotov, "Namibiiskii Urok," *Pravda*, April 12, 1989, 5; A. Nikanorov, "Polozhenie Ostayotsya Napryazhennym," *Izvestiya*, April 15, 1989, 4.

46. Namely, Vladimir Tikhomirov, director of studies at the Africa Institute of the Academy of Sciences, as cited in the *Johannesburg Star*, November 23, 1989. The

diplomats extended direct contacts beyond the ANC and SACP to more moderate forces in the opposition (namely, white liberals and Gatsha Buthelezi's Inkatha movement), and indeed to the South African government itself.[47]

On the other hand, the predominant Soviet public position was that the abandonment of armed struggle should not occur until the ANC itself decided on it.[48] Prominent Soviet writers stressed that the lack of other alternatives left the ANC with little choice but the armed path. Once the alternative of negotiation opened, however, it became difficult to find anything on the subject in the Soviet literature. I would surmise that the Soviet leadership, while unenthusiastic about revolutionary war in South Africa, did not wish to jeopardize its ties to the ANC and so remained silent. The ANC apparently believed that giving up the armed struggle before the grant of such critical concessions as the ending of the state of emergency[49] and the release of political prisoners would remove a principal element of the movement's leverage with the regime. Underlying these justifications was the realization that moderation risked alienating the more radical internal cadres over whom the ANC had precious little control in any case. Awareness of this dilemma was probably a further reason the Soviets did not press the point.

These shifts in Soviet analyses of the content and form of liberation struggles reflected more basic reassessments of the importance of the struggle for liberation in Third World and global politics. Perhaps the most essential Soviet alteration of relevance here was a reassessment of the balance between zero-sum and positive-sum elements of world politics.

The perspective characteristic of the 1970s (and for that matter of the entire history of Soviet foreign policy) was that in essence world politics was dominated by the class struggle between capitalism and socialism. No fundamental compromise or common ground was pos-

---

statement predates the unbanning of the ANC. Ultimately the ANC suspended the armed struggle, pending negotiations with the government of the Republic of South Africa.

47. W. Kuhne, *Africa and the End of the Cold War: The Need for "New Realism"* (Ebenhausen: Stiftung Wissenschaft und Politik, 1990), 10.

48. "Soviet Policy," 6 (see note 31).

49. The state of emergency has now been lifted with the exception of Natal Province.

sible. The two systems were engaged in a conflict that would endure until one side or the other collapsed. Although cooperation on the basis of mutual interest was possible, such cooperation was by definition limited, tactical, and temporary, and did not alter the fundamental political conflict. Nor did it diminish it. The struggle for national liberation was a significant component of this Manichaean struggle between good and evil.

It was Eduard Shevardnadze who announced the official revision of this element of dogma, although his statement drew upon a broad revision in Soviet understanding of international relations that is amply evident in the literature. In the summer of 1988 he noted that the category of class struggle had enjoyed excessive weight in the determination of Soviet foreign policy in the past, that this policy needed to be "deideologized," and that greater attention in formulating policy should be paid to concrete state interests shared by both social systems.[50]

The broader context of current Soviet thinking on international relations is of some relevance here. Although previously the interests of the two social systems were seen to be basically antithetical, the more recent Soviet wisdom was that on a number of key issues (for example, the avoidance of war, nuclear disarmament, the diversion of scarce resources from military to civilian use, global economic health, environmental decay, and Third World development) all states had overriding interests, whatever their social system.[51] It was these mutual interests that seemed to be the focus of much new Soviet discourse on foreign policy and international relations. Although they seemed unwilling to abandon the category of class conflict altogether, Soviet writers dramatically played down its significance,[52] and the balance between peaceful and violent means of national liberation shifted dramatically in favor of the former. That these shifts were viewed with discomfort by many in the Third World left was evident in the heated debates in *World Marxist Review* during 1988–89 on

50. Eduard Shevardnadze, *Vestnik Ministerstva*, 35–36 (see note 3).

51. Vadim Medvedev, in "Sovremennaya Kontseptsia Sotsializma," *Pravda*, October 5, 1988, 4.

52. Georgii Mirsky, "Deideologization of International Relations," *Asia and Africa Today*, no. 4 (1989):13, 15–17; Gromyko, "Sudba Kontinenta" (see note 34).

global versus class values and interests and on the balance between the avoidance of war and the need to use force in the struggle for liberation.[53]

To the extent that processes in the Third World were judged to be important in terms of this struggle between social systems, one would expect that the significance attributed to these processes would have diminished.[54] Moreover, to the extent that conflicts in the Third World impeded efforts to pursue an agenda of cooperative East-West relations, one would expect Soviet advocacy of efforts at resolution or mitigation rather than moves to inflame or take advantage of them.

In a related vein, the category of "world revolutionary process," which was of such significance in assessing the relevance and importance of national liberation struggles, seems to have been altogether abandoned in mainstream Soviet discourse.[55] When Soviet writers did comment on the relationship of liberation revolutions to the global political process, it was often to note that liberation struggles and related conflicts emanated from local causes rather than from the overarching conflict between capitalism and socialism. As Goncharev put it with regard to the Southern African situation, "The current

53. See, for example, "The Communists in Today's World," no. 3 (1988):101–17; "Perestroika in the USSR and the International Communist Movement," no. 9 (1988):99–102; "Peace and Revolution in the Nuclear Age," no. 2 (1989):53–56, 59; "Two Views on the Crisis in Marxism," no. 6 (1989):55–56; Antonio Diaz-Ruiz (CP of Cuba), "A Question of Priorities: National Liberation and Universal Peace—Any Contradiction?" no. 9 (1989):68–70.

54. This diminished significance is blatantly obvious in the major documents of the 27th Party Congress. The contrast between Gorbachev's report there ("Politicheskii Doklad TsK KPSS XXVII Sezdu KPSS: Doklad Generalnogo Sekretarya tov. Gorbacheva M.S.," *Pravda*, February 26, 1986) and that of Brezhnev to the 25th Congress ("Otchot TsK KPSS"—see note 12) is striking.

55. In January 1990 a Soviet scholar told me that one basic development in Soviet analysis of international relations in the past four years was the widely accepted realization that there was no such thing as a concrete global revolutionary process. The closest one gets to an official comment on the world revolutionary process these days is this statement in the 1986 party program: "The alliance of the forces of social progress and national liberation is the guarantee of mankind's better future." ("Programma KPSS," 7—see note 35). As is noted in Chapter 1 herein, this evasiveness extends to the "international communist movement" as well, reference to which has grown increasingly rare in mainstream discourse, and to many of the institutional structures associated with Soviet internationalism, the World Peace Council being set adrift financially, and the *World Marxist Review* (*Problems of Peace and Socialism*) ceasing publication in 1990.

conflict in this area of the world is primarily the result of the development of the internal socio-economic and political process in the region, the natural consequence of decomposition of the exhausted vicious system of social relations itself."[56]

Consonant with the new stress on state interest rather than class conflict, the issue of the Third World remained important in Soviet analysis primarily in relation to the pursuit of concrete economic interest in relations with states. The role of "nonstate actors" such as the remaining liberation movements diminished commensurately.

This brings us to the question of Soviet role. After Gorbachev took office the Soviet role in the Third World shifted from the facilitation of a historically determined revolutionary process to the construction of normal interstate diplomatic and economic ties independent of ideology. With regard to Third World conflicts involving friends of the USSR, the Soviets came to define their role—in rhetoric in any case—as a facilitator of conflict resolution.[57]

The rhetoric was, to a degree, contradicted by actual Soviet practice. I have already noted the Soviet reluctance to write off armed struggle in cases where close historical friends were involved in wars of liberation (for example, Namibia and South Africa). Indeed, the Soviets continued to supply small amounts of arms to the ANC despite the improvement in the general situation in South Africa. But this reflected an understanding of the difficulties of the ANC's situation and particularly a desire to avoid a rupture in relations rather than any belief that victory could be won by force of arms. The Soviets must have concluded, reasonably, that a cessation of arms transfers might undermine the incentives for the South African regime to compromise in negotiation. Presumably this consideration, among others, caused the USSR to accord diplomatic status to the ANC delegation in Moscow at a time of increasing discord between the two on questions of tactics. In the Namibian case, similarly, it appears that Soviet military and technical assistance to SWAPO forces in Angola continued until the 1988 settlement was achieved.[58]

56. Viktor Goncharev, "The Soviet Union and Southern Africa: Issues of Ensuring Regional Security," *Southern Africa Record*, no. 47/48 (1987):78.

57. Shevardnadze, "Vneshnaya Politika," 2 (see note 39).

58. This continuation is consistent with a broader pattern in Soviet relations with the socialist and socialist-oriented states, where, despite the concern about the high cost and low return of relations, the Soviets have until now been willing to continue to

Turning finally to the question of the relationship between struggles for liberation and East-West relations, we must examine this in relation to broader Soviet analysis of the issue of Third World conflict, since to my knowledge the Soviets have said little about wars of liberation in this context. With the advent of Gorbachev, the stated Soviet view on the question of escalation changed substantially. Now the leadership stressed the potential for escalation from Third World conflict—with the resulting danger of nuclear war—as one important reason for negotiating settlements of such disputes.[59]

Given the obviously diminishing weight of Cold War competition in the Third World as a component of East-West relations, it is hard to take this concern at face value. Perhaps the subtext here was a justification for gradual Soviet disengagement from such conflicts and pressure upon their allies to go to the table. To the extent that such remarks applied to insurgencies, the message may have been intended as an effort to deter the United States, since in this period it was in fact the United States that was more deeply involved in the support of antigovernment insurgencies in the Third World (namely, the Nicaraguan Contras, UNITA in Angola, the mujahedeen in Afghanistan, and the opposition coalition in Cambodia).

Whatever the specific motives of such statements, they did generally reflect a heightened sense of the danger of spillover from disagreements in the Third World. This concern was quite consistent with the main lines of Soviet comment on political linkage. Prominent Soviet analysts pointed out that a major failure of Soviet foreign policy during the Brezhnev era was the misunderstanding of the negative effect of Soviet activism in the Third World on American domestic politics and policy toward the USSR.[60] This admission suggested a significant revision in the Soviet assessment of the costs and benefits of involvement in the struggle against imperialism in the Third World.

---

underwrite states such as Cuba and Vietnam (aid to the latter actually increased substantially during the 1986–91 planning period), and to sustain flows of arms. In the Angolan case, the agreement on Cuban and South African forces in Angola and on the independence of Namibia did not stop Soviet arms transfers to Angola.

59. Starushenko, *Problems of Struggle,* 31 (see note 32); Gorbachev, "Politicheskii Doklad," 8 (see note 54); Evgenii Primakov, "USSR Policy on Regional Conflicts," *International Affairs,* no. 6 (1988):1–6.

60. Vyacheslav Dashichev, "Vostok-Zapad: Poisk Novykh Otnoshenii," *Literaturnaya Gazeta,* May 18, 1988, 14.

The obverse of the purported concern about escalation and stress on the potential negative impact of competitive behavior on the central superpower relationship was an apparent belief that cooperation in the management and resolution of remaining Third World conflicts would improve Soviet-American relations. Indeed, the Soviets sought to cooperate closely with the United States from 1987 onward in crisis management and conflict resolution. The 1988 accord on Namibia and Angola was a case in point. Close consultation and joint initiatives in this region continued after the accord as well, as was evident in the late 1990 Soviet meeting with Jonas Savimbi and the American meeting with Pedro De Castro Van Dunem, foreign minister of Angola, in Washington.[61] Also, the Soviets and Americans continued to discuss the Afghan issue (including the question of military assistance to the two sides) as much because the war constituted an unnecessary, stubborn irritant to their own relations as because they desired a complete settlement for the Afghanis. Sufficient progress had apparently been made by the end of 1990 that Shevardnadze announced his expectation of a further superpower accord on Afghan issues at the year-end foreign ministers' meeting in the United States.[62] In the Cambodian case, joint efforts to arrive at a UN-based transitional arrangement[63] again reflected as much a concern to enhance the structure of Soviet-American cooperation in the Third World as to protect the diminishing Soviet stake in the region's affairs.

In summary, there was substantial change in the Soviet attitude toward national liberation revolutions in the Third World. Soviet analysts and policymakers held that the class struggle should be downgraded as an element in Soviet foreign policy, and Soviet practice under Gorbachev reflected this assessment. The struggle for national liberation was accorded far less emphasis in what remained of

61. More recently, the MPLA and UNITA have agreed on a de facto cease-fire to take effect prior to May 15, 1991, and to be followed by a formal accord between the two prior to May 29–31. See *The New York Times*, May 2, 1991.

62. As it turned out, no such agreement was announced.

63. See, for example, the agreement among the five members of the Security Council in August 1990 on a comprehensive political settlement of the Cambodian question, as outlined in "Statement of the Five Permanent Members of the Security Council of the United Nations on Cambodia," issued at the UN on August 28, 1990. The accord is summarized in F. Prial, "Five UN Powers Announce Accord on Cambodia War," *The New York Times*, August 29, 1990, A1, A9.

Soviet policy in the Third World, and Soviet assessment of the current phase of historical development in the Third World reflected increased pessimism about the capacity of national liberation revolutions to lay the basis for a transition to socialism.

The main lines of Soviet policy toward Third World conflicts shifted from support for revolutionary forces to efforts at resolution, even when this implied compromising the struggle and the interests of allies. Soviet analyses of revolutionary movements and regimes in the Third World displayed an increasingly jaundiced assessment of their seriousness and survivability. Indeed, there was reason to question whether the categories of class struggle, revolution, national liberation, and socialist orientation had much relevance at all in Soviet perspectives and policy toward the Third World. Continuing Soviet support of liberation groups such as the ANC, of socialist-oriented states such as Angola, and of socialist ones such as Vietnam and Cuba suggested more a concern about credibility and the difficulty of graceful exit than it did ideological commitment, or a belief that such ties enhanced Soviet power and prestige.[64]

The Sources of Change

The Soviets' reconsideration of "liberationism" and its relationship to the global correlation of forces (including their deemphasis on issues of anti-imperialism and class struggle) did much to restructure superpower relations in the Third World. U.S. concern about Soviet interference diminished radically as a factor weighing on U.S. policy.

How one judges the significance of this depends, however, on how one accounts for the change. If one perceives the change in Soviet perspectives on Third World liberation to be merely a tactical adaptation to a temporarily unfavorable shift in the correlation of forces, then one might expect a Soviet return, if conditions changed, to old

---

64. Indeed, some Soviet analysts were willing to speak of the USSR's abandonment of global power status, the concept upon which such "realist" interpretations of Soviet behavior in the Third World are to a large extent based. See the comments of Sergei Karaganov, as reported by Hella Pick, in "Soviet Hint of Retreat from World Role," *Manchester Guardian*, November 22, 1989, 12.

patterns. If one perceives the shift in the correlation of forces to be deeper and longer-term, then even if these changes in Soviet perspectives were tactical they might be expected to endure. Alternatively, one could assume that the changed perspectives were the result of a learning process, a cognitive response to accumulated experience that could not be adequately explained in terms of traditional Soviet categories of analysis. Then one would expect the reassessment to endure as long as the new cognitive structure explained more adequately than alternative paradigms the Third World and global realities with which the Soviets found themselves forced to deal.[65]

A second question is whether the sources of change were internal or external. If change emanated from the USSR's international environment, then sustaining what many in the West (if not in the Third World) considered to be favorable trends in Soviet policy would depend on sustaining the external conditions that produced them. On the other hand, if the principal causes of change were internal to the USSR, then outsiders would presumably have little leverage over the process.

In all likelihood the changes were both tactical and long-term, and involved both internal and international variables. Regarding external sources of change, it seems plausible that the more militant U.S. approach to the question of liberation may have induced Soviet reconsideration of the merits of supporting Third World struggles for liberation. The case of American support to the Salvadoran government struggling against the FMLN insurgency comes to mind here. If this was so, then a policy of reduced American support for selected regimes faced with insurgencies might cause the more militant Soviet strategy of the 1970s to return.

The other side of this coin concerns the Reagan Doctrine, by which the United States supported insurgencies dedicated to the overthrow of socialist-oriented regimes friendly with the USSR (in the case of

---

65. Such speculation is particularly apropos given the conservative trend in Soviet politics in early 1991, the displacement of many of those most prominent in the restructuring of Soviet foreign policy, and the reemergence of traditional themes such as class struggle in party discussions such as those at the Central Committee plenum in late January 1991. On the latter, see "Communist Party Is Making a Comeback," *Soviet/East European Report* 8, no. 20 (February 15, 1991):1–2.

Nicaragua and Angola, regimes produced by liberation movements). In these instances the superpowers' roles were reversed, the USSR desperately attempting to preserve the status quo and the United States attempting through the support of guerrilla movements to subvert it. These American actions altered the balance of cost and benefit associated in the Soviet mind with the expansion of socialism in the Third World. It is not surprising that Soviet attitudes towards revolutionary violence should have been altered by the effective American use of this instrument against assets of the USSR.

Several other aspects of the external environment also deserve mention. Perhaps most important, the structure of opportunity in the Third World evolved in such a way as to make support of liberation movements a much less promising instrument of policy than in the past. In the era of decolonization, the support of liberation movements struggling against colonial powers for self-determination had been a comparatively cheap and effective means of acquiring influence and weakening Western positions in the Third World. The struggle for liberation had been widely perceived to be legitimate, the capacity and will of the colonial powers to sustain themselves had diminished, and the material needs of liberation movements had been well within the capacity of the USSR and other similarly inclined states to assume. But the era of decolonization was now essentially over. The principal tasks in the Third World became state-building and economic development, which were inherently much more complex and expensive than subverting colonial rule.

Certainly insurgencies continued to arise, and the insurgents often used the rhetoric of national liberation. But the fact that these movements generally opposed sovereign recognized governments altered the balance of risk and benefit for outside states that contemplated involvement. Support of such efforts had no widely accepted imprimatur in the sense that the anticolonial struggle did. Such support risked alienating other regimes that might see themselves as the next target.

Moreover, in the most recent phase of insurgent activity in the Third World, and at the risk of overgeneralization, we seem to have moved from struggle against external colonialism to struggle against internal colonialism. This was clearest perhaps in the ethnically or territorially based insurgencies of Africa (namely, Eritrea and Tigre in Ethiopia, Northern Somalia, the Ovimbundu-based struggle of UNITA), but one might want to include Sendero Luminoso (Shining Path) of Peru as well. Postwar tensions between Shi'i, Sunnis, and Kurds on the one hand, and the struggling regime of Saddam Hussein, on the other, are also illustrative. Where the agenda is ethnically based separatism, as in Iraq, the territorial integrity of the postcolonial state is at risk. This too is a difficult agenda for outsiders to support, given that so many states are vulnerable to this threat. Where the agenda is the overthrow of the dominant ethnic group and its replacement with the oppressed race, as in Peru where Sendero Luminoso has claimed that it seeks to extirpate all manifestations of five centuries of white Spanish rule, the prospect is one of genocide.

Ethnicity raises a further issue which in a way spanned the divide between external and internal causation. As the colonial era receded into history, the role of class (however defined) as an explanation of the political essence of much of the Third World became increasingly obscure. The recent political history of these regions suggests that "subjective factors" (for example, ethnic and clan affinity, and religion) had far more autonomous explanatory value than would have been predicted by Soviet Marxist analysis. To put it another way, the accumulation of experience in the Third World placed increasing pressure on traditional Soviet analysis of Third World politics and thus encouraged conceptual transformation.

The irrelevance of class analysis relates not just to questions of ethnicity and religion, but to a broad array of issues including prospects for noncapitalist development and socialist orientation, the capacity to build and sustain vanguard party socialist regimes in politically nonintegrated societies, and the tension within progressive regimes between nationalist and internationalist preoccupations and commitments. At the extreme, what we saw in the evolution of Soviet perspectives on Third World liberation was a realization that prior ways of thinking about Third World politics had had little if anything to do with recognizable political and social realities there.

The adjustment of Soviet theory and practice reflected also the increasingly severe domestic economic crisis and consequent changes in domestic politics. Quite simply, there were fewer resources now available for use in the Third World. The leadership of the USSR understood this and sought to curb unproductive investment in Third World policy. Support for revolution was not terribly expensive in material terms, but the experience of such support in the 1970s suggested that where such revolutions were successful, they required of the USSR both long-term and potentially expensive material commitments.

Moreover, the leadership appeared to believe that one necessary aspect of the resolution of the USSR's internal problems was the winding down of the arms race (allowing diversion of resources from the defense sector to the recapitalization of the Soviet economic base) and the enlistment of Western technical and economic assistance in addressing the structural problems of the Soviet economy. This, they hoped, would occur with the integration of the USSR into the global economy. Such objectives were difficult to achieve, however, when relations between East and West were tense, in part because of past Soviet support of revolutionary forces in the Third World. The foreign policy dictates of *perestroika,* in other words, favored some distancing of the USSR from national liberation struggles.

This new domestically driven foreign policy was accompanied by important institutional and personnel changes, which also favored the redirection described above. Principal responsibility for the formulation and implementation of foreign policy toward the Third World and in particular socialist and socialist-oriented states shifted from the International Department of the CPSU Central Committee to the departments of the foreign ministry. Those in the International Department who were most closely associated with Third World policy, for instance Ponomarev and Ulyanovsky, retired. The department itself shrank considerably in size, particularly the sections dealing with the nonruling communist parties and the remaining liberation movements.[66] Analysts such as Karen Brutents who were associated with a preference for normal state-to-state relations with Third World actors—independent of ideological orientation and in pursuit of mutual benefit—came to play a far more prominent role in policy formulation. Suslov, the Politburo member under whose aegis

66. Conversations in Moscow, January 1991.

the policy of support for liberation movements developed in the 1970s, died in 1982, and no one assumed his mantle. From 1986 on, the department was run by officials such as Anatolii Dobrynin and Valentin Falin who had long experience in the West and were attuned therefore to the linkage between revolutionary activism in the Third World and East-West relations.[67]

These changes were accompanied by the dismantling or immobilization of important institutions responsible for the training of cadres in the Third World communist parties and liberation movements, such as the Institute of Social Sciences of the Central Committee of the CPSU. It is reported that the likely fate of the Institute is to become a "Center for Constitutional Democracy." It now hosts delegations from the U.S. Congress who impart their knowledge of how democracies work to Soviet legislators and bureaucrats.[68]

In the process of democratizing Soviet foreign policy, moreover, the Supreme Soviet was beginning to more actively oversee the formulation of Soviet policy in the Third World. To judge from developments on the eve of the 1990s (for example, the subpoenaing of data on assistance agreements with radical Third World states and the public criticism of waste in Soviet policy in the Third World), such oversight was likely to have a moderating effect on Soviet policy and behavior.

More profoundly, the USSR was going through a period of intense questioning of its *own* experience of revolution and the building of socialism. The Soviets were criticizing the very elements of their own society (the domestic political monopoly enjoyed by the Communist Party, and the emphasis on the state in economic development), and the external reflection of this self-scrutiny was found in their prescriptions for national liberation in the Third World.[69] If by its own recognition the CPSU had failed to build socialism and nearly ruined its own country by pursuing the orthodox recipes of Soviet Marxism,

67. This characterization of the transition in the CC International Department is consistent with the analysis of Heinz Timmermann in Chapter 1 herein. For a somewhat different view, see Mark Kramer, "The Role of the CPSU International Department in Soviet Foreign Relations and National Security Policy," *Soviet Studies*, 62, no. 3 (July, 1990):429–39.

68. Such a meeting was held at the Institute in January 1991, thus ironically coinciding with the military crackdown in Lithuania.

69. Zevelev and Kara-Murza, "Destiny of Socialism," 4 (see note 27).

it was difficult to continue to sell these recipes as a means of liberation in the Third World. Thus in some degree the revision of perspectives on the question of national liberation was a logical consequence of the internal reevaluation of the Soviet experience. This revision was linked with a reevaluation of the nature of capitalist systems as well, with a new focus on their capacity to reform (as noted by Timmermann in Chapter 1).

In short, the dampening of Soviet enthusiasm for Third World liberationism was a product of a broad array of internal and external factors. Although some of this adaptation may have been tactical and short-term in character (for example, the need to reduce U.S. pressure on existing Soviet positions in the Third World, or possibly the need for a breathing space in the global competition between East and West to reconstruct Soviet power), other components were far more profound and, presumably, more lasting (for example, the cognitive reevaluation of previous Soviet practice in the Third World, institutional change in Soviet policymaking, and the deeply self-critical reevaluation of the experience of socialism in the USSR itself).

Events of the fall and winter of 1990–91, such as the rejection of the Shatalin Plan for radical internal economic reform, the collapse of negotiations on a new treaty of union, KGB chairman Vladimir Kryuchkov's resuscitation of the foreign subversive threat as a pretext for a domestic crackdown, the resignation of Foreign Minister Shevardnadze, the confrontation with Georgia over Southern Ossetia, and the military attacks on government buildings in the Baltics, suggested nonetheless that in Soviet domestic politics, at least, reversal was possible. Apparent Soviet evasion of the conventional forces agreement (for example, the reclassification and redeployment of some ground forces and the removal of tanks beyond the Urals) indicated that such reversal could have important foreign policy consequences.

Prognosis

The developments in late 1990 and early 1991 raised questions about the durability of change in Soviet policy toward the Third

World. To the extent that Soviet perspectives on the national liberation revolution in the late 1980s were a product of the democratization of Soviet politics and foreign policy, they *were* vulnerable to a
reversal of that democratization. But that extent was very limited.

Many other factors moderating Soviet policy in the Third World in
1985–90 continued to operate despite the rightward shift at the
beginning of 1991. Even at the height of the conservative reaction, the
appointment of Aleksandr Bessmertnykh to replace Shevardnadze as
foreign minister suggested that the first priority in Soviet foreign
policy continued to be the quest for external assistance in dealing
with the country's worsening economic situation. The continuing
perceived necessity of good relations with the United States and the
other Western powers severely limited the potential for reversal in
Soviet policy toward revolution in the Third World. The economic
crisis and the consequent shortage of resources for foreign policy
initiatives continued to dictate conservatism in Third World policy;
they imposed constraints on Soviet activism that would persist whatever the evolution of Soviet domestic politics. To put it more baldly,
the Soviet distancing from the Third World left reflected the secular
decline in the power of the Soviet state in world politics.

Moreover, Soviet leaders, whether conservative or reformist, faced
the same accumulated experience in the Third World—an experience
of expensive commitment to ineffectual regimes which were often
resistant to Soviet influence and which contributed little to Soviet
power and position in global politics. This experience suggested caution in the face of any temptation to reinvigorate the internationalist
mission of Soviet socialism.

Finally, although there might have been limited constituencies in
Soviet politics to which a more active relationship with the Third
World left might appeal, the capacity of such a strategy to enhance the
legitimacy of *any* regime in the USSR is difficult to grasp. The traditional Soviet conception of socialism and proletarian internationalism was by 1991 so thoroughly discredited that its reassertion would
only weaken popular support for a conservative Soviet regime, particularly if it involved the reallocation of increasingly scarce resources.
In short, even in the context of early 1991, there was little reason to
expect that a conservative backlash in Soviet politics would produce

any dramatic shift in the Soviet policy trend toward the liberationist left described in this chapter.

The outcome of the attempted coup in August 1991 merely reinforces this conclusion. It dramatically weakened those elements of the central party hierarchy which might have been most predisposed to revolutionary activism in Soviet foreign policy. It so weakened the central government that it may be an anachronism even to speak of Soviet foreign policy. The current evolution of relations between the union and the republics draws into question just how much of the union will remain, and makes it a virtual certainty that if a central government does persist, its powers in domestic and foreign policy will be radically circumscribed.

The principal beneficiary of the coup's failure, Russian president Boris Yeltsin, gave an early indication of his government's perspectives on past Soviet policy toward the Third World left when, immediately after the coup, he called for the termination of Soviet assistance to Cuba. More generally, those currently responsible for foreign policy within the USSR show little interest in or sympathy for the causes and movements discussed in this chapter. Foreign Minister Boris Pankin's announcement of the withdrawal from Cuba of the Soviet brigade long denounced by the United States is illustrative.

It is rare in the discussion of historical events that one can confidently say that a chapter is really over. In this instance, however, it is.

[5]

The Role and Limits of Reform Communism in East-Central Europe: Is Anything *Left* Still Left?

Federigo Argentieri

Ever since the Stalinization of East-Central Europe more than four decades ago, the concept of a political left in that region has undergone a rather complex process of evolution,[1] as will be discussed in the following pages. Today, after the democratic revolutions of 1989 and the legislative, presidential, and local elections of 1990–91, the political spectra of Poland, Czechoslovakia, and Hungary are slowly recovering, *mutatis mutandis,* some of their traditional historical features as well as those of normally functioning democracies of the late twentieth century.

The purpose of this chapter is to analyze the influence of Mikhail Gorbachev's policies on the dramatic upheavals of the region in 1989, to discuss the role and limits of reform communism in these upheavals as compared to those of 1956, 1968, and 1980–81, and finally to reflect upon the political culture, the behavior, and the possible future trends of the left, including an attempt to adequately define that term in the context of contemporary East-Central Europe.

The author thanks colleagues and friends who have assisted him with useful comments and advice: Christie Cochrell, George Evans O'Keefe, Charles Z. Jókai, Bill Lomax, Miklós Molnár, and last but not least, Joan Barth Urban, whose contribution and encouragement have been essential.

1. The concept is discussed in depth in the introduction to Ferenc Fehér and Agnes Heller, *Eastern Left, Western Left—Totalitarianism, Freedom and Democracy* (Atlantic Highlands, N.J.: Humanities Press, 1987), 1–47.

The Road to 1989: Crumbling Foundations
of Soviet Hegemony

Nobody today seriously questions that 1989 marked the end of an entire epoch not only for East-Central Europe, where the major upheavals took place, but for the world. The beginning of the historical period that ended in 1989 can be said to have been the postwar settlement of 1945 or even, from many viewpoints, the outbreak of the Bolshevik revolution in 1917. And since the latter was to a large extent the result of World War I, and particularly of the failure of the Second International to prevent it, the point of departure can be placed as early as 1914.[2]

Whatever its starting point, this historical period was characterized by the existence of communism not only as an ideology or a philosophical trend, but also as a political movement—the Communist (Third) International until 1943, the international communist movement thereafter—and as a system of states which emerged after World War II and was called the "socialist camp," then the "socialist community." The years 1989–91 marked the collapse of the latter and the virtual disappearance of the former, even if some communist parties continue to exist.[3]

In East-Central Europe, as is widely known, communist parties built up totalitarian dictatorships in the late 1940s as a result of Soviet occupation following the defeat of Nazi Germany. The relationship between the Soviet party, army, state bodies, and strategic interests and their respective East-Central European counterparts was always one of coercive submission, although the forms it took changed to

---

2. According to a leading expert on East-Central Europe, "1989 . . . was the year when Europe grew up and shook off the legacy of the Great European Civil War of 1914–1945 and began to redefine itself in its own terms and against the now declining superpowers which had exercised tutelage over it for so long." George Schöpflin, "The End of Communism in Eastern Europe," *International Affairs* 66, no. 1 (January 1990):3. For a different opinion on the beginning of the European "civil war", see Ernst Nolte, *Nazionalsocialismo e bolscevismo* (Florence: Sansoni, 1988). In late 1990 Nolte lectured in Florence on "The World Civil War, 1917–1989."

3. In mid-1991 those represented in the respective parliaments of Europe were the CPSU, whose Central Committee was, however, disbanded by Gorbachev on August 24 of that year, the Czech, French, Greek, Spanish, and Portuguese Communist parties.

some extent under the different Soviet leaders.[4] The subordination
of East-Central Europe to Soviet state and party interests was so
unremitting that two Hungarian experts, in an article on the security
aspects of the region, refer to the "Stalin-Khrushchev-Brezhnev doctrine."[5]

Their point is that, although the terror unleashed under Stalinist
rule from 1948 to 1953 was unique, the substance of the attitude
of succeeding Soviet leaderships toward the so-called satellites did
not change, as was shown in 1955 by the forceful interruption of
Imre Nagy's reform experiment in Hungary, in 1956 by the threats
to Władisław Gomułka's Poland and the armed suppression of the
Hungarian Revolution, in 1968 by the Warsaw Pact intervention in
Czechoslovakia, and in 1980–81 by the palpable threat of another
Red Army invasion of Poland which reportedly was prevented by
General Wojciech Jaruzelski's coup d'état.[6] It is worth noting that the
Soviet interventions or, in the case of Poland (1956 and 1981), direct
threats, took place in spite of the fact that leaving the "socialist
community" had never been on the agenda of the revolutionary or
reformist governments—not even in 1956 Hungary when the Warsaw Pact was denounced and a declaration of neutrality was approved
only after it had become evident that the Red Army, violating all
agreements, had started a second invasion of the country.[7]

After Jaruzelski's coup d'état in December 1981, the impression
among opposition circles in the region was that the East-Central
European countries had virtually exhausted their resources and that
any change in their situation could only come through a change in the
attitude of the Soviet leadership. This point of view was not based on

4. For an extensive elaboration on the history of Soviet-East European relations,
see Charles Gati, *The Bloc that Failed* (Bloomington, Ind.: Indiana University Press,
1990) and Adriano Guerra, "Da Stalin a Gorbaciov" in Federigo Argentieri, ed., *La fine
del blocco sovietico* (Florence: Ponte alle Grazie, 1991), 9–50.
5. Imre Szókai and Csaba Tabajdi, "Il cambiamento di modello sociale in Ungheria
significa anche cambiamento di orientamento della politica estera?" *Magyar Nemzet*,
trans. in *Documenti del CeSPI*, no. 17 (July 1989):14.
6. See *Le Monde*, April 17, 1987, for General Ryszard Kuklinski's revelations in
this regard and Karen Dawisha, "Gorbachev and Eastern Europe: A New Challenge for
the West?" *World Policy Journal* 3, no. 2 (Spring 1986):292.
7. For a detailed account, see George Heltai, "Gli ultimi giorni di Nagy," *l'Unità*,
November 4, 1986. In 1956 Heltai was Hungary's deputy minister of foreign affairs.

wishful thinking, let alone resignation, but was the outcome of an accurate analysis that the democratic opposition itself had been making since 1968 of the main features of the Soviet model, the policies of "normalization," and the situation in the economic field. In other words, there was a growing awareness that the communist system as a whole had reached a dead end and that its stability was therefore far less strongly grounded than it appeared to be.

In late 1981, for instance, János Kis, later the chairman of Hungary's Alliance of Free Democrats, remarked that "if we were lovers of the old-time slogans of the Communist International, we could now triumphantly announce that the proclamation of the state of emergency marks not the end of the Polish crisis, but the beginning of the generalized crisis of the East European System."[8] A little later, Kis likewise wrote:

> After 1956 and 1968 it was enough to reestablish forcibly the authority of the one-party state to restore the *status-quo*, while economic aid from the Soviet Union and the other countries of the Eastern bloc was sufficient to restore living standards and make up for the loss of production. In 1982 the Polish situation will not be so easily resolved for now the whole region battles with the same crisis. Nothing will ever be the same as before, for with the military takeover of power in Warsaw, the entire post-Stalin epoch is drawing to a close.[9]

The events that took place in the first half of the 1980s seemed to confirm this view. The martial-law regime in Poland proved incapable of overcoming the rift that occurred between the state and society, whereas this had been possible—at least to all outward appearances—in post-1956 Hungary and post-1968 Czechoslovakia. At the same time, the Soviet Union itself was clearly experiencing a serious leadership crisis, with aged and sick general secretaries succeeding one another. By 1985 the East-Central European democratic opposition thus seemed ready to assume new responsibilities. As Poland's Adam Michnik put it,

8. Quoted in Bill Lomax, "25 Years after 1956: The Heritage of the Hungarian Revolution," in *The Socialist Register 1982* (London: Merlin Press, 1982), 101.
    9. Ibid.

The Communists like to repeat that the effects of Yalta can only be changed by a nuclear war. This statement, surprisingly expressed by people who are familiar with Karl Marx, is nothing else than wishful thinking: the effects of Yalta can be changed by internal transformations in the Soviet Union and in the other countries of the bloc.[10]

In June 1985 the Hungarian dissidents, composed of four groupings—the creators of *samizdat* literature, the populists, the survivors of 1956, and the reformers inside the regime—organized a meeting in the small town of Monor where they discussed the country's problems and the possibilities for concrete action.[11] A year before, Václav Havel had already expressed what was to become the political philosophy of the "Velvet Revolution" in Czechoslovakia, and of the 1989 events in general, when he said:

Every time I am asked the question whether we [East European dissidents] want capitalism or socialism, I have the impression of a voice coming from the very bottom of the last century. . . . I think that the true question is . . . whether we will manage, in one way or another, to reconstitute the natural world as the real ground of politics, to restore man's personal experience as the original criterion of things, to place ethics above politics and responsibility above usefulness, to give again a meaning to human community and a content to human language.[12]

Kis also seemed to be paving the way for 1989 when he wrote, "We don't need right-wing or left-wing policies, but a policy that would make them possible."[13]

The tightening economic straits of the Soviet bloc were producing not only a revival of opposition movements, but an increasing division within the ruling parties as well. At the end of 1986 in Hungary, for example, a document prepared by the official People's

---

10. Adam Michnik, *Etica della resistenza—Scritti dalla prigione e dalla libertà* (Milan: Sugarco, 1986), 158.

11. See *A monori tanácskozás* and *A vita jegyzőkönyve*, both mimeo and *samizdat*, Budapest, 1985 and 1986.

12. Václav Havel, *Essais politiques* (Paris: Calmann-Lévy, 1989), 238–39.

13. János Kis, *Vannak-e emberi jógaink?* (Paris: Magyar Füzetek, 1988), 12.

Patriotic Front severely criticized the leadership and suggested radical solutions.[14]

The other factor that contributed to the collapse of 1989 was the powerful delegitimizing effect on communist regimes of the "new thinking" in Soviet foreign policy as well as that of *perestroika* and *glasnost* within the USSR. These new currents undermined the self-assurance of the ruling communist parties (even those such as Kádár's Hungarian Socialist Workers' Party that could boast of mildly reformist accomplishments), which was mainly based on the conviction that they could rely on Soviet troops in case of a threat to their powers. At the same time, the new thinking worked to the advantage of the opposition groups, which drew new energy from the visible reduction of direct Soviet interference in their countries' affairs. In the second half of 1989 these two trends gained momentum as a consequence of the significant changes taking place in Poland and Hungary, as well as of the complete withdrawal of Soviet troops from Afghanistan, which marked a clear-cut break with past policies. The momentum became irreversible after the opening of the Berlin Wall in November.

The first five years of Gorbachev's leadership of the Soviet Union can be divided into three periods with respect to its relationship with the Warsaw Pact countries: March 1985 to the liberation of Andrei Sakharov in December 1986, a period that was not marked by any definite differences in approach; December 1986 to July 1988, characterized by cautious and mainly verbal support for reform policies throughout the bloc; and a period of increasing pressure for radical change which occurred without direct interference from Moscow and culminated on December 4, 1989, with the Warsaw Pact's summit meeting in the Soviet capital at which the Brezhnev doctrine was openly rejected and the 1968 invasion of Czechoslovakia was declared to have been a huge mistake.

The turning point, therefore, was the summer of 1988, precisely the time of two important events in Moscow: the 19th Conference of the CPSU, at which Gorbachev's proposals for political reform of the Soviet system won out over his conservative opponents,[15] and the con-

---

14. *Fordulat és Reform*, supplement to *Medvetánc* 7, no. 2 (1987).

15. See Peter Reddaway, "Resisting Gorbachev," *The New York Review of Books* 35, no. 13 (August 18, 1988):36–44.

ference of the Ministry of Foreign Affairs, which assembled the country's entire diplomatic staff plus a number of experts in the military, economic, cultural, and political fields and opened with an introductory speech by Eduard Shevardnadze signaling a dramatic turnabout in the traditional Soviet approach to world politics.[16]

Particularly important was the foreign minister's emphasis on the ethical foundations of politics, the rejection of "class struggle" as a principle of foreign policy, the interdependence of the contemporary world—particularly with regard to environmental and security aspects—and the necessity for all countries, including the USSR, to respect the main principles of peaceful coexistence. In practice, his articulation of these ideas also had an important impact on the "fraternal socialist countries" and especially on relations among them. On this point, Shevardnadze was cautious but unambiguous, and his statements on past errors already amounted to an implicit rejection of the Stalin-Khrushchev-Brezhnev doctrine, especially when he emphasized freedom of choice for every country as a basic element of "new thinking."

The Role and Limits of Reform Communism

A brief comparative assessment of the East-Central European crises in 1956, 1968, and 1980–81 and the 1989 upheavals shows a number of interesting similarities and differences. The variables in these political developments were mainly three: the first could be called an internationally favorable context, consisting of a reform-minded leadership heading the Soviet Union; the second, a popular movement involving all strata of the society; and the third, a reformist wing inside the local communist party. Table 1 indicates the presence or absence of these conditions during the successive post-Stalin crises.

Of course, a number of qualifications should be mentioned. For one

---

16. Eduard Shevardnadze, "Teoria e prassi della nuova diplomazia," in his *Crisi del potere e diplomazia internazionale* (Rome: Lucarini, 1991), 7–50. See also Peter Clement, "Shevardnadze's Foreign Ministry: the Institutionalization of New Thinking," paper presented at the 21st Annual Convention of the American Association for the Advancement of Slavic Studies, Chicago, November 2–5, 1989.

Table 1. Characteristics of post-Stalin crises

	Reform leadership in USSR	Popular protest movement	Reform wing in local CP
Hungary 1956	Present	Present	Present
Poland 1956	Present	Present	Present
Czechoslovakia 1968	ABSENT	Present	Present
Poland 1980–81	ABSENT	Present	ABSENT
Hungary 1989	Present	ABSENT	Present
Poland 1989	Present	Present	ABSENT
Czechoslovakia 1989	Present	Present	ABSENT

thing, although both the Khrushchev and Gorbachev leaderships had an influence on East-Central European events, each behaved in different ways before, during, and especially after the upheavals. For another thing, the absence of a mass movement in Hungary in 1989 did not mean that the people did not participate (in fact they did at Nagy's ceremonial reinterment in June, for example, and when the Republic was proclaimed on October 23), but rather that they behaved more like interested spectators than protagonists.

Similarly, the absence of a reformist trend in the Polish party in 1989 did not mean that Jaruzelski and Czeszław Kiszczak did not move toward the recognition of Solidarity, but that they did so purely out of realpolitik and with no great cultural or political elaboration.[17]

Furthermore, the political orientation of the mass movements, while always profoundly tolerant and democratic, had been much more in favor of "authentic socialism" (including workers' self-management and forms of direct democracy) on the previous occasions than in 1989, when socialism was straightforwardly identified with bureaucratic oppression and therefore altogether absent from the populations' chants and slogans. By the same token, the ideology of reformism inside the party was also different. Nagy and Gomułka

---

17. Probably the only significant document produced by the PUWP between 1982 and 1989 was the one written in 1987 by M. F. Rakowski, its last secretary general, which amounted to little more than the admission of a historical failure. See M. F. Rakowski, "Note su alcuni aspetti della situazione politica ed economica della Repubblica popolare polacca nella seconda metà degli anni ottanta," in *Documenti del CeSPI*, no. 16 (February 1989).

in 1956 and Alexander Dubček in 1968 did not question Leninism or communism, but only Stalinism; whereas Imre Pozsgay in 1989, although trying to establish a connection between himself and Nagy, flatly declared that the system could not be reformed and should be destroyed. Indeed, he called himself a social democrat.[18]

This difference in no way suggests that the popular movements in 1989 were devoid of some of the traditional values of socialism, such as international solidarity, social justice and the like. Rather, these had come to be seen as established pan-European values. What really disappeared in 1989 was the notion of a "third way"—the idea of a democratic socialism that was separate and distinct both from bureaucratic oppression in the East and from Western capitalism, an idea that had been largely present in 1956, 1968, and 1980–81.[19]

This change can be explained by a very simple observation: over the recent decades Western societies had evolved and communist systems had stagnated. Western capitalism proved capable, thanks certainly to pressure from the left, of getting rid of overtly colonial practices and authoritarian regimes (for instance, in Greece, Portugal, Spain, the Philippines, and Chile) and of providing for an extensive network of social welfare as well as for reasonable protection of democratic rights and liberties (at least in Europe and America). Eastern communism, on the contrary, proved to be genetically incapable of reforming itself. It degenerated to the point of adopting the worst practices of imperialism (as in Afghanistan) without being able to increase the standard of living of the people or jettison the antilibertarian and antidemocratic features it had assumed almost since its birth. In short, what really won out in 1989 was the idea of an open society as opposed to a closed one: not only Von Mises' revenge but also Karl Popper's.[20]

18. See Pozsgay's interview with Radio Free Europe in *RFE Research* 14, no. 22 (June 2, 1989).

19. See the anthology by Francesco Leoncini, ed., *L'opposizione all'Est 1956–1981* (Manduria: Lacaita, 1989), which contains many documents on the upheavals of 1956, 1968, and 1980–81, especially on the workers' councils.

20. The expression "Von Mises' revenge" refers to the Austrian liberal economist's prediction in the 1920s that the socialist planned economy would fail, and was coined by British economist Philip Hanson; quoted in Argentieri, ed., *La fine del blocco sovietico,* 125 (see note 4). The expression "Popper's revenge" refers to philosopher K. R. Popper, *La società aperta e i suoi nemici,* vol. 2 entitled *Hegel e Marx falsi profeti*

In this context, it is interesting to analyze the differentiation that occurred within the communist movement throughout its seventy-year history. After extensive political and historical debate over the elements of continuity and cleavage between Leninism and Stalinism, today it is possible to affirm that, although a distinction between the 1917–27 period and the Stalin era remains pertinent, Stalinism represented a logical outcome of Leninism, even if not the sole possible one, and the Stalinist mentality and practices, with minor changes, substantially represented the main trend of communism until 1989.

Concurrent with this main trend, a secondary one developed from the late 1920s onward which could be called "non-Stalinist communism." In the Soviet Union it was represented by personalities like Nikolai Bukharin and Leon Trotsky who, however strong their criticism of the main trend, remained profoundly dependent on it because they always sought legitimation for their platforms in what they saw as "authentic" Leninism as opposed to its Stalinist "distortions." They never questioned the rules of the game set forth by Lenin—from the one-party system to "democratic centralism"—and thereby suffered a resounding political defeat long before Stalin had them assassinated.

After Stalin's death in 1953 yet another communist trend that can be called revisionist, or reformist, made its appearance in East-Central Europe, and expressed itself openly in Hungary (1953–56), Czechoslovakia (1968) and Poland (1956) around the leading figures of Nagy, Dubček, and Gomułka. The last betrayed his original commitments, so much so that he was forced to resign in late 1970 much in the same way as his Stalinist predecessor had been fourteen years before, whereas the first two remained faithful to theirs at the cost of life and twenty years' internal exile, respectively.[21] In ideological

---

(Rome: Armando, 1981). The concept of the victory of the open society in 1989 is also expressed by Ralf Dahrendorf, *1989: Riflessioni sulla rivoluzione in Europa* (Roma-Bari: Laterza, 1990) passim; and also by François Fejtö, "La libertà non è di destra," *l'Unità*, May 12, 1990.

21. On Nagy's life and works, see Aron Tóbiás, ed., *In Memoriam Nagy Imre* (Budapest: Szabad Tér, 1989) and the supplement to *l'Unità*, June 15, 1989, containing articles by Federigo Argentieri, Tibor Méray, Miklós Molnár, and Elek Nagy, as well as Imre Nagy's assessment, previously unpublished in a Western language, of the 20th CPSU Congress; see also Charles Gati, *Hungary and the Soviet Bloc* (Durham, N.C.: Duke University Press, 1986), 127–56. For an evaluation of the Nagy, Gomulka, and Dubček experiences, see also Fehér and Heller, *Eastern Left*, 18–19 (see note 1), and Miklós Molnár, *La démocratie se lève à l'Est* (Paris: PUF, 1990), 171–92.

terms, reform communism in East-Central Europe did not differ all that much from Bukharin's conception for it also sought legitimacy in "true Leninism"; but in practice it marked, contrary to non-Stalinist communism in the Soviet Union, a very clear rift with old methods, old aims, and old mentalities.

The policies of reform communism implied and encouraged a growing articulation of civil society as a strategic and not simply tactical move, so much so that they generated autonomous grassroots democratic movements, such as the workers' councils that developed in the first days of the Hungarian revolution and in Czechoslovakia after the invasion of August 21, 1968, which had no organizational link with the initiatives "from above."[22] Obviously we cannot know what the developments in those countries would have come to had they not been interrupted by foreign military intervention. But it is certain that both communist parties had initiated a process of renewal from the ground up with the purpose of breaking with Stalinism and tuning in completely to the popular movement.

In 1956 Hungary it was János Kádár, who had been elected first secretary of the Hungarian Workers' Party on October 25 (forty-eight hours after the outbreak of the revolution), who announced five days later the dissolution of the party and his full agreement with the restoration of a multiparty system.[23] On November 1 he delivered a significant speech over the radio that underscored the extent to which the party reformers had responded to the grassroots democratization movement:

> Hungarian workers, peasants and intellectuals. . . . In a glorious uprising our people have shaken off the Rákosi regime. They have achieved freedom for the people and independence for the country, without which there can be no socialism. We can safely say that . . . those who prepared this uprising were recruited from our ranks. . . .
>
> In these momentous hours, the Communists who fought against Rákosi's despotism have . . . decided to form a new party. . . . In these momentous hours, we call on every Hungarian worker who is inspired

22. For an interesting development of this viewpoint, see Bill Lomax, "Il popolo trascinò Nagy e Dubček," *l'Unità*, June 30, 1989.

23. *The Revolt in Hungary—a Documentary Chronology of Events Based Exclusively on Internal Broadcasts by Central and Provincial Radios* (New York: Free European Committee, n.d.), 43.

by affection for the people and the country to join our party, whose name is the Hungarian Socialist Workers' Party. A preparatory committee has been formed whose members are: Ferenc Donáth, János Kádár, Sándor Kopácsi, Géza Losonczy, György Lukács, Imre Nagy and Zoltán Szántó. This committee will begin to organize the Party, . . . [which] is prepared to do its share in fighting for the consolidation of independence and democracy. . . . We turn to the newly-formed democratic parties—first of all . . . to the Social Democratic Party—with the request that they help consolidate the government and thereby overcome the danger of menacing countries and intervention from abroad.[24]

As Kádár was pronouncing these words, Soviet troops were invading Hungary again—after announcing their withdrawal.

Kádár himself would be the only member of the leadership of the new party to switch to the Soviet side; the others were to be arrested or deported to Romania. Later on, Lukács and Szántó would accept the accomplished fact of the Soviet invasion, while the remaining four members would not and thus would be put on trial and sentenced, in June 1958, to death (Nagy), life imprisonment (Kopácsi), twelve years in prison (Donáth). Losonczy was to die in prison in December 1957—after a hunger strike and a failed attempt to forcefeed him.[25]

In 1968 Czechoslovakia this same melding of reform from above and democratic mobilization from below was evident. A Central Committee meeting held on May 29–June 1 convened the 14th Extraordinary Congress of the Communist Party for September 9. In his opening speech to the session Alexander Dubček emphasized that

the Communists request that the party get rid . . . of all the deformations of the past and all those who are concretely responsible for them. Communists request from the party secure and convincing guarantees that no return to old bureaucratic methods of management or to the deformations that marked so tragically the 1950s will be possible.[26]

---

24. Ibid., 63–64.

25. Federigo Argentieri, ed., *Il processo Nagy—Il revisionismo comunista alla sbarra* (Roma: Quaderni di *Tempo Presente*, 1987).

26. "Rapport d'Alexandre Dubček devant le Plénum du Comité Central du PC Tchécoslovaque le 29 mai 1968," in Jiři Pelikan, ed., *Le Congrès clandestin—Protocole secret et documents du 14ème Congrès extraordinaire du P. C. Tchécoslovaque (22 août 1968)* (Paris: Seuil, 1970), 19.

During the late spring and the summer, party cells all over the country discussed in unprecedented freedom and openness the political situation and its possible outcomes, and the delegates to the upcoming congress were elected democratically after long debates.

The "Letter of Five," signed in Warsaw on July 15 by representatives of the USSR, Poland, the German Democratic Republic (GDR), Hungary, and Bulgaria, urged the conservatives in the Czechoslovak party to stop the process of renewal, but this pressure only had the effect of strengthening the new course. One of the main aims of the invasion on August 21, 1968, was therefore to prevent the holding of the congress, which took place anyway, clandestinely, the following day.

The week after the invasion, Dubček and the chief leaders of the Prague Spring, who had been taken to Moscow virtually as prisoners, were forced to repudiate the validity of the congress.[27] When the news of this event reached Prague, the Central Committee elected at the 14th Congress responded in the following way:

> Our public opinion reacts with bitterness and disappointment to the communiqué announcing the result of the talks that our representatives held in Moscow. We share those feelings and are fully aware of the gravity of this moment. We give in to force, but will never renounce our demand for sovereignty and freedom.[28]

Gorbachev's *perestroika* represented the decisive culmination of this brand of reform communism. Indeed, it is only in the light of this history that the recent Soviet experience becomes fully comprehensible. In the first three to four years of leadership, Gorbachev adopted elements of Bukharin's and Khrushchev's non-Stalinist policies and followed the course of struggling against the "bureaucratization of socialism" in the name of the "original Leninist values and principles," just as Nagy, Gomułka, and Dubček had done thirty and twenty years before him. By mid-1990 he seemed to have achieved the

27. See Bohumil Simon's eyewitness account of the arrest, the deportation to Moscow, and the "talks" with the Soviets in his previously unpublished report, "Prigionieri al Cremlino," *l'Unità*, August 14, 1988.
28. Pelikan, *Le Congrès clandestin*, 339–40 (see note 26).

aim of defeating the Stalinist system. According to one Italian expert, commenting on the July 1990 CPSU Congress,

> The 28th Congress constituted a crucial turning point, a watershed that definitively marked the irreversibility of the changes that have occurred in the Soviet Union over the past five troubled years. Of course, this does not mean that the Soviet situation is on its way to speedy normalization, or that the huge array of problems the Kremlin leadership faces has suddenly disappeared. On the contrary, the months and years to come will witness disruptive developments and great tragedies. But the 28th Congress will pass into history as the moment of the collapse of resistance by the most important and dangerous group hostile to change— the communist party apparatus. It is now virtually impossible for party conservatives to turn back the clock.[29]

As for the personal political views of Gorbachev, it is difficult to say whether by mid-1990 he had come to realize that the role of reform communism was also over. In November of that year he told the general secretary of the Italian Communist Party (PCI), Achille Occhetto, that he still stood "for socialism, despite the tragedies that marked the past seven decades."[30] Somewhat ambiguously, in an interview with the Spanish daily *El Pais* about the same time, the Soviet leader said: "For me, to be a Communist means faithfulness . . . to democratic socialism. . . . The socialist idea does not exclude either a market economy, or parliamentary democracy, or freedom and human rights."[31] It is obviously understandable that, if only for tactical reasons, Gorbachev was highly unlikely to take a public stand against communism, Lenin, or the Bolshevik revolution. But it is also indisputable that everything he publicly stood for by the middle of 1990 raised questions not only about Stalinism, but about the very roots of the Soviet system at least since January 1918, when the Constituent Assembly was dissolved and disbanded by the Bolsheviks.

29. Giulietto Chiesa, "The 28th CPSU Congress," *Problems of Communism* 39, no. 4 (July–August 1990):24.

30. Information released by Achille Occhetto, following a trip to Moscow, at a meeting of the PCI Foreign Affairs Committee on November 21, 1990, at which the author was present.

31. Text in *la Repubblica*, October 26, 1990.

The rift that opened between Gorbachev and Eduard Shevardnadze on December 20, 1990, and between Gorbachev and many well-known intellectual reformers connected with the progressive weekly, *Moscow News,* on January 16, 1991, after the crackdown on Lithuania, showed that for reasons of his own the Soviet president was not yet prepared to accept the ultimate consequences of his policies: to wit, after the virtual dissolution of the so-called exclernal empire, a profound democratization of the so-called internal one—a development that in early 1991 seemed highly problematic. Many of his closest collaborators wanted just such democratization, however, and in mid-January 1991 one of them even publicly pronounced the fatal sentence, so often heard in the previous decade in East-Central Europe: "Communism is not reformable."[32]

But the events of the following months were to suggest that Gorbachev had had only a tactical retreat in mind. During the Gulf War the Soviet Union remained faithful to the UN Security Council decision of early December 1990 despite strong conservative opposition. And the "Ten Presidents' Agreement" signed in Novoe-Ogorevo on April 23, 1991, on the basis of which Gorbachev and Boris Yeltsin (along with the leaders of eight other union republics) resumed the process of reform and federalization of the USSR, represented a clear defeat for the "hawks" in the party apparatus. Thus by mid-1991 the process of democratization—including respect for the will of those republics that wanted to leave the Union, the problematic introduction of a market economy, and the *dissolution from above* of the Communist Party—had been put on track again. The most dangerous conservative counteroffensive of the first six years of Gorbachev's rule had been rebuffed.

An even more dangerous conservative attack took place in the form of the failed coup of August 19–21, 1991. At that point, the powerful popular reaction had the effect of dramatically accelerating the de-

32. Stanislav Shatalin, the economist responsible for the so-called 500 days plan, wrote, "The country's crisis started neither in 1985, nor in the years of stagnation. Either we realize the mistake made in October 1917, or the socialist movement in our country is doomed to failure." Quoted in Jolanda Bufalini, "URSS, stampa in libertà vigilata," *l'Unità,* January 17, 1991. According to the article (reported from Moscow), Shatalin also wrote, "There is also another thing that must be realized, which is the impossibility of reforming the Communist Party."

mocratization process and obliging Gorbachev, whose political survival was at stake for several days, to cease all equivocation. Only after a humiliating public admission of his mistakes, the disbanding of the CPSU Central Committee, the reaffirmation of his alliance with Yeltsin, and a severe limitation of his powers could the former and last general secretary of the CPSU retain his position as head of a state undergoing profound transformation.

It is therefore possible to conclude this section with the following assertion: the history of communism in this century has been made up of a main Stalinist trend and of a subordinate reform tendency which, although never representing an autonomous political culture, proved capable of peacefully destroying the previous one; it thereby contributed to the birth or rebirth of democratic systems, but in doing so exhausted its historical role.[33] This statement could also be formulated in another way: Stalinist communism drives a country into a dead end, and reform communism extricates it but becomes worthless immediately thereafter. For reformist leaders and supporters, while thinking they were questioning only Stalinism, realized once they were victorious that they had questioned the whole Leninist canon, and hence communism not only as a system of states and a political movement but as a doctrine and a theory as well. They also realized that the only way to prevent the resurgence of dictatorship was to stick to the rules of party pluralism and separation of powers and to a market economy, without which civil society and economic welfare cannot exist. This course applied not only to the ruling or formerly ruling communist parties, but also to the Western brand of reform communism. The strongest representative, the PCI, once the ideas it had been elaborating for thirty years prevailed in Moscow and elsewhere in Eastern Europe, had no other choice but to dissolve itself and become a noncommunist political force.[34]

This background helps explain what happened in East-Central Europe as far as the former ruling parties are concerned. With the exception (so far) of the Czech Lands' party, they all changed their

33. The author has further elaborated on the subject together with Antonio Missiroli and Silvio Pons in "Dal '56 a Gorbaciov: Il paradosso del comunismo riformatore," *l'Unità*, April 19, 1990.
34. See Chapter 2 herein.

names and switched to socialist or social democratic programs and identities. Their varied electoral performances in 1990 can be partially explained on the basis of three elements: first, their historical influence (for example, electoral performance after the war or contribution to the antifascist struggle); second, their contribution to the 1989 transformations; and third, the credibility of their shift to reform communism, a criterion that includes the existence of a reformist wing prior to 1989, their behavior toward the conservative leaders, their readiness to disclose party assets and disband party militias, and so forth.

On the basis of these criteria, Table 2 presents a graphic analysis of the 1990 electoral showings of the erstwhile ruling parties in East-Central Europe. Also included, for the sake of comparison, are those of the former GDR and the formerly Yugoslav republic of Slovenia.

What becomes immediately clear is the relatively low correlation between a party's voter appeal in 1990 and its earlier support, or lack thereof, for the reform process. Only in Poland and Slovenia was the party's electoral showing fully explained by its pre-1990 conduct. Even there, however, qualifications are in order. In Poland only local elections were held in 1990, with completely free legislative elections being scheduled for 1991 (the 1989 ones gave a 65 percent share of the seats in the lower house to the former Polish United Workers' Party [PUWP] and its allies); while in Slovenia the communists profited from the fact that, contrary to their colleagues in neighboring countries, they were never seen by the people as the tools of a foreign power.

As for Czechoslovakia, it seems that the party's strong historical tradition was in itself sufficient to enable it to survive 1989 and 1990 with no significant change of identity and a reasonably respectable performance at the polls. In the GDR, the March 1990 elections amounted to a referendum on Chancellor Helmut Kohl's plan for rapid reunification. This controversial issue contributed to the unexpectedly good performance of the traditionally hard-line communists, who obviously opposed the plan and were supported by those voters whose status or identity was linked to the continued existence of a separate East German state. In unified Germany's first elections of December 1990 the Communists managed to become the fifth party

Table 2. Considerations affecting 1990 electoral performance of former ruling communist parties in East-Central Europe

	Historical influence	Contribution to 1989 transformation	Credibility of reformist commitment	% of vote
Poland	very low	little	little	under 1
Czechoslovakia	high (38% of 1946 vote)	none	little	13.6
Hungary	low (17% of 1945 vote)	decisive	considerable	8.5
GDR	low	little	medium	16.5
Slovenia	high	decisive	considerable	17

(after the Christian Democrats/Christian Socialists, Social Democrats, and Free Democrats), thanks to the collapse of the Greens and to a particularly favorable electoral mechanism, which did not extend to the eastern part of the country the 5 percent rule requiring a minimal electoral showing for parliamentary representation. Thus the real anomaly was Hungary, where the communists' decisive support for reform early on was hardly rewarded by the voters. Perhaps this simply underscores the above-stated conclusion that reform communism had performed its historical role of destroying Stalinism and thereby outlived its usefulness.[35]

From Antitotalitarian Unity to Polarization

The main actors in the 1989 revolutions in East-Central Europe were the people, who on numerous occasions took to the streets, demonstrating their will to put an end to the communist regimes and to create new democratic and pluralistic institutions. Except in Poland, where Solidarity had existed for almost a decade, the demonstrators came to be represented by newly formed organizations: the

35. This conclusion is shared by Pierre Kende, "Miért nem győzött a reformkommunizmus?" in the farewell issue of the Hungarian emigré journal, *Magyar Füzetek*, published by Budapest's *Szazadvég*, no. 3–4 (1990):70–73; and by Bill Lomax, "Hungary—from Kadarism to Democracy: The Successful Failure of Reform Communism," in D. W. Spring, ed., *The Impact of Gorbachev* (London: Pinter, 1991).

Hungarian Democratic Forum, founded in September 1987; the Alliance of Young Democrats and Alliance of Free Democrats, also Hungarian, and formed in March and November 1988 respectively; and Czechoslovakia's Civic Forum/Public against Violence, created on November 19, 1989, two days after the outbreak of the "Velvet Revolution."

A comparative assessment of the transition to democracy in these three countries indicates that in Hungary, contrary to Poland and Czechoslovakia where the opposition was represented by large conglomerations of antitotalitarian unity, the democratic forces were already functioning with separate organizations that retained a united platform against the ruling party only until the last phase of the roundtable negotiations between the regime and the opposition held from June 13 to September 18, 1989. The Hungarian situation reflected the fact that the Kádár regime, quite unlike Jaruzelski's and even less like the Czechoslovak one, could be deemed authoritarian rather than totalitarian; for it had allowed, at least since the mid-1960s, a very limited pluralism.[36]

It is important to emphasize that in Budapest the rift within the opposition occurred almost simultaneously with the rift inside the ruling party. On September 18, 1989, a group of four organizations (the Alliance of Free Democrats, the Alliance of Young Democrats, the Smallholders' Party, and the Social Democratic Party) refused to sign the roundtable agreements. Three weeks later an extraordinary conference of the Hungarian Socialist Workers' Party (HSWP) ended in a split when about 80 percent of the delegates decided to found the Hungarian Socialist Party (HSP).[37] The reason for both rifts was the same. In the case of the opposition, the Free Democrats and their associates (in contrast to the Democratic Forum) refused to delegate

36. For an assessment of the Kádár regime, see Bill Lomax, "Hungary: The Quest for Legitimacy," in Paul G. Lewis, ed., *Eastern Europe: Political Crisis and Legitimation* (London: Croom Helm, 1984), 68–110; Molnár, *La démocratie*, 193–205 (see note 21); Ferenc Fehér and Agnes Heller, *Ungheria 1956—il messaggio di una rivoluzione oltre un quarto di secolo dopo* (Milan: Sugarco, 1983), 224–36; Charles Gati, *Hungary and the Soviet Bloc*, 156–76 (see note 21); and Federigo Argentieri, "Il mito di Kádár 'riformista,'" in *MicroMega* 1, no. 4 (1986):126–34.

37. For a description of the conference, see R. L. Tőkés, "Beyond the Party Congress—Hungary's Hazy Future," *The New Leader*, October 30, 1989, 5–7.

to Parliament, still dominated by the communists, the solution of three important problems: the dissolution of the Workers' Guard (a paramilitary body founded in early 1957 to prevent the possibility of another "counterrevolution"), the disclosure of party assets, and the disbanding of party cells in workplaces. In the case of the ruling HSWP, the reformist wing led by Imre Pozsgay realized that in order to meet these legitimate requests and so be able to compete in free elections, it had to break with the conservatives.

Another political struggle started immediately afterwards. The new HSP, supported by the benevolent neutrality of the Democratic Forum, wanted to hold the presidential election before the parliamentary one and presented Pozsgay as its candidate. The four organizations that had refused to sign the roundtable agreements opposed this move and collected signatures for a nationwide referendum on the issue, which they won on November 26, 1989, by a tiny majority (50.07 percent of the votes). Therefore, it is possible to say that as of October 23, 1989, when the Hungarian Republic was proclaimed on the 33rd anniversary of the outbreak of the 1956 revolution, the political spectrum of the country had already clearly divided into several conflicting forces.

The question arises as to whether the traditional Western categories of "left" and "right" could be applied to these forces at that moment in Hungary's political evolution. The answer is probably yes, although some further elaboration is necessary.

As far as political culture is concerned, from many viewpoints it looked as if Hungary had gone back to the 1930s, when its intellectuals were divided between "urbanists" (pro-Western, business-oriented, European, liberal or social-democratic, often Jewish) and "populists" (nationalistic, rural-oriented, Christian, wary of anything foreign—especially Western political theories and cultural trends—and tending toward anti-semitism). The Alliance of Free Democrats (AFD) appeared to be the heir of the urbanists, and the Democratic Forum that of the populists. This difference also explains the paradox of the different attitudes of the two toward communist power. The AFD, although placed on the center-left, was eager to overcome traditional Hungarian backwardness in relation to the West, which had certainly increased during the communist era, and urged the quick dismantling of the communist party-state. The Forum, on the other hand, was in much less of a hurry because it stood merely for a "Hungarian" outcome, with no particular regard for the European context; therefore, although placed on the center-right, it was indulgent toward the Pozsgay maneuver to win the presidency.

In contrast, no such articulation of the political spectrum took place in 1989 in either Poland or Czechoslovakia. In those two countries the opposition was represented by broad antitotalitarian platforms that peacefully managed to compel the ruling party to relinquish power.

In Poland, after two months of roundtable negotiations (February 6–April 4, 1989), parliamentary elections were held in early June 1989 (see Table 3). The result was clearly defined by the fact that in the newly created Senate, where the vote was free, Solidarity won ninety-nine seats out of one hundred, with the remaining one going to an independent candidate. As already mentioned, the ruling PUWP managed to obtain 65 percent of the seats in the Sejm (lower house) only because such a share had been guaranteed to it and its satellites in the roundtable agreements.

In Czechoslovakia negotiations were essentially held between the people in the streets and the communist government, which surrendered in less than two weeks (November 17–29, 1989). The government received the final blow a few days later when at the Warsaw Pact summit in Moscow, summoned on December 4 to ratify the outcome of the Malta meeting between Bush and Gorbachev, the members openly condemned the 1968 suppression of the Prague Spring.

As of 1990, however, the pace of political differentiation began to speed up, and by the end of the year polarization had become an accomplished fact in both Poland and Czechoslovakia, while in Hungary the political spectrum had evolved to the point where it started to look, albeit still very vaguely, like the traditional Western pattern.

Interestingly, all through the spring and summer of 1990 it was the center-right that took the initiative to disrupt the "conglomerate parties"[38] where they still existed, and to acquire a more European,

---

38. The expression is used by George Schöpflin, "The End of Communism," passim (see note 2).

Christian-democratic or liberal outlook as opposed to a nationalistic and populist one. The center-left, on the other hand, tried to stick to antitotalitarian unity, which in its view would have served as a basis for continued mass support of necessarily severe austerity policies, and was defeated.

In Hungary the Free Democrats, after polling about 22 percent in the first round of the March 1990 parliamentary elections, proposed a coalition government to the Democratic Forum, which had won about 26 percent. The Forum refused, and after the second round decided to form a coalition with the Smallholders and the Christian Democrats, which it found more compatible with its political culture. Shortly after, in late June, the Forum hosted in Budapest a European meeting of Christian-democratic parties. Moreover, the new Hungarian prime minister, József Antall (head of the Democratic Forum), never made a secret of his excellent personal and political links to both Germany's Chancellor Kohl and Italy's Christian Democratic prime minister, Giulio Andreotti.[39]

By autumn Hungarian political developments had become clearer after the local elections of September 30 and October 14, and especially after the "gasoline revolution" of late October.

The local elections were notable on two accounts. There was, first, the disturbingly low participation (about 42 percent) of the electorate, probably caused by inevitable dissatisfaction over the increasingly poor economic situation. But the contest also represented a brilliant outcome for the Alliance of Free Democrats, who, either alone or in coalition with Fidesz (Alliance of Young Democrats), won mayoralties in Budapest and other major cities, thereby harvesting the fruits of a consistent and responsible opposition policy.

The "gasoline revolution" further clarified the political evolution in Hungary. Nobody questioned the fact that the Gulf crisis, combined with the need to pay for Soviet oil in hard currency as of January 1, 1991, made a price hike inevitable. However, the way the government

---

39. Antall was an honored guest at the Italian Christian Democrats' annual festival in Cagliari; for his speech, which among other things described the Hungarian Democratic Forum as "a party based on Christian Democratic values," see *il Popolo*, September 18, 1990. See also George Schöpflin, "Conservatism and Hungary's Transition," *Problems of Communism* 40 (January–April 1991):60–68.

Table 3. Parliamentary elections in East-Central Europe, 1989–90

Country/date	Type of legislature	Party (alliance)	Number of seats	
			Sejm	Senate
Poland, June 4 and 18, 1989	560-member bicameral National Assembly	Citizens' Parliamentary Caucus (Solidarity)	161	99
		Polish United Workers' Party (PUWP)	173	–
		United Peasant Party (PUWP ally)	76	–
		Democratic Party (PUWP ally)	27	–
		Former proregime Christian groups:		
		PAX	10	–
		Christian-Social Union	8	–
		Polish Catholic Social Union	5	–
		Independent and Unaffiliated	–	1
		Total	460	100
Hungary, March 25 and April 8, 1990	386-member single chamber	Hungarian Democratic Forum	164	
		Alliance of Free Democrats	92	
		Independent Smallholders' Party	44	
		Hungarian Socialist Party (ex-communist)	33	
		Alliance of Young Democrats	21	
		Christian Democratic Party	21	
		Agrarian Alliance	1	
		Independents	6	
		Single candidates representing two parties	4	
		Total	386	
Czechoslovakia, June 8–9, 1990	300-member bicameral Federal Assembly	Civic Forum/Public against Violence	168*	
		Communist Party of Czechoslovakia	47	
		Christian Democratic Union/ Christian Democratic Movement	40	
		Movement for Self-Governing Democracy/ Society for Moravia and Silesia	16	
		Slovak National Party	15	

Table 3. (cont.)

Country/date	Type of legislature	Party (alliance)	Number of seats
		Coexistence/Hungarian Christian Democratic Movement	12
		Liberal Democratic Party	2
		Total	300

Source: Report on Eastern Europe, July 13, 1990, 40–41.

*Of the 170 mandates obtained by the Civic Forum/Public against Violence in the election, two are now held by the Liberal Democratic Party, which ran under the Civic Forum's umbrella but has since set itself up as an independent group.

established it overnight, without consulting either the opposition or the social groups most affected (entrepreneurs and unions, for example), and especially the fact that the hike amounted to 60 percent of the previous price, provoked severe social disturbances. The government's attempt to reply with a campaign of "law and order" ended only after a negotiated reduction of the hike to 32 percent.[40] The AFD's criticism of the government was twofold: its economic incompetence and demagoguery in postponing the hike until it became imperative, and its authoritarianism in imposing it abruptly with no prior consultation.[41]

In Poland it was Lech Wałesa who decided during the spring that a united Solidarity had become useless. The reasons for this, both personal and political, have been carefully analyzed by others.[42] After trying to prevent the rift, the center-left replied by forming the Civic Movement-Democratic Action (ROAD) in opposition to Wałesa's Center Alliance.

40. Alfred Reisch, "The Gasoline War: Order or Chaos?" *Report on Eastern Europe* 1, no. 45 (November 9, 1990):6–10; Karoly Okolicsanyi, "The Economics of Gasoline Price Increases," ibid., 11–14; George Fletcher, "The Day Budapest Shut Down," *The New York Review of Books* 37, no. 19 (December 6, 1990):48.

41. Fletcher, "The Day Budapest Shut Down," 48 (see note 40).

42. Timothy Garton Ash, "Eastern Europe: Après le Déluge, Nous," *The New York Review of Books* 37, no. 13 (August 16, 1990):55–57; Luisa Vinton, "Solidarity's Rival Offspring: Center Alliance and Democratic Action," *Report on Eastern Europe* 1, no. 38 (September 21, 1990):15–25.

Until the autumn an apparent paradox juxtaposed the Hungarian situation against the Polish one. In the former the left criticized the right for not being determined enough in dismantling communist structures, whereas in the latter it was the other way around. Developments in Hungary in autumn 1990 showed, however, that the Free Democrats were correct. For following the "gasoline revolution," the Antall government switched from a three-year economic plan of "gradual recovery" to a much more radical one, scheduled to last six months.[43] In contrast, during the 1990 presidential campaign Wałesa and his team accused the Mazowiecki government of dragging its feet despite the fact that it had approved and implemented Leszek Balcerowicz's plan for a rapid transition to a market economy. This was plain demagoguery, for the new Polish executive formed in early 1991 after Wałesa's election as president followed exactly the same policy as its predecessor, even keeping Balcerowicz himself at his post as finance minister.

In Czechoslovakia, a similar process was taking place at the same time. Finance Minister Václav Klaus, who proudly called himself "a conservative," was elected chairman of the Civic Forum on October 13, 1990, and thereupon expressed his intention to oust as soon as possible the members of *Obroda* (a socialist-oriented club composed mainly of veterans of the Prague Spring) as well as the Trotskyite Left Alternative, both of which were founding members of the Civic Forum.[44] The parliamentary caucus was thus divided between a Democratic Right that supported Klaus and Civic Association, which, almost exactly like ROAD in Poland, opposed what it called "the artificial left-right division" and stood for the continued unity of the Civic Forum.

Is Anything *Left* Still Left?

From a conceptual point of view, the numerous debates that took place beginning in the second half of 1990, both among specialists

---

43. See note 40.
44. Massimo Boffa, "Praga, dalla libertà alla realtà," *l'Unità*, November 17, 1990.

and East-Central European political actors, about the definition of left and right and the post-1989 elections pointed to the existence of broad disagreements. At a conference in France held in mid-September, for example, the Czech emigré historian Karel Bartošek said that "the left is whatever opposes dictatorship and oppression, the right is the other way round." Yet the Hungarian-French sociologist Pierre Kende expressed another view.[45] In early 1991, according to him, the logic of Bartošek's opinion would have placed the former ruling parties—with some exceptions such as Hungary's HSP—on the right, led or provisionally supported by Gorbachev, and *all* the new political forces on the left. This would include people like Shevardnadze on account of his resignation speech on December 20, 1990,[46] Boris Yeltsin, and the Soviet establishment intellectuals who in mid-January 1991 sharply condemned the crackdown on Lithuania, denouncing "the regime that doesn't want to leave the scene"[47] and provoking the anger of Gorbachev himself.

This writer holds still another view: that distinctions must be made, in the history of this century, between a democratic and a nondemocratic right and a democratic and a nondemocratic left, each of these having further internal differentiations. Franco's Spain, Mussolini's Italy, and Hitler's Germany were quite different from each other, though all belonged to the category of nondemocratic rightist regimes. By the same token, Kádár's Hungary, Husak's Czechoslovakia, and Stalin's USSR could be termed nondemocratic leftist regimes, although they differed from each other, too.

The year 1989 represented for the nondemocratic left something similar to what 1944–46 represented for the nondemocratic right, that is, the emergence of broad national alliances of virtually the entire political spectrum against totalitarianism or its remnants.[48]

45. Pierre Kende, "S'abstenir de tout classer," *La Nouvelle Alternative*, no. 20 (December 1990):4. The author quotes Bartošek and expresses the intention "d'ajouter une note de prudence."

46. Shevardnadze, *Crisi del potere*, 145–48 (see note 16).

47. *Moscow News*, January 16, 1991. The text was signed by many former supporters of Gorbachev such as Tenghiz Abuladze, Yevgenii Ambartsumov, Aleksandr Bovin, Oleg Bogomolov, Tatyana Zaslavskaya, Stanislav Shatalin, Nikolai Shmelyev, and Aleksandr Tsipko.

48. The same point is made by Bill Lomax in "Hungary Today—Has the Spirit of 1956 Been Laid to Rest?" *Planet*, April–May, 1990, 3.

Although this is not the place to elaborate on the differences between communist and fascist regimes, one point should be made which is that a communist dictatorship is more destructive than a fascist one of civil society in all its dimensions: private initiative, sense of responsibility, entrepreneurial spirit, grassroots spontaneous organization—whatever represents the backbone of a modern free society. And the need to reconstruct all this has strongly influenced and will continue to influence the political evolution of postcommunist countries.

Now that nondemocratic regimes are disappearing from East-Central Europe, the main distinction is between the democratic left and the democratic right. The forces that emerged from the 1990 elections can thus be grouped into three main categories. The first is the center-right, which as previously mentioned is subdivided into a populist-nationalist trend and a liberal–Christian democratic one. The former includes, for instance, the Slovak National Party and some intellectuals of the Hungarian Democratic Forum like István Csurka. The latter is represented by people like Tadeusz Mazowiecki, Václav Klaus and József Antall. The Polish case is particularly interesting in this respect, for Lech Wałesa and his Center Alliance could be placed somewhere between the above two trends, whereas Mazowiecki would have preferred a closer association with the social-liberal left of the former Solidarity activists Adam Michnik, Bronisław Geremek, and Jacek Kuroń, who not only supported his government and his unsuccessful presidential race but also contributed to the foundation of the Democratic Union, which took place on December 16, 1990, and consists of ROAD and the Democratic Right, the two main supporters of Mazowiecki.

The second group is composed of the remnants of the former ruling parties, which have a rather weak parliamentary representation and are struggling with a deep identity crisis, the causes of which have already been suggested. Irrespective of the ups and downs of political contingency—for example, the fact that in Poland the candidate of the former Communist Party polled over 9 percent in the first round of the presidential race, thereby considerably improving his party's poor performance in the local elections; or that the present Czech Communist Party is deeply divided between belated Eurocommunists and diehard Stalinists; or that Imre Pozsgay in November 1990 left the

HSP, which certainly weakened that political group[49]—these parties, as well as the old communist trade unions, seem doomed to a marginal role for a long time to come. They are unable to represent any but those who are nostalgic for old times and who, for different reasons, are afraid to lose the lumpen-welfare provided by communism.

The third, and by far the most vital and interesting group, is made up of the parties, political groups, and trends that have their roots in the former democratic opposition of the 1970s. Its spiritual and political leaders are such talented people as Havel, Kis, and Michnik. Though all of them flatly refuse the label "left," it is not arbitrary to apply it to them—not only because the right has been doing so since the winter of 1989–90, but also because they definitely seem to prefer *"liberté, egalité, fraternité"* to "God, homeland, family." They have nothing in common with Stalinism, just as Churchill had nothing in common with Hitler, but many of them (including Kis and Michnik) once shared the illusions of reform communism.

Their leftism is much more grounded in ethics, personal responsibility, and tolerance than in traditional Marxism, with the theory of which all of them settled accounts long ago. In many ways their outlook reminds one of the antitotalitarian commitment of such intellectuals as George Orwell and Ignazio Silone, who placed themselves beyond communism but also took a critical stance towards social democracy. For Kis and Michnik, who come from countries whose *political* Europeanness has been, and still is, questioned to some extent, the main task is to look westward, to catch up not only economically but also socially and culturally with the European Community countries. Václav Havel, who was never a Communist and comes from a country that was in 1938 the fourth industrial power in Europe, is more of a maverick and criticizes not only totalitarian communism but also the "emptiness" of Western democracy. In his view, the latter tends to diminish personal responsibility and to alienate the individual. This explains his antiparty rhetoric, which in 1991

---

49. See Edit Oltay, "Imre Pozsgay Resigns from the Hungarian Socialist Party," *Report on Eastern Europe* 1, no. 48 (November 30, 1990):6–8. In mid-September of the same year Pozsgay told this author during a private meeting in Modena, Italy, that his main task since the elections had been to "cool down the revanchist sentiments" of his party.

placed him in a difficult position after the forceful initiatives of Klaus to remove democratic leftists from the Civic Forum.[50]

The problem for this third political tendency—following the collapse of the communist regimes to which it contributed so greatly—is that, however much it is aware of the necessity to reconstruct a civil society, the democratic right is convinced that it is more qualified for this task. Thus the right may have a notable psychological advantage, which has also become a political one.

As for the reconstituted social democratic parties, which polled disastrously in the elections, their political situation can be summed up briefly. Their main platform is a welfare state, but since there is presently no economic welfare of any kind, their role is obviously marginal. And it will remain such as long as economic recovery, or at least the most urgent part of it, is not achieved.

So the answer to the question raised in the subtitle of this chapter is yes, much of the *left is* left in East-Central Europe after 1989, but it is safe to predict that its political role as such will be small until the main foundations of a civil society have been reconstructed. To quote the former Polish dissident and labor minister in Mazowiecki's government, Jacek Kuroń: "I'll be on the left, a moderate left, in a capitalist system. Before that, I'll build up that capitalist system."[51]

50. For the political writings of Havel, Kis, and Michnik, see notes 10, 12, and 13.
51. Quoted in *La Nouvelle Alternative*, no. 19 (September 1990):25.

Afterthoughts in Light
of the August 1991 Coup

Joan Barth Urban

The failed coup of August 19–21, 1991, marked the end of Mikhail Gorbachev's attempt to reform the existing Soviet and CPSU structures and the start of the revolutionary transformation of the USSR. The putsch itself was the culmination of the schism between the reform wing of the Soviet Communist Party and its hard-line faction that had been developing at least since 1987. Immediately after the coup's defeat, reform communists united with the democratic opposition led by Boris Yeltsin in a joint effort to crush the power of the CPSU apparatus and to create a new union of democratic and sovereign republics. The post-coup readiness of Russian reform communists to join forces with Russian democrats tended to obscure the fact that most leading figures in the democratic movement had themselves belonged to the CPSU as recently as the 28th Congress in July 1990. The contrast between this situation and the East-Central European political landscape after the revolutions of 1989 could hardly have been greater. Finally, those August days of horror, then of joy, represented a personal tragedy for Gorbachev and his vision of a "humane, democratic socialism"; yet this in no way diminished his place in history. Paradoxically, it seems that precisely his socialist convictions had impelled him to open the Pandora's Box of *glasnost* and *perestroika,* of free speech and grassroots politicization, which ultimately brought about the collapse of communism and the Soviet empire.

The Schism behind the Coup

The schism between the Soviet Communist reformers and hard-liners that led to the August 1991 coup can be viewed as a recurrence at the very core of the CPSU of the split between social democracy and Leninism that had torn the European Marxist movement asunder at the time of the Bolshevik Revolution and the founding of the Comintern.

The social democratization of the CPSU's reform wing had for all intents and purposes been achieved by 1990, as Heinz Timmermann has described in Chapter 1, and provided the theoretical backdrop for the abrogation of the CPSU's constitutionally guaranteed monopoly on power in March of that year. Gorbachev's establishment of a preferential relationship with the Italian Communist Party (PCI) was, as I have related in Chapter 2, a logical corollary of the Soviet reformers' search for contacts and common positions with European social democracy, with which the PCI was already closely aligned. It also reflected the ongoing pull of communism's internationalist mystique, or ideologically conditioned urge to find allies in the global arena to buttress one's political position at home. This internationalist mystique had, historically, formed the matrix of Moscow's ties with the global left.

At the same time, the legalization of a multiparty system and the parallel crystallization of organized factions among the Soviet Communists themselves led to the emergence of a wide spectrum of left-oriented groups ranging from social democrats to CPSU reformers to pro-Beijing Leninists. One could, therefore, no longer speak of "Moscow's" relationship with the global left. Instead, multiple transnational linkages were developing between Soviet groups of varying political outlooks, leftist and otherwise, and their like-minded colleagues in the world beyond the USSR.

The rapid creation in the Soviet Union of several social democratic parties greatly complicated the CPSU reformers' quest for a special relationship with international social democracy.[1] On May 14, 1990,

---

1. For details on the new social democratic parties, see Eberhard Schneider and Heinz Timmermann, "Neue Demokratische Parteien in Russland, der Ukraine und Weissrussland," *Aktuelle Analyse des BIOst* (Cologne), no. 36 (July 17, 1991):1–8.

for instance, the Social Democratic Party of Russia held its inaugural congress. One month later the CPSU's Commission on International Affairs, headed by Aleksandr Yakovlev, met to consider the impact of such developments on the party's cooperation with European social democrats, given the interest of the latter in the new Soviet social democratic formations. Although the published summary of the discussion suggests second thoughts on the part of some, Yuriy Krasin, rector of the CPSU Central Committee's Institute of Social Sciences, remained the same outspoken advocate of CPSU overtures to Western social democracy that Timmermann has described. Despite European socialists' vacillations toward the CPSU, Krasin insisted, "We under no circumstances should change our general strategic line" of partnership with international social democracy.[2] All the while, the CPSU reformers staunchest foreign supporter, the PCI, was about to transform itself into a noncommunist party of social democratic bent.

The factionalization of the CPSU led to open political conflict at the 28th Congress in July 1990, with the hard-liners in the party apparatus seeking to shackle, if not unseat, Gorbachev, and the Democratic Platform group and other reform communists rallying to his defense.[3] With the help of Boris Yeltsin, Gorbachev managed to preserve his position and his freedom of action, only to see Yeltsin resign from the party at the close of the congress. Numerous Democratic Platform members followed his example in succeeding weeks with some of them regrouping as the social democratic Republican Party of Russia in November 1990 and others choosing—as did Yeltsin—to remain without party affiliation.

A portentous consequence of internal disarray was the absence from the 28th Congress—for the first time in the post-Stalin era—of official foreign communist delegations.[4] Their presence at previous CPSU congresses had played a vital part in the Kremlin's projection of its internationalist mystique. Now, however, the CPSU's transna-

---

2. "O sotrudnichestve KPSS s sotsial-demokratiei na sovremennom etape: S zasedaniya Komissii TsK KPSS po voprosam mezhdunarodnoi politiki 15 iyunya 1990 g.," *Izvestiya TsK KPSS*, no. 11 (November 1990):90.

3. Giulietto Chiesa, "The 28th Congress of the CPSU," *Problems of Communism* 39, no. 4 (July–August 1990):24–38.

4. Moscow Television Service in Russian, 1700 GMT, June 29, 1990 (FBIS-SOV, July 2, 1990, 19).

tional linkages no longer represented the concerted policy of a united leadership but had become intertwined with the party's internal struggle between reform and reaction.

Nowhere was the linkage between CPSU factionalism and international alignment more evident than in the entente that developed between the Soviet party's hard-line Leninists and the leadership of the Chinese Communist Party (CCP). In Chapter 3 Harry Gelman has described how during the winter and early spring of 1990, behind closed doors, General Secretary Jiang Zemin called Gorbachev a traitor to socialism and paramount leader Deng Xiaoping predicted the Soviet president's eventual ouster, telling one party meeting that "we should place our hopes on . . . the broad ranks of genuine Bolsheviks." Premier Li Peng's state visit to Moscow in April 1990 was widely seen as a step in the continued normalization of Sino-Soviet relations. In fact, however, it was apparently only a cover for the subsequent expansion of ties between Beijing and the CPSU hard-liners.

As it turned out, the very next month a CPSU delegation spent ten days in the PRC studying the work of the CCP's "control-disciplinary organs."[5] The Soviet delegation was led by none other than Boris K. Pugo, at the time head of the CPSU Central Control Commission, later the Soviet minister of the interior, and ultimately a ringleader of the August 1991 coup who preferred suicide to arrest on charges of treason after its defeat. In September 1990 a CCP delegation paid a ten-day return visit to Moscow, holding "meetings and talks" with Pugo and three other high-ranking CPSU officials later to be arrested for orchestrating the August coup: Gennadiy Yanayev, Oleg Shenin, and Boris Boldin.[6] The Chinese visitors on that occasion were not received by Gorbachev. Finally, in May 1991 when Jiang Zemin became the first CCP general secretary to visit the USSR in thirty-four years,[7] his meetings with Gorbachev and other Soviet government officials were followed by a two-day stay in Leningrad where he was

5. The visit took place May 22–31, 1990; see "Mezhdunarodnye svyazi KPSS," *Izvestiya TsK KPSS*, no. 6 (June 1990), 159.

6. The visit took place September 17–27, 1990; see "Mezhdunarodnye svyazi KPSS," *Izvestiya TsK KPSS*, no. 10 (October 1990), 120. The Chinese delegation also met with Central Committee secretaries Valentin Kuptsov and Yuriy Manayenkov as well as Politburo member Stanislav Gurenko, first secretary of the Ukrainian CP.

7. Technically speaking, when Mao Zedong visited Moscow in 1957, he occupied the position of CCP chairman, which was later abolished.

hosted by the hard-line first secretary of the Leningrad regional communist organization, Boris Gidaspov.[8] When the independent Moscow news agency Interfax announced the schedule for the Chinese leader's visit, it reported that it had "failed to get any explanation as to who masterminded the program."[9]

In other words, as the CPSU reformers became more isolated in what remained of the world communist movement, the Soviet hard-liners received the encouragement and no doubt the advice of the Chinese Communist leaders responsible for the bloody crackdown in Tienanmen Square in 1989. Whatever their visions of socialism, the orthodox Soviet and Chinese communists had in common a commitment to Leninism as a prescription for centralized single-party dictatorship.

It is hardly surprising, then, that on August 19, 1991, CCP leader Jiang Zemin welcomed Gorbachev's overthrow as a "good deed" for the Soviet people and the international communist movement.[10] The Portuguese and Greek communist parties likewise backed the coup attempt, as did the North Koreans and Vietnamese, while the French Communist Party was ambivalent.[11] (In contrast, the former PCI, now reconstituted as the Democratic Party of the Left, fervently condemned the putsch from the start.[12]) Just as the CPSU hard-liners had exposed their Leninist-Stalinist character to their compatriots and the world, so too did the rump of the once-menacing world communist movement.

On August 24, 1991, President Gorbachev called upon the Central Committee of the CPSU to disband itself, resigned as its general secretary, and ordered the sequestration of party property.[13] These steps portended the political marginalization of the movement founded by

8. For Gidaspov's hard-line views, see Roy Medvedev and Giulietto Chiesa, *Time of Change: An Insider's View of Russia's Transformation* (New York: Pantheon, 1989), 308.

9. Moscow *Interfax* in English, 1811 GMT, May 14, 1991 (FBIS-SOV, May 15, 1991, 14–15). For Jiang Zemin's visit to Leningrad, see *Pravda*, May 20, 1991, 5.

10. Quoted in Lena H. Sun, "Chinese Battening Hatches," *The Washington Post*, September 11, 1991, A25.

11. Steven Greenhouse, "French Communist Chief Attacked for Stance on Soviet Coup," *The New York Times*, August 27, 1991, A11.

12. See the extensive coverage in *l'Unità*, August 20–22, 1991.

13. For the texts of Gorbachev's statement and decrees, see *The New York Times*, August 25, 1991, 14.

Lenin and even its eventual merger, at least in Russia, with right-wing, xenophobic nationalism.[14] Viewed in the historical context of Marxism in the twentieth century, the crackdown on the CPSU also represented the defeat of Leninism by its traditional competitor on the left, social democracy.

"We Can't Go on Living like This"

These concluding comments began with the suggestion that Gorbachev's reformism stemmed, at least partially, from his socialist convictions, from his sense of the disparity between everyday life in the Soviet Union and the CPSU's socialist goals as he understood them. Time and again he affirmed his belief in socialism. Already at Moscow State University, recalls the former Czech reform communist Zdenek Mlynar, "Gorbachev took Marxism very seriously," which "was a rare thing among Soviet students."[15] And as late as November 1990, as Federigo Argentieri notes in Chapter 5, the Soviet leader told the PCI general secretary, Achille Occhetto, that he still stood "for socialism, despite the tragedies that marked the past seven decades." Clearly his ideas on how to achieve socialism as well as his understanding of the term itself changed over time. In a striking essay published in late November 1989, he spoke of "humane socialism," "democratic socialism," and defined its essence as *the concept of man as an end rather than a means.*"[16] He also adopted the slogan of the 1968 Prague reformers, declaring that "the new face of socialism

14. Suggestive of such a merger was an appeal signed by twelve hard-line communists, including two of the men arrested after the coup, which was published in the conservative communist daily *Sovetskaya Rossiya* on July 23, 1991, and included the following statement: "The Motherland, the country, our great power—passed down to us for preservation by history, nature, and our great ancestors—is dying, falling apart and sinking into darkness and nothingness." See David Remnick, "Hard-Liners Appeal to Military to Prevent Soviet 'Humiliation,'" *The Washington Post,* July 24, 1991, A23.

15. Mlynar was one of Gorbachev's college roommates. The quotation is in Robert G. Kaiser, *Why Gorbachev Happened: His Triumphs and His Failures* (New York: Simon & Schuster, 1991), 29. Of the many works that have appeared on Gorbachev, Kaiser's is surely one of the most perceptive.

16. Mikhail Gorbachev, "Sotsialisticheskaya idea i revolyutsionnaya perestroika," *Pravda,* November 26, 1989, 2; emphasis added.

is its human face."[17] To be sure, late November 1989 was the time when the "Velvet Revolution" was sweeping hard-line communist rule from Czechoslovakia, thus a time when political realism dictated emulation of the Prague Spring. These remarks nevertheless suggested a key to understanding Gorbachev: precisely because he did believe that socialism should serve the people, or provide for general well-being, he launched *perestroika*. He took a hard look at Soviet reality and held his nose in disgust.

Gorbachev's quest for a reconciliation between the CPSU and the PCI from the time of his coming to power provides circumstantial evidence of this idealistic bent. A cynical view holds that the Soviet leader saw the PCI only as a bridge to social democratic power brokers in Western Europe, but while there is a kernel of truth here, the matter is far more complicated. Perhaps as a result of witnessing the 1984 funeral of Enrico Berlinguer, which was attended by well over a million Italian Communist supporters along with the entire noncommunist political establishment of Rome, Gorbachev displayed respect, even deference, toward the PCI leaders and sought to understand the nature of their socialist vision. Ironically, just as foreign communists had for decades looked to Moscow for ideological reinforcement, in the second half of the 1980s the leader of the CPSU appeared to turn to the largest nonruling communist party in the West for somewhat the same reason. He may well have thought to himself that if competent, reasonable, nonmarginalized individuals in prosperous Italy could opt for socialism, it must indeed have some historical validity. Whatever the case, Gorbachev's rapprochement with the PCI should be seen in part as a search for kindred spirits in a shared quest for "socialism with a human face."

How he arrived at this juncture may only be surmised. His 1972 travels in Italy as a guest of the PCI doubtless brought home to him a basic psychological difference between ruling and nonruling communist cadres: namely, while the former were often motivated by little more than careerism, the latter had made a conscious and often risky ideological choice. To state it somewhat differently, the path to upward social mobility in Catholic, entrepreneurial, pro-American Italy

17. Ibid.

was not normally associated with communist activism. Certainly outside the "Red Belt" of north-central Italy PCI members had fewer prospects than others for attaining political office or influence—in sharp contrast to the USSR, where communist party membership was the prerequisite for both professional advancement and political clout.

Later, as first secretary of the Stavropol regional communist organization from 1970 to 1978 and as a member of the CPSU Secretariat and Politburo thereafter, Gorbachev surely became familiar with the PCI's Eurocommunist heresy, with its condemnation of Moscow's use of military force abroad and violations of human rights at home. Indeed, he admitted to reading PCI historian Giuseppe Boffa's two-volume *History of the Soviet Union* in its limited, restricted Russian edition. He thus knew that the Italian comrades understood the flaws in Soviet society and yet remained, nevertheless, committed socialists. Where better to turn, then, for moral support and encouragement in his struggle for *perestroika?*

The argument that there was any ideological basis for Gorbachev's conduct runs counter to the assumptions of two major tendencies among Soviet-watchers in the West: those who have maintained that CPSU leadership groups from the Stalin era onward were motivated primarily by power calculations and those who have viewed Marxism-Leninism as a determining force in Soviet policymaking. While proponents of the second view were disoriented by Gorbachev's rejection of doctrines presumed immutable, such as democratic centralism and single-party rule, proponents of the first attributed the twists and turns of the Soviet leader's domestic policies on the eve of the 1990s to his urge to retain power, whatever the cost to political conviction or erstwhile allies.

The readiness of Western observers to explain Gorbachev's behavior in terms of political expediency was particularly evident during the fall and winter of 1990–91. That was a time, it will be recalled, when *perestroika* seemed to have been shipwrecked on the shoals of ethnic and national liberationism, when hard-line Leninists in the military-ideological complex launched a counteroffensive to preserve central Soviet power and the command economy and to reimpose control over the electronic media. The widespread view in the Western (and Russian) democratic press was that the Soviet president was caving in to their pressure to save his own political skin.

This interpretation of his conduct may have been one reason for Gorbachev's remarkable outburst in late November 1990 to a gathering of prominent cultural figures in Moscow. He professed to them his commitment to socialism despite the fact that one grandfather had been banished to Siberia and the other imprisoned and tortured during the 1930s, and despite the fact that he and his good friend Eduard Shevardnadze had agreed on the eve of his designation as CPSU general secretary that the Soviet people could not "go on living like this." He insisted, moreover, that he was not a dictator, that if that were his goal he would never have launched *perestroika;* for, he protested, "I already had [dictatorship] in my hands. The general secretary of the CPSU Central Committee was a dictator with no equal in the world and nobody had more power than he, nobody, you see."[18] In other words, he seemed to be pleading for his listeners to trust his commitment to genuine reform precisely because he was genuinely committed to socialism.

From our knowledge of Gorbachev's relationship with the PCI we also get an insight into his educability on the issue of social democracy. What I called, in Chapter 2, Gorbachev's "courtship" of the PCI took place in 1985–86, well before he and the reformers around him contemplated an ideological rapprochement with social democracy. In his report to the 27th Party Congress he remained downright disdainful toward it, and even in mid-1987 he still argued in favor of a world conference attended exclusively by communist parties. Only gradually did he agree to the PCI's idea of holding a meeting of communist, social democratic, and other left-oriented parties during the November 1987 celebration of the seventieth anniversary of the October Revolution. As Gorbachev told the Italian Communist general secretary on that occasion, "We have done as you wished. . . . We must admit that the PCI has argued for some time that this is the path to follow, and it seems to us that it produces good results." Thereafter, as we have seen, establishment theorists took the lead in reassessing in

---

18. Moscow Domestic Service in Russian, 1215 GMT, November 29, 1990 (FBIS-SOV, November 30, 1990, 47).

a highly positive manner the history and contemporary role of international social democracy. Gorbachev underscored the volte-face made on this issue when in his November 1989 essay, quoted above, he admitted to the CPSU's former negative attitude "to the very term 'democratic socialism,' which was identified with the expression of an . . . opportunistic line in the socialist movement."[19]

The Russian Paradox

The question to which we turn by way of conclusion concerns the future of reform communists in the Soviet Union. Will theirs be the fate of reform communists in East-Central Europe? There, as Argentieri explained in Chapter 5, reform communism constituted merely a transitional stage on the path to Western-style pluralist democracy. Not only that, but in free elections the former communist parties were reduced to vestigial rumps, losing out to anticommunist forces of the center-right and center-left. And even *reform* communists were relegated to the sidelines of public life as a wave of popular anticommunist sentiment swept the dissidents of yesteryear—the likes of Václav Havel and Lech Wałesa along with their closest colleagues from the opposition—into one high office after another.

To repeat, will the post-coup USSR follow in the footsteps of Poland, Hungary, and Czechoslovakia? As of September 1991, the newly liberated Baltic republics as well as Georgia, Armenia, and to some extent Moldavia were rather closely emulating the East-Central European pattern. In the peripheral European areas of the Soviet Union, communism had been seen as the force opposing nationalism in the public mind, just as it had been in the USSR's East European empire. As a consequence, the populaces were unwilling to sanction a role for any communists of recent vintage, reformist or otherwise. The situation was less clear in Bielorussia and the Ukraine, and prudence dictates silence on the question of Soviet Central Asia. But in the Great Russian heartland a paradoxical scene was emerging in which reform communism plainly represented a transitional stage

19. Gorbachev, "Sotsialisticheskaya idea," 2 (see note 16).

on the way to emergent pluralist democracy but a pluralist democracy in which *breakaway reform communists* were poised to play a preeminent role. Barring a total economic collapse and a xenophobic populist-Leninist backlash, it seems that these trends might well continue.

The Russian Republic, comprising half the population of the USSR and three-fourths of its territory, constitutes of course the linchpin in any future resolution of the crisis precipitated by the disintegration of the Soviet Union. In Russia, moreover, developments even before the August 1991 coup reinforced the paradoxical trend of erstwhile reform communists playing a paramount role in the evolving postcommunist order. Gorbachev himself conceded to Harvard political scientist Graham Allison in late June that "we have left one system of government, and now the structures of the government and the economy cannot remain long in the *transition stage*. We have to move to a new system."[20] At the same time, the Russian elections of June 12, 1991, underscored the centrality of reform communists in this process. Boris Yeltsin won almost 60 percent of the vote to become the first directly elected president of the Russian Republic, and Anatoliy Sobchak and Gavriil Popov became the popularly chosen mayors of Leningrad (St. Petersburg) and Moscow, respectively, with even larger mandates.[21] Yet all three men had resigned from the CPSU less than one year earlier, after the 28th Congress, and Yeltsin had made his career in the party apparatus just like Gorbachev. Similarly, most of the leading figures in the post-coup democratic circles—men such as Ivan Silayev, Arkadiy Volskiy, and Aleksandr Rutskoi—had left the ranks of the CPSU even more recently.

This trend of breakaway reform communists becoming articulate democratic politicians was highlighted on the eve of the August coup when two of Gorbachev's closest *perestroika* colleagues, former foreign minister Shevardnadze and presidential adviser Yakovlev, resigned from the party and established a Democratic Reform Movement aimed at competing with the CPSU in the next Union-wide

20. Quoted from Allison's notes on a June 25, 1991, meeting with Gorbachev by David Remnick in *The Washington Post*, June 26, 1991, A14; emphasis added.

21. *Izvestiya*, June 20, 1991, 1; cf. *Report on the USSR* 3, no. 25 (June 21, 1991), 33–34.

elections.[22] The contrast between this phenomenon and the postcommunist developments in East-Central Europe or the Baltics, Georgia, and Armenia could not have been greater. It reflected the extent to which communism in Russia had, after World War II, become an indigenous and national, if spent, force. And it suggested at least one ray of light in an otherwise clouded outlook for the future: unlike in East-Central Europe and the USSR's European borderland republics, there could be little ground for vilifying communists per se in postcommunist Russia.

22. For the creation of the Democratic Reform Movement, see Francis X. Clines, "Soviet Reformists Decide to Create Opposition Group," *The New York Times,* July 2, 1991, A1 and A6; for Shevardnadze's letter of resignation from the CPSU, see *The New York Times,* July 5, 1991, A7; for Yakovlev's resignation, see David Remnick, "Reformist Yakovlev Quits Communist Party," *The Washington Post,* August 17, 1991, A17.

Index

Library of Congress Cataloging-in-Publication Data

Moscow and the global left in the Gorbachev era / edited by Joan Barth Urban.

    p. cm.
    Includes bibliographical references and index.
    ISBN 0-8014-2726-6 (cloth : alk. paper). — ISBN 0-8014-8008-6 (paper : alk.
paper)
    1. Soviet Union—Foreign relations—1985–   2. Communism—History—20th
century.   3. Soviet Union—Relations—Communist countries.   4. Communist
countries—Relations—Soviet Union.   I. Urban, Joan Barth, 1934–
DK289.M68   1992
327.47—dc20   91-57898